The Diversity Advantage

HOW AMERICAN BUSINESS CAN
OUT-PERFORM JAPANESE AND
EUROPEAN COMPANIES IN
THE GLOBAL MARKETPLACE

JOHN P. FERNANDEZ
WITH **MARY BARR**

LEXINGTON BOOKS
An Imprint of Macmillan, Inc.
NEW YORK

Maxwell Macmillan Canada
TORONTO

Maxwell Macmillan International
NEW YORK   OXFORD   SINGAPORE   SYDNEY

Library of Congress Cataloging-in-Publication Data

Fernandez, John P.
The diversity advantage : how American business can out-perform
Japanese and European companies in the global marketplace / John P.
Fernandez with Mary Barr.
p.   cm.
ISBN 0-669-27978-1
1. Organizational effectiveness—Social aspects—Cross-cultural
studies.   2. Human capital—Social aspects—Cross-cultural studies.
3. Corporate culture—Cross-cultural studies.   4. Minorities—
Employment—Cross-cultural studies.   I. Barr, Mary.   II. Title.
HD58.9.F46   1993
331.13'3—dc20   93-23793
                                                                                          CIP

Lexington Books
An Imprint of Macmillan, Inc.
866 Third Avenue, New York, N. Y. 10022

Maxwell Macmillan Canada, Inc.
1200 Eglinton Avenue East
Suite 200
Don Mills, Ontario M3C 3N1

Macmillan, Inc. is part of the Maxwell Communication
Group of Companies.

Printed in the United States of America

printing number
2   3   4   5   6   7   8   9   10

*This book is dedicated
to Louis K. O'Leary,
a dear friend and mentor,
to whom I owe a great
deal of my successes.*

Contents

1

Introduction

As corporations in the United States, Japan, and the European Community position themselves to become leading competitors in the emerging global marketplace, it is increasingly clear that a key to their success will be their ability to develop diverse, well-trained work forces that can function effectively as high-performance teams and produce quality products and services at a competitive price. The crucial first step in developing such teams is teaching increasingly diverse groups of employees to understand and value different races, ethnic groups, cultures, languages, genders, ages, religions, sexual orientations, levels of physical abilities, and family structures. Only by assisting employees to respect differences will the corporations be able to build trust (which is the key factor in building diverse, high-performance, quality-oriented teams) and to develop in the employees the skills and tools to deal effectively with diverse customer bases, diverse stockholders and diverse influences in a highly competitive marketplace.

Although Japan's population is fairly homogeneous, its low birthrate will lead to a declining population and a need to utilize women and foreign laborers more effectively. In addition, it will continue to expand its businsess operations overseas. The European Community's population is much more diverse than Japan's in terms of ethnicity, culture, language, religion, and to a lesser extent, race. The EC is also faced with low birthrates that have already begun to create shortages of labor in key areas. For the EC to be successful, many of its predominantly small and midsize corporations must merge and try to capture customer bases not only in the EC but throughout the world, where there is considerably more diversity. The United States has by far the most diverse population in terms of race, ethnicity, religions and culture; however, the global marketplace is even more diverse in all of these areas. For many American corporations to survive and prosper in the 1990s, they must more effectively utilize diverse populations in the United States and in the world.

In this book, we put forward the thesis that despite the problems with diversity experienced by the United States, it is uniquely positioned among the three economic powerhouses of the 1990s (the others being Japan and the emerging EC) to grasp the competitive advantage. All three are dealing with the growing realities of increasingly diverse work forces and customer bases in the global marketplace, but only the United States has a history and philosophy embracing diversity. As will be seen, the European countries and Japan have a limited history of embracing diversity—except in a superior role through conquest and colonization—and today are opposing the increasing variety of their population. The United States, meanwhile, has spent decades creating programs and laws to respect and utilize such diversity. We maintain that U.S. success in the new global marketplace rests in the rich cultural, ethnic, and racial mix of its population, which will make it better able to adapt to foreign markets and global customer bases.

Japan and the separate EC countries, as noted above, take pride in and are staunchly attempting to protect their homogeneity, with stringent restrictions against immigration and a denial of certain rights and freedoms to nonnationals. Japan, in particular, believes that homogeneity is largely responsible for its phenomenal success in recent decades; Japanese leaders have even expressed the opinion that the United States has been hampered by the influence of "inferior" minorities. In fact, former Prime Minister Yasuhiro Nakasone said that Americans have lower average intelligence than the Japanese because of the large numbers of African and Hispanic Americans. Yuji Aida, Japanese specialist in European Renaissance history and professor emeritus at the University of Kyoto, wrote that

> it is only a matter of time before U.S. minority groups espouse self-determination in some form. When that happens, the country may become ungovernable. . . . Within one hundred years, and probably much sooner, most Americans will be people of color. For the first time since the United States came into being, Caucasians will be a

minority. Illiteracy may become widespread, and many Americans will not speak standard English. . . . Blacks and Hispanics will not be able to run a complex industrial society like the United States unless they dramatically raise their sights and standards in the next forty years.

This view is indicative of the intolerance and ignorance spreading not only between Japan and the United States but globally among disparate cultures concerning cultural diversity. It illustrates the current sorry state of understanding among world economic leaders, where members of purportedly advanced societies blame economic, political, and other problems on the diversity of a culture and argue that homogenization is the cure to these ills.

Just as troubling, supposed allies, at the first sign of difficulties, have often reverted to childlike tactics of name-calling, usually by pointing out the differences between themselves and their rivals in terms of skin color, ethnicity, and culture. Former French Prime Minister Edith Cresson, in discussing a feared Japanese invasion of European markets, referred to the Japanese as "ants." A CIA report released in 1991 described Japan as an "immoral, manipulative and controlling culture" trying to dominate the world through its economic power. Such comments are further examples of the recent bashing caused by economic rivalry among the United States, Japan, and the European Community. These issues are only some of the multitude of problems discussed in this book; many divisions to be discussed exist not only between countries but within countries and corporations.

Opinion polls portray a growing tide of global intolerance and ignorance. In December 1990, a survey in Britain revealed a major and increasing worry about the possible increase in illegal immigration that European unity might bring. A study on racial attitudes found that 90 percent of the British believed the English discriminated against people of color. A majority of French nationals polled (53 percent) felt that Islamic girls should not be allowed to wear their native dress to school, and another poll revealed that 72 percent of them in 1990 (up from 65 percent in 1985) believed there was a significant amount of racism in France. Neo-Nazi and fascist attacks against Third World immigrants and Jews in Europe have skyrocketed.[1] Germany has seen the strongest xenophobic and racist reactions, the most notorious of which was the firebombing of a Turkish home, killing an elderly woman and her two grandchildren. Calls for a more unified Europe have been drowned out by a surge in nationalist movements that instead threaten to divide it further. For example, rising nationalism in Denmark led to a vote denying the Maastricht treaty, which calls for more economic, political, and social unity; the French public barely approved the treaty after an all-out campaign by the government to support it. The Catalonians in Spain, meanwhile, are moving toward a separate and independent state. But the worst examples of negative ethnocentrism in Europe are the civil wars that have erupted in the former Yugoslav republics. (The Yugoslav republics are not EC members but could be possible candidates at a later date.)

A year before the Los Angeles riots in 1992 touched off violence in communities across America, white Americans in several polls displayed a remarkable lack of knowledge regarding the plight of African Americans: 75 percent said that racial trouble in their community was unlikely (only 2 percent thought any trouble existed at all), and 66 percent (compared to 37 percent of African Americans) believed that African Americans were treated as well as whites.

In Japan, the city of Kawguchi banned Pakistanis from teaching since they were believed to be "dirty" carriers of communicable diseases and to be associated with crime. In September 1990, the new minister of justice, Seiroku Kajiyama, compared prostitutes in Japan to African Americans. Koreans living in Japan are faced with discrimination in jobs, housing, and marriage and have only since the late 1980s felt fairly comfortable using their Korean names. Until recently, the Japanese still required persons of Korean descent living in Japan to carry identification cards, and many are denied citizenship despite generations of residence in Japan.

Women are also discriminated against in the three economic blocs. The U.S. has the best record among the three powers in providing women equal and fair opportunities. Women's status in the European nations is comparable to what it was in the United States in the 1950s and early 1960s, whereas their status in Japan is like that in the United States in the 1930s.

Below is a brief summary of some of the key current and future diversity issues that Japan, the United States, and the European Community face. Also included are our opinions on how these issues will affect the competitiveness of these three powers.

Japan

Japan will lose its competitive edge in the global marketplace during the 1990s and the early twenty-first century, in part because of its changing demographics and its inability to change rapidly the elements of racism, sexism, ethnocentrism, and xenophobia in its culture. Centuries of isolationist history have allowed many Japanese to develop a sense of superiority toward and distrust of foreigners that still persists. Foreign employees of Japanese-owned companies throughout the world complain of a "cement ceiling" that keeps them out of higher management positions and excludes them from important decisions. By the year 2000, the four hundred thousand Americans who in the early 1990s worked for U.S. subsidiaries of Japanese companies will grow to one million. But unrest is growing among these workers; American workers, especially in management, are filing more and more lawsuits against their Japanese employers because of perceived discrimination.[3] The problem is costing Japanese business money in terms of lost productivity, as well as lawsuits—in 1990, the Quasar television company, a subsidiary of Matsushita, was penalized $2.5 million by a federal court in Chicago for discrimination on the grounds of national origin when it dismissed sixty-six American managers but retained all Japanese managers. Discrimination by Japanese employers is also a problem in other countries.

At home, Japan is facing these incontrovertible demographic truths. Until the economic slowdown that began in 1991, Japan was experiencing a labor shortage of 100 placements for every 147 jobs; since the recession, the ratio has become almost even. (There are still 114 jobs for every 100 men, but there are only 92 jobs for every 100 women.) Demographics are against Japan in the long term, however, and the labor shortage will emerge in more serious forms in the coming years. They key reasons for this are that their population is aging more rapidly than that of any other industrialized nation; and they are suffering an extreme birth dearth which shows no sign of letting up. The women who could fill the work force void, though, will be mostly recruited as "office flowers" who in most cases must retire upon marriage. The equal employment law that passed in 1986 under international pressure contains no sanctions against violators. Furthermore, the immigrant labor pool is being discriminated against as Japan passes ever more restrictive immigration laws.

Japan is also faced with rising discontent at home. Its success has created wealth primarily for a select few, causing the Japanese have-nots to resent the haves. Japanese workers may actually earn more than their American counterparts, but their salaries are worth less: the same amount of money buys twice as much goods and services in Cleveland, for example, as in Osaka. And Japanese must save heavily to cover their retirement, since existing plans are insubstantial.[4] The Japanese are, all in all, working too hard; a Ministry of Labor report states that the average weekday of a working couple mostly consists of sleeping, eating, working, cleaning, and child care, with very little time allotted to leisure.

The growing have-not class is virtually unable to buy a home. Despite a significant decrease in real estate prices in the early 1990s, property is still prohibitively expensive. Skyrocketing housing prices in the 1980s resulted in young families living in tiny one- or two-bedroom apartments that are a long commute from work. Many young couples are forced to live with parents because even apartments are unaffordable; this living arrangement discourages many from having children. In fact, Japanese wives aged twenty-five to thirty-four stated that the primary reason (with 37 percent concurring) for limiting the number of children they had was "that their homes were too cramped and their incomes too small to give a child the kind of upbringing they would like." One Japanese professional explained the problem as follows:

> "People feel so much pressure on the job that they work until nine, ten o'clock at night," said Kunio Kitamura, a Tokyo obstetrician who closely follows the birthrate problem. "Then they have another hour and a half home on a train, because most people can't afford a house anywhere near the office. You probably can't get a seat, and the train is full of drunks, singing and throwing up. After all that, who has the strength to get in bed and make a baby?"[5]

The traditionally subservient Japanese worker, however, is now showing signs of rebellion. As the number of university graduates has jumped from 5 percent of the population to 37 percent since the early 1960s, workers who once perceived themselves as servants of a company now see themselves as professionals with skills to sell on the labor market. This new breed of young and well-educated workers have earned themselves a popular label—the "new human species."[6]

As of 1992, despite generations of cultural socialization to do otherwise, one in five Japanese workers has been making a deliberate effort to separate work from personal life.[7] Consequently, workers are leaving their companies at midcareer for better pay, more freedom and creativity, and reduced working hours. The stigma traditionally attached to workers who leave jobs is slowly fading as the new emphasis on competitiveness forces companies to court these job-hopping workers. The extensive amount of time Japanese have spent traveling and working abroad, along with the introduction of satellite TV, are believed to be largely responsible for these changing attitudes.[8] In 1991, one in ten Japanese workers switched jobs after returning from a stay in the United States, compared to one in a hundred a decade earlier. Many choose U.S. and European companies as their new employers because of better pay, promotions based on merit rather than seniority, greater personal freedom, and more creativity and decision making. It should be noted that the economic slowdown in Japan in the early 1990s has forced many companies to begin to adopt such Western managerial strategies as pay for performance, restructuring, and downsizing.

Internationally, Japan is facing an increase in anti-Japanese sentiments. Former Harvard economist Robert Reich, who became the U.S. secretary of labor in 1993, has written that Japan is replacing the Soviet Union in American eyes "as a means of defining ourselves, our interests, our obligations to one another." According to one Japanese military historian, "America has always needed an enemy to pull itself together. Now that the Soviet threat is gone, that enemy could become Japan."[9] The fact is that many Americans, Europeans, and Asians are viewing Japan's increased economic power with growing wariness. In a nationwide survey by the Chicago Council on Foreign Relations in the fall of 1990, 60 percent of Americans considered Japan's economic strength as a "critical threat" to U.S. interests. Americans' dislike of Japan, however, seems to be at least partially racially motivated, unlike anti-Soviet sentiment, which was directed at communism but not at the Soviet people. Japan also faces hostile attitudes from Europe, as the EC is determined to keep the Japanese from taking over the European economy in the same way as the EC perceives has happened in the United States. Japan's Asian neighbors are its closest trading partners, but they view Japan suspiciously and with much resentment; the wounds of Japan's World War II imperialism have not yet healed.

The 1990s economic recession in the United States, Europe, and Japan has not helped to improve American and European attitudes toward the Japanese. Other reasons for hostility range from jealousy over Japan's economic success to anger and resentment over its attitudes of racial superiority and sexism. Unless Japan begins to address the grievances of its overworked and underappreciated work force, to open its markets, to become more proactive in minority and immigrant rights, and to give its female and foreign employees equal opportunities, it will lose out to more astute American and European competitors.

Europe

The twelve-member EC (Belgium, Denmark, France, Germany, Greece, Ireland, Italy, Luxembourg, the Netherlands, Portugal, Spain, and the United Kingdom) is the largest trading bloc of the industrialized world. The EC, however, was formed not out of the love of European countries for one another but out of the fear that without such an alliance, the United States and Japan would dominate the separate nations' economies. A mere three hundred directives will be insufficient to overcome the thousand-year history of conflict and tension existing among these twelve independent and richly diverse nations.[10]

The recent cross-Channel squabble between the French and British is testimony to this fact. Former French prime minister Edith Cresson criticized English men for being less virile than the French, stating that the former are "not interested in women." Much more serious antipathy exists between Britain and Ireland, where there is long-standing animosity over Britain's former role as ruler of Ireland, as well as the current situation in Northern Ireland. Fears lingering from the two world wars have resurfaced with Germany's reunification, as the rest of Europe makes conjectures concerning the potential future power of the new Germany. Tensions also exist within countries, as in Belgium, where there is increased political and cultural animosity between the Dutch-speaking north and the French-speaking south. Increasing regional divisions are evident in Italy between the prosperous northern and the poorer southern provinces. Spain has had a long-standing and strong separatist movement among the Basques and a similar movement in Catalonia. There is also the situation of the Bretons in northern France, whose rights to a separate linguistic and ethnic identity is still being threatened.

These cultural and political differences among and within EC countries will affect competitive business operations. One British and Italian joint venture, for example, has experienced recurring clashes based on subtle yet disparate concepts of what constitutes an effective meeting. In general, many Italians are comfortable with more than one person talking at the same time, several issues being dealt with simultaneously and heated, direct discussions. Most British prefer one person talking in a calm, controlled manner about one issue at a time.

It is our belief that the EC will also have problems achieving a dominant position because of difficulties dealing with differences in race, ethnicity, religion, language, culture, and gender.[11] Like Japan, the EC is experiencing a severe decline in births and a rapid aging of its population. Therefore, as the twenty-first century approaches, the EC will have to find new sources of workers to keep its economic machine running; however, the EC countries are reacting as if their small existing immigrant populations (averaging 3 percent) represent a tidal wave. Only 5.2 percent of the German, 3.8 percent of the French, and 3.3 percent of the British populations are from non-EC countries. Conversely, the United States in the 1980s accepted almost 50 percent of the legal immigrants in the world. When immigration has been allowed in European countries, it has been only for a short period of time and to meet individual national needs. Although immigrants arrive in Europe from many sources, however, the share from developing countries is on the rise. In order to protect their cultures against the "impurity" of these nonwhite immigrants, many in the EC are proposing more restrictive immigration laws and even repatriating immigrants—against their will—to their countries of origin.

Despite their small numbers, foreign workers have become vital participants in certain sectors of some EC economies. Immigrants represent about 14 percent of industrial workers in Germany (19 percent at Mercedes Benz), 17 percent in England, and 25 percent in France and Belgium. In France, immigrant workers make up 35 percent of the construction and public works labor force, 18 percent of service and commerce, 15 percent of mining and material and 13 percent of the auto industry. Nevertheless, these countries seem to consider foreign laborers as negligible, and plans continue to repatriate these workers and their families.

Furthermore, hate crimes in Europe against Third World immigrants are on the rise. A young woman from Mali who entered a French police station to present her papers was searched and handled so roughly that her wrapped dress fell off, leaving her nearly naked while several male policemen taunted her. When a fifteen-year-old African boy had his front tooth smashed by the French police, the youth reported that one of the policemen had pushed him away when he bled, saying, "You probably have AIDS." In Germany, attacks on foreigners surpassed two thousand in 1992, versus less than one thousand in 1990. Seventeen foreigners were killed in 1992. Neo-Nazi computer games have been circulating in which Jews and Third World immigrants are hunted and killed. In Italy, Spain, and other EC countries, racial hate crimes have been on the rise as well.

In the case of women, legislation in EC nations calling for equal treatment in the workplace has specifically addressed the issues of pay, working conditions, employment and training, promotions, career guidance, and social security benefits. Although the EC has forced member nations to pass laws providing equal employment opportunities, some laws contain traces of sexism, and most possess no real sanctions; in many countries, they are ignored. European working women are often channeled into traditional female occupations, and few of them are in key line management positions.[12] If they are in such positions, it is usually at the lower levels. In a few EC countries, some service sectors virtually exclude women. The Banco (Bank) Commercial Portuguese (BCP), for example, employs only seven women out of a total of one thousand seven hundred employees. Until recently, English women were refused admission to certain departments of the military School for Officers, and English men were not permitted to enroll in training courses offered by the military School of Nursing for Officers. Italian women constitute 34 percent of the working population, but hold only 3.3 percent of executive posts. Sixty percent of Greek working women are employed in the public sector; however, they hold only 11 percent of high-level positions.

For the EC to be competitive in the global marketplace of the 1990s, its member states must put aside their nationalistic, ethnocentric, and racist attitudes. They must recognize the demographic problems created by lower birthrates and an aging population. They must see their women as full, equal partners in all aspects of their societies.

United States

The United States is ethnically a very diverse nation. By the year 2040, one-half of the U.S. population will be African American, Hispanic/Latino American, Native American, and/or Asian American. Women will fill 65 percent of the new jobs created during the 1990s; by the year 2000, nearly one-half of civilian workers will be female.

It is apparent that the United States has considerable diversity problems related to different race/ethnic groups. Minorities represent almost three in ten persons in the U.S. population, but few people of color have made it to the middle and upper ranks of corporate America. Only about 8 percent of middle-level managers and less than 2 percent of upper-level managers were people of color in the 15 major corporations we have studied. In professional sports, an area where African Americans have supposedly excelled, African Americans represent 72 percent of the basketball players but only 11 percent of the head coaches; in football, they are 60 percent of the players but only 7 percent of the head coaches; and in baseball they represent 18 percent of the players and 8 percent of the managers (despite the fact that African Americans have been playing in the league for more than forty years).[13] Although only 8.8 percent of white Americans lived below the poverty level in 1989, 28 percent of African Americans and 23.3 percent of Hispanic/Latinos were below that level. In fact, African Americans showed little improvement in this regard from 1974, when 28.6 percent were below the poverty level, and Hispanic/Latinos actually lost ground, as 21.9 percent were below poverty level in 1974.[14] In 1989, 21.6 percent of all whites had less than twelve years of education, compared to 35.4 percent of African Americans and 49.1 percent of Hispanic/Latinos.[15] Currently, African Americans and whites of high school age are completing high school at the same rate, although Hispanics still lag far behind. In terms of income, the 1989 median income for white households was $31,435, whereas that for all nonwhite households was $22,813: $36,784 for Asian households; $24,156 for Hispanic/Latino households; $20,025 for Native American, Eskimo, and Aleut households; and $19,758 for African American households.[16] Thus, African Americans and other people of color (with the exception of some Asian groups) have far to go before achieving financial and educational equality.

In an April 1992 poll, 53.7 percent of African Americans said that racism in America was about as common as it was ten or twenty years earlier.[17] Fifty-seven percent of African Americans in another 1992 poll said race relations in the United States were generally bad. Still another poll that year asked youths aged fifteen to twenty-four for a response to the statement "Racial and ethnic discrimination was a problem in the past, but isn't a problem anymore." Only 16 percent of young African Americans strongly agreed, and 21 percent somewhat agreed; 11 percent of white youths agreed strongly, and 27 percent agreed somewhat; and 8 percent of Hispanic youths agreed strongly, and 28 percent agreed somewhat. The numbers agreeing with the statement never added up to more than 38 percent for any group—not even close to a majority. Clearly, young people perceive that discrimination is still a problem.[18]

Asian Americans, although possessing the highest median income of any minority and although having the most positive image with white Americans, are victims of jealousy and prejudice as their numbers increase and "mainstream" Americans perceive that Asians are taking their jobs. Members of all Asian groups also have been victimized by attacks spurred by anti-Japanese sentiments.

People of color in America must also come to terms with their biases toward other people of color and toward whites. These prejudicial attitudes are apparent in the following quotes from participants in our workshops:

[I need] to overcome the fear I have when I walk in the African American community. (Asian/Hindu, middle-level, male)

When I see an African American person, I feel they are less likely to be intelligent and serious about work. (Hispanic, middle-level, male)

Have some problems with Asian males. I have been affected by having an insensitive, biased [against blacks and Asian females] manager. I now feel I have to work harder when a male Asian is on the team to prove that I belong. (African American, lower-level, female)

Attitudes such as these have contributed to misunderstanding and, ultimately, violent behavior between groups. In Philadelphia, Los Angeles, Chicago, and New York, African Americans and Hispanics have attacked Korean store owners; other Asian Americans have been attacked and reviled by African Americans, Hispanics, and whites primarily for no reason other than their Asian origins. There have been increasing trends of interracial violence involving African Americans and Hispanics, including the highly publicized brutal attack on a Central Park jogger, a white woman, by a gang of young men of color. Asian gangs have also attacked African Americans and Hispanics for intruding on their "territory." These incidents illustrate the hostility people of color, especially those who are poor, feel toward other ethnic groups; however, such violent attacks are counterproductive and inexcusable.

Hispanic/Latino Americans also hold discriminatory stereotypes of the disparate ethnic groups within their own umbrella group.

> Cubans and Puerto Ricans come to California and try to take over. Mexicans have been here for centuries. (Hispanic, occupational [non-management], male)

> Puerto Ricans need to get educated and work hard like us Cubans. They have a lot of advantages but don't use them. (Hispanic, middle-level, male)

Lumping together such diverse groups as Argentines, Chileans, Costa Ricans, Cubans, Dominicans, Mexicans, Puerto Ricans, and Spanish as one is contravening reality as these people themselves perceive it. Some of the Hispanic respondents in our studies and seminars had serious objections to considering themselves members of a minority or as people of color.

U.S. women in 1992 made only 72 cents for every dollar earned by a man; at their current pace, women will not reach pay parity with men until 2017. In fact, American women with college degrees are earning roughly the same amount as men with only high school degrees. The U.S. Labor Department's report on "glass ceilings," released in the spring of 1992, revealed that such ceilings were much more prevalent and lower than had been thought. The report concluded that its original directive to concentrate its analysis on the executive suite and highest levels of management was irrelevant, because there were few if any women at these levels. Another report found that fewer than 0.5 percent of the highest-paid officers and directors of the top one thousand U.S. companies are women. Only 2.6 percent of executive positions (vice president and up) at Fortune 500 companies are held by women. Women have made virtually no gains in the upper echelons of management since the early 1970s; men held 99 percent of senior management positions then, and still hold more than 97 percent now. The fact that women can receive less pay and advancement even when they are more educated and experienced than men exposes as a fallacy the rhetoric that women are not getting ahead because they have yet to accumulate enough experience and education.

The percentage of children in two-parent families with both parents working outside the home grew from 29 percent in 1970 to 61 percent in 1990. In 1991, almost 25 percent of all children were born to single women. As a result, some corporations are increasingly responding to the needs of working mothers, and state governments have been commended for their implementation of such family-friendly policies as on-site day care centers, flextime, and family leave. Such policies are the exception rather than the rule, however, and are seen by some as light years ahead of those of many private-sector organizations. When the Families and Work Institute surveyed 188 firms to determine the level of family-friendly policies employed by the companies, only four companies scored marginally well, with scores hovering around 179 points out of a possible 610. The average score was 68 points.[19]

Despite the gloomy picture just described, the United States internationally is in the forefront of awareness on issues of race and gender. Because of its expertise with immigrants, racial minorities, religious minorities, and women, the United States is better positioned to accept the aged, the disabled, and those with various sexual orientations and create the world's most competitive and dominant economic power. Also, women, minorities, and foreign nationals have risen higher and in greater numbers in U.S. corporations (in the United States and overseas) than in Japan and Europe.

Nevertheless, the United States must take the next step. Although it possesses the best laws in the world to protect the rights of all citizens, it must now move from the philosophical and legal to the proactive and personal. U.S. citizens must, in short, walk their talk. Each individual must recognize that he or she is part of both the problem and the solution to diversity problems negatively affecting our competitiveness. In the corporate world, this means linking managing diversity to team building and quality efforts. We believe that managing diversity (in other words, getting groups of diverse people to form high-performance quality-oriented teams) is not only right but smart.

Without total acceptance of diversity and a business plan that completely integrates it into corporate strategic plans, a corporation cannot succeed in the global market. In this book, we will present more extensive details of the situations in Japan, the European Community, and the United States regarding women, people of color, and immigrants as they relate to labor, business, and economics to give the reader a comprehensive overview of each economic power's situation. Most importantly, we will provide our formula for achieving a completely productive work force—one that merges the three tenets of managing diversity, team building, and total quality management. Despite the fact that this is a corporate strategy, it meticulously deals with diversity on the personal level: corporations are made up of people, and it is their attitudes, opinions, and biases that shape both corporate and community culture. Therefore, people are the most important bottom-line cost for an organization. To be competitive, companies must seriously concentrate in both the short and long term on developing value systems and human resource practices that respect the people upon whom their success depends—and in the future, those people and the customer base are going to grow increasingly more diverse.

In short, only by embracing diversity as a part of national and international policy can a country or common market survive economically and politically. Only by each individual embracing diversity on a personal level can communities survive. And only by integrating diversity into team building and quality efforts can corporations likewise survive. This book will not only detail the problems posed by diversification on community, corporate, and global levels but will provide definite and solid solutions to those difficulties.

2

Racism, Sexism, Ethnocentrism, and Xenophobia

In order to understand the problems that race, gender, and ethnicity will create for the three major economic powers, it is important to understand racism, ethnocentrism, sexism, and xenophobia. These are four of the most powerful forces influencing the ability of societies to have efficient, competitive economies.

Most of us are socialized to have some degree of discomfort with people who are different than we are. Comprehensive data throughout this book demonstrate that these beliefs exist in all three economic powers and in all facets of their populations' lives, and that presumably rational, objective people harbor a large supply of stereotypes and dislikes about those who are different. Women, people of color, and minority ethnics have painfully unique problems in trying to become full and equal members of the societies in which they live and/or the corporations in which they work. There is some evidence that white males in Japanese companies are suffering discrimination, and that European companies discriminate against Americans. The latter also seems to be true for European men in American companies (but to a lesser degree). In addition, it is clear that male European managers have better advancement opportunities in companies of their own national origin than in companies owned by other European nations. The negative impact of these beliefs on a society and its corporations is evident throughout the chapters which discuss women and the major race/ethnic groups in America, Europe and Japan.

Definitions and Problems

We define *racism, sexism,* and *ethnocentrism* as cultural ideologies that define males and specific ethnic groups as inherently superior to women and other specific ethnic groups (e.g., Koreans in Japan) solely based on their race, gender, or ethnic origins. Whites, men, and usually (but not necessarily) dominant ethnic majorities wield the power in societal institutions to develop, spread, and enforce the very myths and stereotypes that are the basic foundations of these hostile negative beliefs, in the minds of not only the oppressors but also many of the oppressed. These myths and stereotypes are used to maintain and justify the oppressor's dominant social, economic, and political positions. They are deeply rooted in the very structure and fabric of different societies. They are not solely a matter of personal attitudes and beliefs. Indeed, it can be argued that these negative beliefs are but accessory expressions of institutionalized patterns of power and social control.

Underlying these beliefs are power struggles between the dominant groups, who seek to maintain privileged positions in society, and the out-of-power groups, who are determined to change the status quo. Even while they control society's major institutions, the oppressors have a great fear of losing their hegemony. This drives them, consciously or unconsciously, to nurture myths and stereotypes about the oppressed in order to preserve the status quo, much in the manner that Machiavelli and other astute observers of society noted hundreds of years ago.

We suggest that racism, sexism, and extreme ethnocentrism are defensive adjustment mechanisms used by whites, males, and other in-power groups to deal with psychological and social insecurities and anxieties. They are psychological disorders that more often afflict those who are interested in preserving systems than those interested in tearing them down. Too often, though, the oppressed groups also use these beliefs and stereotypes to relive their psychological stress. By accepting and internalizing racist, sexist, and ethnocentric assumptions, the oppressed groups can explain and justify their subordinate societal position.

The origins of *xenophobia* are similar, although "hostility to foreigners should be understood not primarily as a personality characteristic, but rather as a social and political 'tidal current' whose ebb and flow can be influenced politically and limited by the action of social groups and governmental authorities and their definitions of violence."[1] While racism, sexism, and extreme ethnocentrism fragment groups within a nation, xenophobia can bind a country's major ethnic groups together through fear and hatred of all things foreign. For example, young German men (especially the economically disadvantaged) have come together to attack violently all foreigners and foreign ideas, including not only nonwhites but also many white immigrants from Yugoslavia and other eastern European countries.

Xenophobia contributes to nationalism and to the philosophy of isolationism. Xenophobia's nature in Japan and the European Community has not been greatly modified as sexism, racism and ethnocentrism have in the United States. Instead, it continues to inspire and justify bloody ethnic and religious struggles and unfair immigration laws, as it always has. The failure of the EC's proposed unhindered border passage between member nations, the increase of violence among ethnic groups in what was formerly Yugoslavia, and growing hatred toward foreign immigrants, especially in Germany, indicates that xenophobia is on the rise in Europe.

The degree and extent of xenophobia in a country often parallels its economic and social status. As of the first half of 1993, many countries' economies are in severe states of recession. Traditional social networks are breaking down, and the nature of many cultures is changing. Instead of accepting and adapting to this change, many cultures look for a scapegoat; foreigners conveniently fill this role. A society convinces itself that the foreigners and the alien culture are what is destroying the old order, and its people respond with hatred and violence.

Opportunistic politicians and the lack of strong moral leadership have fanned the latent fires of xenophobia in Europe as well as in Japan. Wilhelm Heitmeyer believes that many Europeans are susceptible to these trends because of increases in freedom and mobility and a decrease in family ties and class structures:

The individual today not only can, he also must increasingly shape his life by himself; in the final analysis, it is he alone who must bear the risks of failure. Anxiety caused by the risk of failure and isolation as consequences of harsher individual competition are major sources for feelings of estrangement. . . . Experience of powerlessness can be traced back to the individual's overpowering competitive experiences that threaten his social status and subject the isolated individual to the experience of "the strongest always wins." Since powerlessness narrows an individual's alternatives, violence can become a subjectively meaningful means (or even an end in itself), for it creates clarity in unclear situations.[2]

In addition to overt negative hostile beliefs (which are minimal in American society, but more evident in Japan and Europe) are the covert forms of these beliefs; they are rampant in all societal organizations regardless of country. It is these subtle forms that are the greatest hindrances to competitiveness in each of the economic powers.

Neoracism, Neosexism, and Neoethnocentrism

As the consciousness of Americans, Europeans, and Japanese has been raised (Europeans to a more limited extent than Americans, and Japanese to an even more limited extent than Europeans), increasing numbers of people have grown to oppose overt racism, sexism, and ethnocentrism—not eliminating the latter feelings but just modifying them to be more palatable to others and to themselves. The modified forms are in most cases subtler and more sophisticated than their predecessors, but we believe they are just as harmful. For our purposes, we will label them *neoracism, neosexism,* and *neoethnocentrism.* (Note that by definition, xenophobia is always overt.)

An example of neoracism and neosexism is the lack of social mobility of many people of color, ethnic minorities, and women. Though our data show racism, sexism, and ethnocentrism to be the key factors in the lack of mobility, the dominant-group bureaucracy will cite lack of experience, of numerous opportunities, of political skills, or of cultural compatibility (an excuse that many Japanese and some Europeans use frequently). They will say the people of color, women, or subordinate ethnic group members' attitudes are not the right ones for higher levels: the latter have to polish their image, improve their style, or "smooth out the rough edges."

The new sensitivity to sexual harassment is another example of neosexism. Some male employees find the more subtle forms of sexual harassment to be indistinguishable from acceptable male behavior. Instead of changing their behavior, these males simply avoid dealing with female coworkers by "unintentionally" excluding them from formal and informal groups related to work and social activities. Women therefore suffer from exclusion from these groups, which are important for career advancement.

Britain and Denmark's lack of desire for a stronger European monetary and political union are examples of neoethnocentrism. Another example is the arguments for and against German becoming the third official language of the EC. They are based not on necessity, (that is, usefulness and cost), but on the fact that many French and English dislike and fear the German nation.

Many Japanese companies also display characteristics of neoethnocentrism. For example, non-Japanese Asian managers face exclusion from the inner circles of many Japanese companies that limit access to important executive positions. These actions are usually explained in terms of the non-Japanese needing more skills and experience. In reality, however, only Japanese employees will be considered for these positions, because these companies believe that no other group can be trusted with the sensitive information to which the positions give access.

Institutional Racism, Sexism, and Ethnocentrism

Inertia, the reluctance to change, tends to pervade bureaucracies. Their rate of change is naturally slower than that of the individuals who make up the organizations or the groups of individuals who maintain them. Bureaucracies tend to captivate these groups and use them in a way that defies individual influence (that is, they become systems or entities somewhat apart from the people whom they serve). Institutional racism, sexism, and ethnocentrism are based on these systems.

Institutional beliefs are bureaucratic regulations, policies, and practices that in and of themselves exclude people who are different. They were established in times in the United States, Japan, and Europe when discrimination was more acceptable. Even though they were not established to do so, they provide a mechanism for discrimination.

The corporate "old boy" network graphically illustrates a bureaucratic system of institutionalized sexism, racism, and ethnocentrism that remains functional today. Historically the old-boy network was used to find and select candidates for higher-level public and private jobs. Since the network in America was primarily white, middle-class,

Protestant, and male, when used as a recruitment tool and/or a source of talent for promotion, it unintentionally excluded people who did not fit those characteristics. Currently the old-boy network remains functional at higher management levels; upper management remains predominately white and male even in companies with a good mix of minorities and females at lower levels. Japan's old-boy network is much more overtly ethnocentric; indeed, many Japanese men openly argue the merits of helping all Japanese males over other race and gender groups. European countries' networks are white and male, but depending on the country, the network can be primarily one ethnic/religious/linguistic group or another.

The continued lack of women in nontraditional jobs illustrates still another example of institutional sexism. In many situations, there still exist stereotypical beliefs that women cannot do "men's" work and that women are much better off in staff jobs than line jobs. It will be seen throughout the chapters of this book on women in the three economic powers that they are placed and steered institutionally into traditionally "female" jobs. This is very much the case in Japan, less so in EC countries, and least of all in the United States; but even in the United States, where the situation is the most equitable for women, the problem is still chronic.

Development of Attitudes and Behaviors

A discussion of how people develop these negative attitudes can be instructive in discovering methods to solve these issues.[3] Racism, sexism, ethnocentrism, and xenophobia are developed and nurtured by all societal institutions controlled by the dominant group. Babies begin life with a sense of kinship to all human beings regardless of race, gender, skin color, ethnic origins, language skills, and so on. Most infants and very young children are open, loving, and comfortable with people who show them love, attention, and caring. But children can also learn racist, sexist, ethnocentric, and xenophobic attitudes and behaviors at an early age. Families, schools, churches, government, the media, and other social groups and institutions socialize the population by communicating what is good behavior and what is bad. They teach us what to expect of ourselves, our friends, and our families; in short, they teach us how to relate to society.

As a result of their socialization, children learn how to be people of color or whites, Basque or Catalonian, Japanese or Koreans, men or women, or Nazis or Democrats. They acquire a sense of the worth of their social group and of themselves during their earliest contact with other members of their family, their peers, and their teachers; from what they read; from conversations they overhear; and from their daily observations. T. F. Pettigrew, a leading psychologist on racial prejudices, makes some relevant comments that can also apply to sexism, ethnocentrism, and xenophobia: "The emotions of racism are formed in childhood, while the beliefs that are used to justify them come later. Later in life, you may want to change your 'isms,' but it is far easier to change your intellectual beliefs than your deep feelings."[4] An example of what Pettigrew is saying is that many whites can change their intellectual beliefs that African Americans are intellectually inferior to whites and thus perceive them as equals; however, many often react somewhere between slight discomfort and violence when their children choose to marry one. An example related to sexism is when men say they believe women should be treated fairly in their companies, but either have negative reactions when they have a female supervisor or oppose corporate efforts to assist employees with child care problems. (Our research studies over the years indicate that women are still the primary child care providers.) An example of ethnocentrism is when Japanese companies come to the United States to open a factory with reservations about American workers, but sincerely believing that the Japanese management style will be totally accepted. When American workers begin to express their individuality, some Japanese managers began to feel angry that these "inferior" Americans are not behaving well. Finally, an example of xenophobia is that natives of many European Community countries often recognize their dependence on foreign labor, especially for the menial labor that others find unattractive, and yet have a deep hatred for immigrants and blame increased crime and poverty on them.

Language and Language Conflicts

A great deal of ethnocentrism is centered around language. As the reader shall see, language issues are becoming a considerable source of conflict and inefficiency in the increasingly diverse work forces throughout the world. Language lies at the very heart of culture, as its first and most obvious artifact. It not only includes the names of things and of people and describes their movements in space and time, but makes possible the abstractions that govern people's behavior and their beliefs, values, and attitudes. It is those abstractions (like friendship, loyalty, trust, permanence, and quality) that make business possible within any culture. To go global means to be able to find common understanding of what those abstractions mean in other languages and other cultures. A leading international consultant writes that "the way executives use language acts as either the grease that slides this adaption into place or the grit that keeps it from fitting. The global executive is, if anything at all, a global communicator, using spoken language, written language, and nonverbal communications to the advantage of his or her business."[5]

As countries form economic trading blocs and as corporations become more global through expansions and acquisitions, work forces will move more readily from one country to another. As plants move from one country to another for cost and other economic reasons, and as countries require foreign firms to establish plants on their soil in order to do business, the issue of accepting and understanding different languages becomes critical to corporate success.

In our seminars over the past five years with more than ten thousand employees, many born outside the United States, the most frequent problems they indicated having with people different from themselves were in the language and cultural areas. Sixty-seven percent of the employees we surveyed in 1988 were bothered when they heard other employees speak in a language they did not understand; in a study we conducted in 1993, the figure was 60 percent.

We have noticed that many Americans like the sound of a French accent, thinking it is beautiful. Likewise, they find the English accent aristocratic, and the German accent elegant. Many of these same people, however, complain that Spanish accents do not have nice tones, and that Asian accents are too harsh and too hard to understand. As a white, female lower-level manager said, "I have problems tolerating foreign accents. I tend to enjoy an English accent, but dislike Spanish accents."

The constant battle between the Germans, French, and English over German becoming a third official language of the EC and the division between French- and Dutch-speaking residents of Belgium indicate that language is an issue in Europe as well as the United States. In Japan, it is very clear that Japanese is the official language. This creates problems because of the difficulties of non-Japanese in learning the language and the fact that in Japanese companies based outside the country, Japanese frequently speak in their own language despite their knowledge of the host country's language.

The following comments reflect a range of reactions from hostility toward people who speak foreign languages to legitimate concerns about the problems of working effectively with people to whom English is a second language. We should note that 70 percent of the employees who speak English as a second language in our studies are from Asian countries; we believe this fact leads to the significant negative reactions from Americans.

> I tend to be apprehensive when dealing with people with a foreign accent. This is due to (1) the inability to clearly understand what they are saying and (2) having doubts about them actually saying what they mean. (African American, lower-level, female)

> I have a problem with severe foreign accents. I believe if a person chooses to live and work in this country, they should make the effort to speak the language fluently. (white, middle-level, female)

> The major problem is that in language. I sometimes emphasize that everyone in the U.S. should speak English since that is our recognized language. I have encountered situations where I have not helped or been patient with non-English speaking people because of my bias. (white, middle-level, male)

> I have a real hang-up with people who do not speak English. I have enough problems dealing with people, without having to be subjected to the misunderstandings that this causes. "When in Rome, do as the Romans do"!! (white, lower-level, female)

> I lose patience with people who speak very slowly. (Asian, middle-level, female)

> One issue would be dealing with people that have a heavy accent. Sometimes I tend to lose interest in what they're saying and drift off. [I find myself] making excuses or not including certain people in out-of-work functions, unintentionally, by just saying "they wouldn't be interested in that." (white, middle-level, female)

My most important issue is accepting a language barrier. I know I avoid people I have a difficult time talking to or understanding. There are signs in Spanish; I don't know why they won't learn English. (Hispanic/Latino, occupational, female)

I don't so much mind employees who speak in a language I do not understand, but the loudness of these conversations becomes annoying. (African American, lower-level, male)

I have problems, sometimes, with foreign accents, sometimes due to my hearing. It bothers me sometimes when people speak in foreign languages in public situations. It is like whispering if someone seems impolite. (white, lower-level, male)

I have problems and feel when I talk with Asians on the telephone I can't communicate with them. (Hispanic/Latino, occupational, male)

A corporation will be less competitive if employees avoid or discount the input of employees who have accents. No society can be competitive in a global marketplace if it becomes intolerant of people speaking a foreign tongue and/or if the society's people are so ethnocentric that they are reluctant to learn additional languages or to speak these languages when it is appropriate.

In the United States, the vast majority of the population speaks English fluently or at least has some working knowledge of the language. In the interest of basic practicality, immigrants and other residents who speak foreign languages use English when imparting most public information. There are large segments of some states and especially some cities, however, in which the use of foreign language is the normal way to conduct business and personal affairs. For example, Florida's Dade County possesses a large Spanish-speaking community, as does New York City. Health services, driver's guides, and voting instructions in these areas are printed in both English and Spanish. No one in the 1990s would argue that the United States should use a language other than English as the primary mode of communication; however, we believe that important signs, materials, and public information should be printed in several languages to make their messages clear to everyone (as has been done in Dade County, in New York City, and on airlines throughout the EC). In certain situations and communities, speaking in a foreign language is much more productive for business purposes than speaking in your native tongue. For example, President John Kennedy captured the German people's hearts when he began a speech in broken German.

People can miscommunicate even when they speak the same language:

> Even English speaking countries don't speak American. One American banker was asked to be an after-dinner speaker in Australia. He blundered in his first sentence, when he said he was "full." When he heard the nervous laughter, he changed that to say he was "stuffed." In Australia, "full" means "drunk" and "stuffed" means being on the receiving end, so to speak, of sexual intercourse.[6]

New statutes in the United States seeking to limit all public discourse to English have nothing to do with the mere practicality of English use; they have more to do with U.S. fear of foreigners taking over the country. Many forget that not long ago their ancestors arrived in America speaking their own native tongues. Visitors to the United States are expected to enter the country equipped with a full knowledge of English, yet interestingly, many Americans visit other countries (Mexico, for example) and expect to hear and speak English. This extreme ethnocentrism is dangerous, given the emerging global marketplace. With more rapid modes of transportation being developed and business deals being cut globally, Americans will increasingly find themselves in other countries and will find more foreigners in the United States. Therefore, they should not only get used to hearing languages other than English but actually learn these languages and become familiar with other cultures in order to maintain a competitive edge. In short, to be successful in the global village, one should adopt this dictum: "The language of business is your customer's language, whatever it is."[7] The EC, recognizing the importance of language to its success, has developed numerous programs to make school-aged students and other citizens (especially in corporations) multilingual.

Despite these efforts and the fact that many more Europeans are multilingual than are their counterparts in the United States, in Chapters 6 through 9 we will demonstrate that ethnocentrism regarding language is playing a crucial role in some of the conflicts that limit the EC's ability to function effectively. Also, as will be discussed in Chapter 5, Japan until recently banned the use of the Korean language for Koreans living in Japan, despite the fact that many of these families have resided there for generations.

Of the three major economic forces that will be competing in the 1990s, Japan and Europe have an advantage over the United States because much higher percentages of European and Japanese children learn other languages (often English) early in their school years than do American children. They also study languages for more than just one or two years. Many U.S. students cannot speak, read, or write any foreign language correctly, regardless of their national origin or native language. In order to balance these differences and make the playing field more level, the United States could utilize its large number of first- and second-generation immigrants who are fluent in both their native tongue and English. One problem that must be overcome is corporate America's reluctance to accept and make full use of these foreigners, especially those from Third World countries. The Europeans and the Japanese are dealing with even more intense ethnocentrism; all three economic powers should adopt strategies to make their populations multilingual.

Different Cultures

Human culture, for our purposes, can be defined as the product of learning, particularly that resulting from experiences with people and institutions. Societies determine their cultures by developing workable solutions to the problems of living in their indigenous environments. For example, a society's culture—its family patterns, social strata, religion(s), political system, clothing, music, and laws—is determined by geography, climate, language, history, and neighboring cultures. Within cultural groups, individuals develop values; values held by the majority of the group are called norms. An understanding of these aspects of individual and group cultures can help diverse peoples to deal more constructively with each other.

When one discusses the concept of a truly diverse work force, there are numerous cultural issues that must be raised. "Accepting diversity" means much more than being able to look at another employee whose race, ethnicity, or gender differs from your own and feel comfortable. It can mean listening to an accent or to speech in a different language. It can also mean accepting people who dress differently and eat differently. Culture manifests itself not only in language, clothing, and food but in literature, music, art, architecture, and religion, among other things.

Perhaps a more difficult aspect of accepting diversity is learning to value and respect different cultural styles and morality norms. For instance, body movement varies in different cultures and relates different messages. Americans generally greet each other with a hearty handshake, whereas Japanese bow respectfully. Most Americans find public kissing distasteful while the French, both men and women, warmly meet each other with a series of pecks on the cheek. European companies with businesses located in the United States often make the assumption that their American employees have European ancestry and, therefore, will share a similar culture. Conversely, the American employees assume that businesspeople from European companies will speak English fluently—which can be true, but even if the company uses correct pronunciation and grammar, the connotations of the words in European culture may differ from those in American culture. These assumptions lead to miscommunication. In a survey conducted by Lamalie Associates, 60 percent of the 242 American executives interviewed responded that there was mutual misunderstanding between themselves and their foreign employees. Their responses when asked about the disadvantages of working for foreign companies are listed in Table 2–1.

Unless one understands different cultural norms and values, actions and behaviors will be misunderstood, which can greatly inhibit cor-

TABLE 2–1

Disadvantages Working for Foreign Companies

Difference in culture/lack of understanding of U.S. culture	35%
Turf problems/differences in organizational structures	35%
Lack of understanding of U.S. markets and business practices	29%
Communication/language	26%
Lack of career growth potential	14%
Compensation policies and control/lack of incentives	12%
Slower and more difficult decision-making processes	12%
Increased reporting	9%
Distance from management	8%
Travel	6%

porate competitiveness. Over the past twenty years we have conducted numerous surveys on diversity and other corporate human resource issues; the comments we are about to discuss come from surveys conducted between 1988 and 1993. Although participants in our surveys were never asked specifically about foreign culture, their responses paint a picture of conflict and intolerance in such areas as hygiene, dress, food, religious holidays, praise, eye contact, modesty, and aggressiveness. The two questions the following comments were in response to are as follows:

> Some people believe that in our society, everyone is socialized into exhibiting one or more of the following: sexism, racism, ageism, ethnocentrism, intolerance of foreign accents, other religions, sexual orientation, and so on. What do you believe are the most important issues that you must deal with about your own reactions to people who are different than you? Put another way, what problems do you have in accepting and dealing with people who are different than you?

> What are the major diversity issues you believe you must deal with in the work environment because of your age, gender, race, religion, native language, sexual orientation, family characteristics (child/elder care responsibilities), and/or physical and mental limitations, and so on?

The comments suggest a host of potential problems that U.S. managers must learn to recognize and solve.

> I feel people from foreign countries should learn to speak our language better. I have a hard time understanding them. Understanding their religions and life-styles. (white, occupational, female)

> Inability to "warm up" to culturally different people—not being myself—walking on eggs to avoid offending others in the belief that they are super-sensitive, or I am insensitive. (white, lower-level, male)

> Uncomfortable around Orientals, Indians, etc., because I don't speak their language or culture. I feel I may offend them because I don't understand them, especially if they are not very friendly. I find it hard to carry on a conversation even though I want to. (white, middle-level, female)

Whites don't understand the reasons for pluralism efforts and don't want to; they are too damn arrogant. It would help them understand themselves and their feelings toward pluralism. (Hispanic/Latino, lower-level, female)

I feel more intimidated by the white males than other groups. I'm more willing to take leadership roles [and] speak up in groups with fewer white males. (Asian Indian, lower-level, female)

Certain ethnic groups [Asians] tend to stick together more so than others, thus shutting out other people. (Hispanic, occupational, male)

Instinctive prejudice against Asians and/or Persians because of hygiene and language barriers. (white, middle-level, male)

Conservative personality, unwilling to advertise ourselves, lack of social skills. (Asian, middle-level, male)

I accept relationships among races for other people, but I couldn't marry a black man. (white, middle-level, female)

How would I deal with my children marrying a different race? How would I respond to a black or female supervisor? These are problems for me. (white, upper-level, male)

I can have an uncomfortable feeling among people who are different in any way when white males are in the minorities. (white, occupational, male)

My attitude toward women. My dislike about Japanese. My opinion about certain people after some interactions will hold fast. (Asian Indian, middle-level, male)

I sometimes prejudge people when they are quiet and nonaggressive, at first, and conclude they are not going to be as competent as others who sound off more. This tends to occur much more with women and Asians. (white, lower-level, male)

I have no background living or growing up in, say, a black family or Hindu society and have preconceived ideas based on my culture, family, etc. that I use daily. I usually don't question these. (white, occupational, male)

White men seem to be given more responsibilities and are expected to perform better. This may trigger stress on individuals who are not that capable. This may cause a lot of alcoholism, which is prevalent in white male managers. (Asian, occupational, female)

We should send all the "spics" back where they come from. Now they want all signs in Spanish. What next, they want my wife? (white, occupational, male)

Notice that no one specific race, gender, or corporate level has a monopoly on having difficulties with different cultures.

Conclusion

In this chapter we defined racism, sexism, ethnocentrism, and xenophobia. The fact that individuals in every society are socialized from birth into certain negative beliefs becomes evident from our definition. These negative beliefs are often promoted by the group in power to continue dominance over such segments of society as women, racial minorities, smaller ethnic groups, and foreign immigrants. Individuals also retain these beliefs (and often exhibit them in acts of violence) because of personal fears and insecurities. We also discussed the newer, subtler forms of racism, sexism, and ethnocentrism that have emerged in societies now familiar with the language of discrimination; instead of tackling and destroying problems of discrimination, those in power have decided to sidestep the issue by creating less blatant forms of bias. We further covered the institutionalization of racism, sexism and ethnocentrism, discussing how bureaucracy has claimed these beliefs as an inseparable part of its workings. Long after the ideas of the people making up a bureaucracy become enlightened, the old practices, policies, and procedures remain so entrenched that many years of effort are necessary to obliterate them.

In this chapter we also discussed the fact that language is the basis of culture and of how people define themselves. Global company employees must not only deal with their racism, sexism, ethnocentrism, and xenophobia but become more tolerant and better listeners. All must work on elements of their cultural backgrounds that are racist, sexist, ethnocentric, and xenophobic. They must recognize that negative behaviors toward people who are different can influence their own effectiveness, as well as their company's effectiveness in being competitive internally with workers and externally with customers, influencers, and stakeholders.

In the global marketplace, people must become multilingual and learn to understand and appreciate different races, ethnic groups, genders, cultures, religions, languages, and so forth. It is important to remember that although there are many cultural differences among peoples, there are also cultural similarities, and ultimately we are all members of the human race.

3

Putting Japan in Perspective

As we work with numerous small, medium, and large companies in the United States and overseas, we are continually amazed at the positive and negative stereotypes about the Japanese business structures, society, and people. This chapter will provide some information to put the Japanese in a more realistic perspective. This in turn will assist the reader in understanding how the Japanese social and economic systems will affect the country's ability to understand and value increasingly diverse work forces and customer bases. What will become clear in the next three chapters is that for Japan to survive as an economic power, it must figure out how it will deal with falling birthrates and a rapidly aging population. It must find ways to deal with its xenophobia, ethnocentrism, racism, and sexism in order to utilize diverse workplaces effectively, both domestically and internationally. The Ministry of Health and Welfare indicates that Japan's population will peak at 130 million in 2011 and decline to 70 million by 2090 if the fertility rate drops as far as is expected. Where will it find the workers and customers to fuel its economic machine?

Japanese Business Practices

We are frequently asked, by Americans in our diversity learning classes and by leaders of major corporations, why diversity is so important. The Japanese are extremely successful with their ethnic homogeneity, many of these questioners note, and they certainly do not utilize their women in the workplace. In order to understand how Japan has been so successful despite its very inefficient manner in utilizing 50 percent of its population domestically and many foreign employees in its international operations, one must have some sense of Japan's business practices.[1]

Japanese business tactics are often called predatory or adversarial by their competitors. The Japanese say they are just practicing free trade, where the highest-quality and lowest-priced product wins. What is the truth of the matter? As in most cases, it is a little bit of both. Japan's brand of capitalism is different from Europe and the United States in five different ways: the extremely close alliance of business and government; the links between Japanese companies known as *keiretsu;* the Japanese strategy for developing products; the weak role of the Japanese shareholder; and the loyal and docile role of the Japanese worker. Some of these tenets of the Japanese way, however, have begun to erode.

The first tenet, close alliances between business and government, is in our mind a key to Japanese success. Whereas the U.S. and European governments subsidize some businesses directly or indirectly, the Japanese government has rigid bidding systems and oligopolistic and monopolistic practices. The Japanese government also subsidizes worker businesses through protective tariffs, low-interest loans, and a long-term commitment of billions of dollars to develop strategies and high-quality products that are priced appropriately to gain significant market share. This relationship is eroding because of the numerous scandals in Japan about shady financial deals and other unethical business practices involving some of Japan's top leaders in government and business. In addition, this alliance is being broken as foreign trading partners—particularly the United States and the European Community—pressure Japan to be "fair" and impose regulations akin to those used by developed nations in the West.

Japanese business is made formidable on the international market and impenetrable in the domestic market by a second key difference, the system known as keiretsu, in which Japanese companies form extensive, stable ties with other companies and plan long-term strategies. The U.S. business approach is, conversely, every company for itself, with most very focused on the short term; the U.S. government is pressuring Japan to break the keiretsu system.

Another reason for Japanese success is their completely different approach to product development: When developing new products, Americans develop the product, add up its cost, include overheads and profit, and thus arrive at their selling price. The Japanese, however, start with the price that allows them to gain the biggest market share and then develop a product that will match the cost. This practice depends, in part, on cutting such things as employee wages and shareholders dividends to keep the price of the product down, as well as on direct and indirect government subsidies. With an increasingly demanding work force, this process may not be as effective in the future. As a result of the economic slowdown, a shortage of cash, and the increasing cost for research, Japanese companies are seeking joint ventures or alliances with foreign companies to remain competitive; for example, IBM, Toshiba, and Germany's Siemens have formed an alliance to develop a new computer chip. These new alliances will require the Japanese to deal more with the issue of working with diverse people as equal partners rather than as subordinates to the Japanese economic juggernaut.

The fourth major difference, the weakness of Japanese shareholders, is evidenced by the fact that they have received around 30 percent of posttax corporate earnings, compared to 50 percent to 60 percent in the United States and Britain. After recent financial scandals in which large shareholders were given special treatment and had their losses covered, however, small shareholders are demanding higher percentage yields and fair treatment. The fifth key element, docile and loyal workers, is also going by the wayside as newer workers demand more freedom, pay, leisure, and comfort on the job.

In the 1980s, the Japanese ran a trade surplus of $533 billion. This shows no sign of decreasing in the 1990s, even in a world recession. One European executive has complained that "the Japanese should stop trying single-mindedly to produce the best goods at the cheapest prices to win the biggest market share." Surprisingly, perhaps, Japanese top executives like Akio Morita of Sony are agreeing. Morita admits that formerly Japan was interested in doing anything to gain market share, noting that a very small percentage of national income went to wages, and employees worked long hours. Morita has been joined in his call for a change by Jaishi Hiraiwa, the chairman of Keidanren, Japan's most powerful business federation. Like Morita, Hiraiwa has called for Japan's large companies to stop expanding their exports and increasing market share, asking that they instead raise shareholder profits and workers' living standards. Moreover, the increasing anger of foreign competitors who have been undercut and the increasing demands and irritation exhibited by Japanese workers dictate that Japan change its style to one of shorter working hours, higher wages, higher dividends, fewer products and longer product cycles. Whether Japanese industry truly adopts this new policy remains to be seen. Those who recognize and accommodate the new realities will have more satisfied and productive employees and will promote a better image for Japan among its competitors.

Despite successes, the 1990s worldwide recession has significantly affected all of Japan; even some of its largest and most successful companies have been feeling the squeeze. Yamaha, the world's largest musical instrument maker, has had such economic woes that its president, Hiroshi Kawakami, resigned in February 1992 after the company asked for the voluntary retirement of seven hundred workers (a move that provoked labor disputes). Japan's biggest carmaker, Toyota, reported a decrease in sales in the latter part of 1992, and 1993 sales were not much better.

The chiefs of Japanese companies in financial turmoil are feeling the pinch. CEOs of such giants as Hitachi, Fujitsu, IBM Japan, and Japan Airlines have been tripping over each other in an apparent contest to see who can absorb the deepest pay cut. Some are cutting their base pay by 35 percent or more. During the recession, the keiretsu companies have been trying to stay strong by forcing the prices of their suppliers down. One supplier to Nissan and Honda said his orders had dropped 10 percent and that his contract prices were down by 20 to 30 percent. Japan's 875,000 small manufacturing companies, which employ an average of ten employees, are powerless against the demands of large automakers to lower prices.[2]

Corporations are facing major restructuring. Isuzu dropped out of the auto marketing market in December 1992, and Daihatsu, which recently stopped exporting its minicars to the United States, may be taken over by Toyota. Consumer electronics firms such as Sansui and Iwatsu are also facing takeovers. And even those companies not facing takeovers are now recognizing that high financing costs are limiting their abilities.[3] Japan watchers say they will be interested to see how the nation reacts to this recession. An entire generation has been reared in "an era of steadily expanding Japanese prosperity and confidence." What profound psychological reaction could this first setback produce in the national psyche?[4]

A noted expert on Japan, Kenneth Courtis of Deutsche Bank in

Tokyo, purports that Japan will overtake the United States as the world's largest manufacturer by the mid-1990s and will surpass the United States shortly after the year 2000 as the world's largest economy. Courtis feels that, despite the recent recession, Japan will soon experience a new period of "explosive expansion" and that Japan's massive investment in upgrades and new equipment (25 percent of its GNP this decade, compared to 11 percent in the United States) will pay off royally. Robert Samuelson, however, argues that Japan cannot soon equal the U.S. economy. Japan's population (127 million) is about half that of the United States (253 million); therefore, for Japan's economy to surpass that of the United States, Japanese productivity would have to double U.S. productivity, and currently it only equals about 80 percent of the U.S. level.

We believe that Japan has some fundamental problems in terms of the people issues (especially regarding diversity) that must be resolved before it becomes the world's largest economy. To understand these problems, it is important to understand some aspects of Japanese culture.

Japanese Culture

Except for a brief period in the sixteenth and seventeenth centuries, Japan was an isolated, closed society until the 1850s. During this long isolation, Japanese religious tenets and various Japanese leaders installed a sense of superiority in the nation's people. The Japanese developed a very strong us-versus-them mentality. Since being forced to open their borders, the Japanese have maintained their sense of group superiority. The closed group has made many outsiders marvel at and praise Japan. In a survey done about the cultures of various societies, Japan rated highest in terms of group orientation.[5] As the reader will see in Chapter 5, this group-oriented culture has negatively influenced its ability to utilize and interact effectively with foreign employees both in Japan and in other countries.

The economic miracle in Japan has not benefited a considerable segment of Japanese society. The Japanese elite convinced common citizens to sacrifice for the nation, to work hard, and to help Japan be successful, promising that once Japan achieved that success all Japanese would benefit. As a result, more and more Japanese who have been "left out" are questioning such altruism. The dramatic rise in doubting the concept of sacrifice can also be attributed in part to the ten million Japanese who have traveled abroad. They have seen that in some ways the "degenerate" societies of the West have many more people benefiting more equitably from their economies than the Japanese. In Japan, the good jobs are found in only a few major cities, which many employees cannot live in because of the high costs. In contrast, in the United States, top job opportunities exist in dozens of cities with affordable living standards. Japanese citizens are beginning to understand that they are paying prohibitively high prices for goods because of extremely restrictive trade tariffs, a distribution system that is archaic, and price rigging that adds tremendous cost to goods. For example, the price of a Japanese camera in New York City is about $380, but the same camera in Japan would cost $550. Japanese beer is more than 40 percent more expensive in Japan than the United States. Japanese must pay five times higher prices for rice, the basic staple in their diet, than they would have to pay if Japan would allow its importation. A 1991 survey found that the most urgent problems the Japanese wanted their government to address were land and housing (32 percent) and the cost of living (29 percent).

This growing have-not class is beginning to understand that the limited amount of land tied in with government land policy, along with the rapid increase in home prices until the 1990s, has left many of them totally unable to buy homes. In Tokyo during the 1980s, a square meter of land cost $2,400. Housing in Tokyo as of 1992 cost seventeen times the annual pretax income of the average Japanese owner, compared to a ratio of five times for Western homeowners in houses twice the size.[6]

Home ownership in Japan has become nearly impossible, with some mortgages actually running ninety years. Seventy-one percent of Japanese believe the gap between those who own homes and/or land and those who do not will grow to become a major societal problem. And even beyond the housing crisis, Japan has serious problems. Because of the country's emphasis on producing goods for the outside world to consume and its mission to buy into other nations' economies, many internal Japanese infrastructure needs are going unmet. More than one out of two Japanese households remain unconnected to a municipal sewage system, and Japan has the lowest percentage of paved roads of any industrialized nation.

The Japanese have-not class has become increasingly aware that it is not true that 90 percent of them are middle class, as the Japanese press likes to claim. They recognize that only a small minority has really prospered because of the Japanese economic miracle. Many of them are becoming aware that Japan has sacrificed the welfare of its common folk in order to support the business of the elite, and that while many day laborers are no longer provided with insurance coverage, the upper middle class is buying more luxury imports than ever before.[7] A *Business Week* survey of 10,000 Japanese found the following sentiments:[8]

47 percent agreed that Japanese should review its economic structure

47 percent agreed with the U.S. position that Japan should open up its markets

57 percent believed changes in the above two areas would improve their quality of life and life style

60 percent believed Japan should open its doors to foreign rice

In addition to the social and economic conflicts between the haves and the have-nots, Saskia Sassen writes that Japan is suffering more and more from the social ills common in the United States, including homelessness, vandalism, crime, and urban decay. And the gap is widening between the haves and the have-nots; working- and middle-class Japanese are experiencing lower salaries and job insecurity. Sassen writes that because the wealth promised for hard work has not materialized, many Japanese have lost patience with the powers that be, resulting in "declining social cohesiveness." Sassen argues that the challenge for Japan (and the United States) is to make certain that economic growth involves the low income sectors of the population now excluded. Future national success can only be maintained if the entire population benefits from that success, and this includes not only Japanese men but also women and the slowly increasing numbers of immigrants.

Japanese Workers

The fractures that are becoming evident in Japanese society are becoming evident in the Japanese worker. The reader will find that many changes are taking place in traditional practices such as lifetime employment for Japanese men (there is no such thing for women and immigrants) and that workers are demanding more leisure, freedom, and comfort in return for their hard work. What we are about to discuss are the general traditions and practices in Japanese top-tier companies, which employ only about 30 percent of Japanese workers. These traditions apply almost exclusively to Japanese men; they do not apply to the 70 percent of the Japanese work force (not only Japanese men, but also many more women and immigrants) who work for small or medium-sized companies.

In Japan, loyalty to the company has been a strong tradition. This loyalty is said to come from the group orientation of Japanese society, the constant emphasis in the Japanese workplace on teamwork, and the lifetime employment system. In most cases, workers are placed into teams and are rewarded or rated not individually, but as a team. All employees are trained to do each task within the team so that they can rotate to different tasks and fill in where necessary. Workers receive pressure to perform well not only from their supervisors but from their peers within the team.[9] In addition, to lose a job in Japan is "personal disaster and a serious social disgrace."[10] Those unfortunates who are let go find it difficult to find employment of similar rank and pay elsewhere. These people are seen as a "burden to their families."[11]

Up until the 1990s, when the world recession greatly affected Japan's economy, Japanese top-tier companies were loathe to fire employees (more accurately, Japanese male employees), and an individual company would only do so a handful of times in a year. Transgressions worthy of meriting firing generally had to be extreme, such as chronic absenteeism or committing a criminal offense. Traditionally these companies have expended their recruiting time and money on aggressively courting young, male university graduates to their ranks. In 1989, companies fell short of their goal for inductee members by 618,770. Despite this shortfall, however, women were not recruited to fill these positions, and those who were recruited were relegated to support staff positions.[12] Although the recession in the latter part of 1992 and 1993 has changed the basic shortage of young women (there are more women seeking jobs than there are jobs available), there are still 114 jobs available for every 100 men.

Unemployment in Japan has been consistently low and remains so despite the slowdown in the economy and resultant layoffs. The most compelling reasons for this are undemanding (or "cooperative") unions; female, immigrant, and retired labor pools that can be employed and dispersed at will; and labor compensations in the form of adjusted bonuses and perks. Unions lower their demands in economic hard times. Women, foreign workers, and older workers are brought into the market when needed and are let go during a crunch; they are not counted among the officially unemployed. A very large portion of workers' pay comes in bonuses, which can be adjusted according to the state of the economy so that layoffs can be avoided. The Japanese also disguise unemployment by transferring workers to subsidiaries instead of laying them off. When workers are laid off they often become self-employed (fully 30 percent of Japan's labor force is self-employed), and in difficult times many of their small businesses go bankrupt. Therefore, low unemployment in Japan could be considered as something of a myth. If the female, foreign, and elderly "discouraged workers" were counted, unemployment in the United States and Japan would be virtually equal.[13]

Japanese employees work long hours—in 1960 an average of 2,432 hours, which by 1989 had declined to 2,159 hours. In 1989 one of Japan's largest unions set a goal to cut average working hours to 1,800 per year by 1993; at that time, Japanese were working 500 hours more per year than workers in Germany and France and 200 hours more than Americans. In 1992 the average dropped for the third straight year to 2,009 hours (compared to 1,924 hours in the United States and 1,655 in western Germany). The number of hours Japanese really work, though, is even higher; a recent survey found that 55 percent of employees worked overtime that was not paid for or reported. The Ministry of Labor recently raided a large financial institution and found that one-third of the employees worked large amounts of overtime that was unpaid and unreported.

Some Japanese are reluctant to change their workaholic behavior because they feel pressured to work long hours. Yoshinobu Sano, who works in a Tokyo bank, said, "My boss doesn't want to go home, because his boss doesn't want to go home. And I can't go home until my boss goes home. It's not written down—it's psychological."[14] To balance such pressures, the government has even released a report, entitled "A Study on How to Take Proper Rest and Recuperation," suggesting that Japanese leave their work at the office and take more extended vacations. The government's interest in promoting relaxation is attributable to the need to slow down production because of the weak economy. The government has met with much resistance from some workers in getting them to take more leisure time. Said one worker, "Rather than saying we don't know how to enjoy life, it's better to say there was just no tradition of doing that here." In the summer of 1992 a Japanese court ruled that an employer could make people work longer hours during the week in order to make up for the time lost when Saturday work was eliminated.

Workaholism is a part of Japanese life, with many stories being reported in the press about people literally dying at their desks from overwork. One estimate is that more than twenty-five thousand healthy Japanese die each year because of working too hard. The trend, cited above, toward decreased working hours has stopped because of the downsizing efforts of many Japanese companies, which have required fewer employees to work longer hours.

The Japanese also have long commutes to work. Because of high real estate costs, many face a commute of between ninety minutes and three hours on packed trains to their workplaces from areas with affordable housing. As a result of the long work hours and other work realities, Japanese are not as satisfied with their life or work as Americans. Robert Levine, chair and professor of the psychology department at California State University at Fresno, compared Japanese and American attitudes on quality of life. Overall, 81 percent of Americans and 67 percent of Japanese were satisfied with their quality of life. When one looks at specific aspects of life, however, the differences are greater; for example, 87 percent of Americans were satisfied with their leisure time, compared to only 47 percent of Japanese. Levine attributed these differences to the conflict between traditional Japanese teachings to accept one's lot in life versus a newfound affluence that made self-denial more difficult to accept.[15]

Lifetime Employment

Lifetime employment in Japan is a practice in which a firm hires employees fresh out of school and trains them extensively at substantial cost, in the belief that these employees will stay with the company until their retirement at age fifty-five (or, as the government is now urging, sixty or sixty-five). Lifetime employment is meant to engender a commitment from Japanese male employees to the company: because their futures are linked with that of the company, employees will work harder to ensure the company's success, and thus the security of their jobs.[16] This practice is also meant to cut down on turnover costs such as recruitment, training, and unemployment compensation.[17] Until recently, very few Japanese male workers in top-tier companies were laid off, instead being shifted to different jobs during economic hard times. This could be done because these male workers were given specific job descriptions but were trained on a variety of tasks over a period of time to make them versatile.[18] It should be remembered that lifetime employment is merely a practice and is not a legal commitment,[19] and that only large companies have the ability to offer such stability without being severely overrun by the cost.

Even before the current recession, lifetime employment was something of a myth, as it existed only for a small portion of the Japanese male population. Many workers in the shipbuilding and steel industries were laid off during the economic downturns suffered by those industries in the 1980s. For example, in 1989 Kawasaki cut back 5,000 employees, and Kobe Steel 6,000. In 1992 other companies announced reductions in force or layoffs. Oki Electric will cut 2,000 jobs (or 7 percent of its work force) by 1995. Sanyo plans to eliminate 2,000 of its 29,000 jobs in the same time period. Mitsukoshi, a famous Japanese department store, plans to cut management positions from 2,600 to 1,000. JVC, a consumer electronics firm, plans to cut its 13,500-member work force by 3,000. Meanwhile, Nissan plans to cut 4,000 out of 55,000 jobs. And unlike some U.S. layoffs, once a worker is let go, he or she usually does not return.[20] Furthermore, part-time and expendable portions of the work force are laid off during recessions; these workers are usually the elderly, women, and immigrant workers at smaller subcontracting firms used by the larger company. Instead of laying off Japanese male employees, Japanese companies sometimes seek volunteers to leave the company; however, the volunteers are carefully interviewed so as not to lose the "good ones."[21]

Changes in Employee Attitudes

Despite cultural socialization to do otherwise, one in five Japanese workers now makes a deliberate effort to separate work from his or her personal life.[22] Consequently, more and more workers are leaving their companies at midcareer for better pay, more freedom and creativity, and shorter working hours. Although the stigma traditionally attached to workers who leave jobs still remains, companies are now changing their attitudes because of the labor shortage of *key skills* and are actively courting these job-hopping workers.[23]

In a 1989 survey, although many workers chose more money over increased leisure time (48 percent), 42 percent preferred hours to be shortened even if there was some decrease in income. By 1992, 47 percent of new recruits in Tokyo firms preferred shorter hours to higher pay, and 72 percent supported (and only 18 percent opposed) the implementation of a two-day weekend throughout all industries. The number one reason given for supporting an extended weekend was to allow people to live more comfortable lives (36 percent); none of the other reasons came close (number two, with 11 percent, was "because that is the trend the world over").[24] These figures show that many Japanese are no longer willing to sacrifice their personal satisfaction, desires, and compensation for the good of the company. They want to enjoy the fruits of their hard labor. For Japanese to want more free time even at the loss of income is nearly revolutionary.[25] Other worker attitudes indicative of change are as follows: 73 percent believed that raises and promotions should be awarded on ability, not seniority (the traditional way of paying employees); 28 percent thought that lifetime employment was still very desirable, and 45 percent felt it was somewhat desirable; and 58 percent said that they would like to change jobs if it allowed them to realize their abilities or increase their income.

One reason for the changing attitudes of Japanese workers, noted earlier, is that they have now spent more time traveling and working abroad.[26] Once they return, those Japanese who work abroad increasingly are interested in joining foreign companies; it is often difficult to return to the Japanese market, as those who leave are perceived as traitorous. There are also many disadvantages to joining U.S. companies: less stable jobs (until recently), ostracism from the Japanese expatriate community, and difficulty adjusting to the individualistic, short-term goal orientation of the U.S. work force. Nevertheless, in the words of one Japanese citizen working in the United States for a U.S. company, "For me, the U.S. companies have a very good atmosphere. . . . It takes too much time to reach a decision at Japanese companies. . . . I don't think I can endure [working in Japan again]."[27]

Japanese companies are also facing increasing competition from U.S. and other foreign companies for their limited talent pool. A 1988 Ministry of Labor survey found that 56 percent of the new hires of 1990 foreign-based multinational firms in Japan were people making midcareer job changes. Foreign companies can offer, on average, 10 percent higher salaries and more flexibility and freedom, as well as merit-based promotions. U.S. and other foreign companies are also more attractive to Japanese women, as they offer greater opportunities for this group.

Increasing numbers of Japanese are clearly unhappy with their present situation. When Sumitomo Bank surveyed five hundred men in their forties and fifties, only 4.6 percent said they would choose their present jobs again if given another chance, and only 12.4 percent said they were very satisfied with their current jobs. Many cited dissatisfaction with low pay, limited holidays, and extensive overtime.[28] One bank worker said he envied Western attitudes toward work and leisure and added, "I want to do many things, but I don't have the time to do anything."

Yoshi Noguchi, managing director for the Pacific Rim for Paul Ray and Carrie Orban International, an executive search firm, noted that he is increasingly receiving calls from Japanese executives both in Japan and the United States who have grown disenchanted with the Japanese management system. These executives increasingly feel that the Japanese management system works well for the company but not for employees and their families. Noguchi argues that until recently this system worked well because Japanese culture is characterized by tight control systems that

> minimize diversity and risk too. . . . But more Japanese executives are beginning to believe the system stifles freedom of choice and creates a psychological imprisonment against creativity and independence—the very ingredients must be unleashed to maintain Japan's competitive position. Japanese companies must promote more opportunities for career advancement and increased compensation based on individual accomplishment, reward risk-taking and promote greater flexibility for leisure time and family. . . . Japan's future lies with fostering and encouraging executives with vision, courage and creativity—the corporate mavericks. Regrettably, Japan today rejects the very people who could become the greatest agents of that positive change.[29]

Many Japanese workers are losing their humble attitudes as the number of university graduates has jumped from 5 percent of the population to 37 percent since the early 1960s. Although workers were once called the "servants" of the company, they now perceive themselves as talented people who will go to the company offering the best career opportunities.

Companies are slowly adjusting their policies to new economic, social, and demographic realities. For example, Japan is faced with what to do for its baby boomers, who have expected to be promoted on the basis of seniority into middle and upper management positions; however, as a result of this generation's large numbers and corporate downsizing and restructuring brought about by the recession, 90 percent of companies surveyed by the Japanese Trade Union Confederation said that they will have to change their seniority-based promotion system. In addition, 18.8 percent of these companies are considering implementing a merit-based promotion and performance evaluation system. Toray Industries is introducing a "hybrid system" combining the advantages of Japanese seniority-based pay raises with Western merit-based pay raises.[30] Honda has introduced a merit-based system that will gradually pay primarily for performance rather than seniority. With the new work-force realities, the seniority-based system of reward only creates gridlock for those competent, ambitious employees who are becoming more "self focused." Some Japanese companies are dealing with this problem by creating a multitrack system that allows employees to be moved horizontally through job rotation as well as vertically through promotion.[31] All of these changes could benefit the better utilization of Japanese women, who are at a great disadvantage with the current seniority system; when they leave a company, primarily for family responsibilities, they must begin at the bottom of the seniority list if they return to the work force.

The Japanese are also facing the growing phenomenon of the *madogiwa zoku*, or "by-the-window tribe." These are middle-aged Japanese male employees who are perceived to no longer have use in the company, are given very little responsibility, and are kept on only because of lifetime employment policies. These workers are a financial drain on the company because of their substantial paychecks (due to their seniority) and reportedly large numbers. No one knows how many by-the-window employees there are, because companies do not like to acknowledge this trend, let alone measure it.[32]

A final exchange in the Japanese labor-management scene is the shift in the capabilities that employers desire of their workers. Whereas in

1985, the number one quality valued in a worker was diligence, today dynamism is much more highly sought after. A 1990 report by Recruit Company of Japan surveyed the employees and management of various Japanese firms and found that in the changing environment of internationalization, the information society, accelerated market cycles, and diversification of values, employees required "intelligence and dynamism in order to cope." In other words, employers for the first time were recognizing the value of employees who think. Strangely enough, the same report states that workers are resisting this change in values: after years of following commands, the new paradigm seems a bit alien.[32]

Conclusion

Japan has enjoyed great success at home and abroad. Much of that success is due to its commendable efforts to produce high-quality, low-cost products. The Japanese also owe much of their success, however, to unfair trade barriers, an extremely close relationship between business and government, and methods that undercut competitors while underpaying workers and shareholders. Japan must begin to deal more fairly with its trade partners and its workers, not only out of a sense of propriety but also because the economic realities of its current recession demand that it do so. Subsequently competitors like the United States, as they become more quality oriented, will have a chance to catch up with Japan in terms of price and quality of products, in part because the United States will have sufficient numbers of qualified workers being used in a more efficient manner to sustain its economy.

Clearly the labor policies of Japanese companies will change to accommodate the new attitudes of workers, as well as the changing economic realities in Japan. Lifetime employment is deteriorating as the economy slows, and travel has opened the eyes of many Japanese to the more leisurely life-styles of foreign workers, resulting in increased job hopping. These employees are demanding the rewards of their efforts, which have made Japan a leading economic power. Japan's top-tier companies will also find that labor tension will increase as workers demand more leisure and money and as women and foreign immigrants demand equal rights with Japanese men. All in all, the homogeneous, sacrificing face previously presented by the Japanese work force is changing to a more diverse and demanding one. Japanese business and government leaders must adequately respond to these demands or jeopardize their survival in the increasingly competitive global marketplace.

4

Japanese Women

Women led Japan at various times in its early history; the last woman was Empress Kohen (A.D. 749–758). During the Tokugawa era (1603–1868), Confucian philosophy ascribed inferior characteristics to women and placed them in subservient positions to men, and the killing of baby girls was a common practice. In the Meiji era (1868–1912), although baby girls were not killed and the government prohibited the selling of girls and women, females were still sold and placed as indentured servants in the first decades of the twentieth century.[1] Thus it is not surprising that in the 1990s, Japanese women are very much in a position like that of American women of the late 1930s. Their role in the Japanese work force has been very restricted; they are seen as cheap, expendable short-term labor and as office decorations. Because of their particular cultural socialization to assume a submissive position (by Western standards), Japanese women do not have a strong equal rights movement. We do not wish to perpetuate stereotypes of the Japanese woman as geisha or household drudge; however, even Japanese women who study the sociological, psychological, and economic situation of Japanese women acknowledge the generally subservient role forced on Japanese women compared to U.S. and European women. Nevertheless, international pressure, an intense labor shortage in the 1980s, and another expected shortage after the global recession evaporates have brought and will continue to bring Japanese women into the work force in large numbers. As this chapter illustrates, many barriers still exist despite a 1986 equal employment law, although numerous opportunities and changes are arising because of that same law, as well as in response to long-term competitive needs.

Japanese Women's Ideas of Equality

Some chroniclers of Japanese mores claim that Japanese women have "developed forms of autonomy in the domestic sphere that can only be looked upon as an advance beyond their condition of semi-servitude in much of pre-war Japanese society," and that Japanese women have a different sense of equality that is exercised in the incredible power they purportedly wield in the domestic sphere over the education of their children, the career choices of the husband, and the disposal of household income. We believe, however, that this is a blunted sort of power and that the above statements are either propagandizations or rationalizations. Until women have direct power by occupying prominent positions in government, universities, and business representative of their numbers, they in no way approach equality to their well-represented male counterparts.

Traditional Role of Japanese Women

Japanese women have a long fight ahead to break out of the traditional roles to which they have been relegated. A recent poll of Japanese businessmen shows that they still prefer women to be "cute, cheerful, and modest."[2] When Yuka Hashimoto was hired into entry-level management by Fuji Bank, she was promised that her future was to be determined by her talents and would not be restricted in any way. Even as a career-track woman, however, she serves tea to colleagues and clients alike—a chore that is never asked of a male worker. Hashimoto would not think of refusing the task, as such behavior would result in a negative mark on her record and limit her promotability.[3]

Most Japanese women who have joined the work force have gone the route of the "office lady" (or OL). Office ladies are strictly clerical workers with no promotability. They are hired with the unwritten understanding that they will retire in approximately three years upon their marriages. These women wear actual uniforms: white checkered at Toray (a Japanese fabric maker), and jade at Sanwa Bank. They are trained in such skills as bowing and using a pleasant phone voice. (The Japanese prefer soft, high voices in women.) Corporations recruit college graduates right along with high school graduates when hiring office ladies. Their jobs entail photocopying, serving tea, and "creating a pleasant atmosphere." This atmosphere relies on the women being "office flowers," and those who are young and attractive are much more desirable for hire than older, less attractive women.

Women are discriminated against because, historically, their work life is very brief. In a society where to remain unmarried is highly suspect, the median age for females to marry has been twenty-four (recently increasing to twenty-five). Women retire immediately after marriage so as not to shame their husbands; a husband who could not support both himself and his wife is considered a poor breadwinner. Most companies maintain a mandatory retirement age for women of twenty-eight, whether or not they married. Women normally graduate from college at about twenty-one or twenty-two years of age, and thus three years is the normal amount of time an employer could expect them to work. Companies see little point in investing important training monies in employees who would retire so soon.

Women's traditional education choices have also injured their chances of promotability. Most female college graduates have a liberal arts background, and therefore large numbers of women are competing for the same jobs in the few fields that offer them any future. The mass media, education, and government jobs they vie for are able to pit these women against each other, resulting in lower wages and an overall undervaluing of the college graduate female labor pool. In fact, corporations would rather hire women with *less* education. Since a woman generally retires by her late twenties, high school graduates (who can be hired at a younger age than college graduates) have a longer work life. Moreover, a college education is really unnecessary for the job responsibilities of an office lady, and college graduates may have unrealistic ideas about promotions, assignments, wages, and equality that are perceived as disruptive to the office.

Businesses defend their practices of discriminating against women for management positions by saying they will lose massive training dollars when these women retire to marry. Women have often been targeted during restructuring and layoffs because—as claimed by Nomura Securities when it planned to eliminate two thousand employees, most of whom were women—female workers tend to quit sooner anyway. These corporations, however, generally discourage women from staying on beyond marriage. One young female office worker stated that during orientation, "we had a lecture for the girls before we had our interviews. They told us if we were from a four year college, we must agree to work for at least three years. I mentioned that I wanted to continue working after marriage, but they said that would really be difficult, that most girls quit after they get married."[4]

The careers of most Japanese women have centered around the education of the children. Women strictly monitor the education of their children, tutoring them at home and closely overseeing their extensive homework. Education is the "key to social mobility and status," but to get into the best universities one must pass a rigorous entrance examination. Thus a mother's role is to ensure that her children, particularly her sons, get into the right university, because only from there can a young Japanese hope to secure a job in the most prestigious corporations.[5]

In Japan, women are expected to devote themselves to marriage and family above all else. Since Japanese businessmen must spend amazingly long hours entertaining clients and making contacts, the onus of raising a family traditionally falls almost entirely on the female. In fact, it is precisely these long hours of socializing necessary to success in the Japanese business world that also keeps women out of management positions: men feel very uncomfortable socializing with women as business equals, and women far from envy the endless nights in bars that steal away one's personal life. Of course, the increasing number of women trying to break into the corporate realm may testify to the lure to some of such a life, or perhaps it is a rebellion against the even worse drudgery of being confined solely to the home.

A Japanese Ministry of Labor report reveals the idea that no one works harder or longer than the Japanese male to be a myth—the Japanese housewife does. She works longer hours per day (eleven hours and sixteen minutes as compared to ten hours and one minute, including travel time) and has less leisure time (two hours and forty-three minutes compared to three hours and thirty-six minutes per day) than her husband. Also, employed married women are still responsible for 90 percent of the housework. The only way for wives to escape housework is to live in a three-generation family, where relief would be provided by the wife's or husband's mother (see Table 4–1).[6]

Ageism is also practiced by the Japanese corporate world against women. Women are pressured to quit, whether they are married or not, once they have aged beyond the *tekireiki,* or proper age for marriage (approximately their mid-twenties). The main reason is that older women can function only on a practical level and not as office flowers; therefore, their value is diminished. Also, when women become older

TABLE 4-1

Who is Responsible for Housework? (number = %)

	Weekday	Holiday	Nuclear family	Three-generation family
Wife	63.6	85.4	90.0	34.7
Husband	1.2	1.5	2.0	0.0
Wife or husband's mother	28.5	7.7	4.2	59.1
Children	0.2	0.0	0.0	0.0
Other family members	3.3	0.0	0.0	3.2
Other	3.2	5.4	3.8	3.0

and are seen only as workers and not decorations, men in the office perceive them to be threats. One older woman worker reported that the men treated middle-aged and older women severely and were purposefully unhelpful to these women.[7]

Japanese women receive similar pressure from all aspects of their society. Education, family, religion, government and finance all point to marriage as the only respectable option for Japanese men and women. Once within a marriage, a traditional "good" wife will never let a husband fend for himself. For a husband to have to clean his own laundry, cook his meals, or do his ironing would be a great source of shame and guilt for the traditional Japanese wife.

This sexist role system has become so deeply ingrained that it will be difficult to discard; however, future Japanese success is dependent on how quickly a new perspective on the role of women can be adopted. Because of its rapidly aging population and the continuing baby bust, Japan must open its eyes to its large, well-educated, and untapped pool of female labor to compete in the 1990s and beyond. Japan's young work force will reach its peak in 1995 and decline thereafter; the 8.7 million young workers of 1995 will decrease by 35 percent by the year 2010 to 5.8 million workers. Japan is rapidly becoming the most aged nation in the world. In 1993, 11 percent of the population is sixty-five or older. In 2000, the proportion will be 17 percent; in 2025, an astounding 25 percent. The United States at that time, even with its aging baby boomers, will have only 18 percent of its population over sixty-five. Japan's percentage of elderly will equal the most aged European nations, Germany and Sweden, by the early twenty-first century and will surpass them soon after. Each senior citizen in Japan is now supported by 5.3 workers, but by 2035, that number will be a mere 2.3. Meanwhile, the Japanese birthrate has dipped to an all-time low of 1.57 children per woman in her lifetime. In order to maintain its population, a nation must maintain a rate of 2.1, but by 1996 Japan's birthrate is expected to fall even lower, to 1.35. Also, the current Japanese life expectancy of 75.5 years for men and 81.3 years for women is 4 years longer than American rates (Japanese life expectancy is, in fact, the highest on earth). As shrinking numbers of workers support a larger portion of elderly persons, many serious problems could develop. Young workers will bear a heavy tax burden as health and social programs explode in cost; labor shortages will increase; and the 14 percent savings rate that has provided the capital for Japan's growth will decrease as senior citizens spend the money they saved for retirement.

Clearly, Japan must learn to utilize its female, elderly, and immigrant work forces to support its aging population and retain its economic strength. Currently, there is an eligible female work force of close to six million people that is not being utilized. Japan must learn to value and promote this asset.

1986 Equal Employment Law

The constitution that Japan drew up with the help of the United States after World War II includes an equal opportunity clause; however, there was no effective legislation created to enact or enforce this clause. The 1947 constitution, in conjunction with the Labor Standards Law of 1947, "eliminated the legal barriers to sexual equality in employment in Japan." The law sounds wonderful as it provided "regulations about equal pay, working hours, night work, menstruation leave, maternity leave, holidays, employment of minors, dangerous work, restrictions on underground work." This law went too far, however, in that it restricted the amount of female overtime and night work and therefore made it very disadvantageous for women to compete for certain jobs. Since 1966, forty judicial decisions have been made declaring mandatory retirement upon marriage unconstitutional. But the practice has persisted, exemplifying the Japanese proclivity for passing laws and making judgments but not backing them up with enforced penalties.

The United Nations Decade of Women, 1975 to 1985, ended with the development of a treaty (the Convention on the Elimination of All Forms of Discrimination Against Women) banning all discrimination against women, including in the workplace. All member nations were to sign; to refuse would be politically injurious. Japan therefore signed and subsequently drew up a domestic law, effective in 1986, to prove the seriousness of its commitment to women's rights. This law was strongly opposed by Japanese corporations, and the fact that the law contains no penalties for violations perhaps reflects the corporate pressure applied to legislators. In order to please both labor and management groups, the government prohibited some actions (like discrimination in new employee training, retirement, and dismissal) and merely requested that corporations "make an effort" toward equal opportunity in recruiting, hiring, and promoting women.[8]

Despite its weaknesses, the law is perceived as a giant step for women, and the government has further tried to improve the situation of women by issuing videos instructing managers on the effective and advantageous use of women in the work force, as well as by encouraging corporations to employ more women. The Ministry of Labor has issued statements encouraging men to do more housework, and the government has also passed a law allowing one year of maternity leave with pay.

The 1986 law resulted in dramatically increased hiring of women with college degrees into career-track jobs by corporations attempting to solve their labor shortage problems and improve their image internationally.[9] And the government prohibition on female overtime has been lifted for so-called professional women. Although this means that women who are doctors, engineers, researchers, and reporters will be able to work late nights, holidays, and Sundays and thereby advance their careers, the majority—those who fill clerical or service jobs—will experience no benefit from the new policy.[10] In fact, most women's groups in Japan did not endorse the 1986 law, as they felt it would effect little if any change. Finally, it should be noted that equal opportunity has a long way to go; as of 1991, women were only making sixty-one yen for every one hundred yen that men made.[11]

Barriers Women Face

Among the many barriers to women's success in Japanese society and businesses[12] is the fact that they represent less than 2 percent of the members of Japan's lower house of Parliament, which is where real power is supposed to be concentrated. In the Diet or the upper house, they represent 13 percent (a respectable number compared to the U.S. Senate), but the Diet is basically a toothless tiger. In addition, the fewer women in politics belong to various parties, cooperating very little, and they are generally ignored by men.

In an October 1991 *Fortune* article entitled "Iron Butterflies," nine Asian women were profiled as an emerging trend of female executives in the East. Although Japan is by far the most economically and technologically sophisticated and advanced nation in the region, not one of the nine women was Japanese. Japan only received mention in the introduction, where it was noted that even though the Japanese word for wife means "inside the house," 38.3 percent of the work force is now female. Most of these women, however, do factory or secretarial work, and they rarely become managers or supervisors. Only 1 percent of female workers (as compared to 8.1 percent of male workers) rise to management. And four years after the start of their careers the attrition rate for college graduates is 11 percent for men, compared to 45 percent for women. Although women generally leave for the traditional reason of family responsibilities, many also cite the difficulty of bucking the system. Said one twenty-eight-year-old former public relations officer, "In the end, large companies are a male-oriented society. It's not a place for women to work for life."

The so-called madonna boom of 1989, caused by the political success of Socialist party leader Takako Doi, evaporated with the 1990s recession. Although women were briefly courted politically and corporately, the number of female candidates in the July 1992 Diet election fell by half, and Japanese companies have trimmed recruitment and management programs for women. It seems that in times of economic woe, women have been the first victims; for example, Toyota planned to reduce its hiring of male high school graduates by 7.4 percent in 1993 while cutting its female high school intake by 25.6 percent.[13]

Beyond the setbacks suffered because of the recession, women continue to face the traditional discrimination despite the new law. Some companies, such as Sumitomo Bank, require career-track women to wear the same uniforms as the office ladies (secretaries). Other banks force females—whether professional or clerical—to retire if they marry within the organization, so as to avoid the difficulty of transferring both husband and wife in case of relocation. The problem many companies have is that they see female employees as one homogeneous group. They fail to separate those who will leave upon marriage from the increasing number of Japanese women who are devoted to their careers, according to Moriko Nakamura, president of the Japanese Association for Female Executives (JAFE). She complains that companies have assumed all women are on the marriage track.[14]

Women trying to break out of the mold still face the obstacle of their male supervisors questioning their level of commitment to the job, as well as the propriety of women even being on the job. One Japanese male manager stated that women "think they can quit if things get too tough. You wonder if they're seriously trying to commit themselves." A twenty-six-year-old former securities salesperson tells the story of how her four years of long hours and top-notch sales records were relatively meaningless to her boss, who assumed she would marry and retire.

Finance Minister Ryutaro Hashimoto in 1992 blamed Japan's seriously low birthrate on the education of women. He implied that Japan should encourage women not to obtain higher education but rather to stay home and have babies. Hashimoto subsequently made conciliatory remarks when it was recognized that his comments were detrimental to his party's efforts to attract female members; however, he did not change his stance.

Hashimoto's remarks reflected growing Japanese fears about the aging population and the future inability of a shrinking youthful work force to support them. Neither were his remarks idle ones: many suggestions have been considered for solving the "birth dearth," including tax incentives to have more children and the restriction of birth control devices. In March 1992, the Japanese government announced that it would continue a long-time ban on birth control pills, which would remain available only through prescription for treating irregular menstruation and other disorders. The government cited fear that use of the pill would discourage condom use and lead to the spread of AIDS. Many experts criticized this explanation as ironic, since the Ministry of Health had made no effort to educate doctors or laypeople about AIDS. Family planning organizations were planning to protest the ban because they felt it restricted the rights of women, their freedom of choice and access to safe and effective birth control.

The Liberal Democratic party alienated some women voters in 1990 when a high-ranking member attacked a prominent female politician, announcing that voters "should be suspicious of Takako Doi, leader of the Japan Socialist Party, because she is unmarried and has no children." Doi and her party fared poorly in the next election; one can only conjecture that such slurs may have been a factor.

Even in the rare instances where women have risen to positions of power, they have met great resistance from Japan's traditional, male-oriented society. In January 1990, Mayumi Moriyama, the first woman chief cabinet secretary, asked to present the Prime Minister's Cup at the New Year Grand Sumo Tournament in Tokyo, as normally done by the person in her position. Her request touched off volatile responses due to the fact that in the two thousand years of the sumo tradition, no woman had been allowed to enter the ring. For her audacious request, Moriyama was accused of being a publicity-seeking busybody, and it was reported that Prime Minister Kaifu was embarrassed by her actions. Some have seen Moriyama's appointment merely as an attempt by the Liberal Democratic Party to placate and woo female voters. Also, she is reportedly not always notified of government policy that she should normally be informed about or play a role in forming. However, Moriyama did have her supporters in the incident, who defended her pioneering spirit in the cause of female equality.

Not only are women hired at lower wages than men, but they fall further behind as educational levels increase: in a comparison of salaries of women and men (aged forty to forty-four) with the same amount of service, the female employees' wages were 26 percent lower for those with junior high school education, 29 percent lower for senior high school graduates, and 35 percent lower for college graduates.[15]

When middle-aged men are hired into new jobs, their past work experience receives some consideration in salary determination. Middle-aged women, however, are not afforded the same allowance; when they reenter the work force after raising their children, they start at the same wage as new eighteen-year-old female hires. Japanese wage increases depend largely on time of service and level of responsibility, and female workers who interrupt their careers for marriage and family do not accumulate seniority or responsibilities. Women also are employed in large part by Japan's smaller businesses and industries, which happen to offer lower wages and benefits. College placement services often advise women to seek employment in smaller, less prestigious companies because they have a "greater opportunity to distinguish themselves."[16]

Since most women are perceived as short-term workers, they are excluded from job training for long-term employees, and this exclusion from long-term training makes them unpromotable. The cost of the first two years of training only begins to pay off in the third year, when many female college graduates are expected to retire. Akira Kurose, personnel manager at Sumitomo Bank, says the training investment most companies expend on their employees does not pay off for ten years![17] As of 1990, the sobering fact was that 52 percent of Japanese companies did not promote women at all.[18] Reasons given presently for unequal pay and promotion for women are their lack of comparable education (24.1 percent of male workers are college graduates, compared to 4.8 percent of women) and their dropout rate (for marriage and childbirth), which precludes their achievement of seniority.[19]

One might argue that the United States has been just as guilty of gender discrimination as Japan, if not presently then in the past. The United States now can claim 33.3 percent of its administrative and managerial workers as women, however, whereas Japan can claim only 6.1 percent. Even a 1991 Japanese Ministry of Labor survey of women in managerial positions has Japan lagging woefully behind, with the United States at 10.8 percent; Canada at 11.1 percent; Germany at 1.4 percent; and Japan at 1.0 percent.[20] In fact, so few women achieve top executive status that those who do are famous (notorious, perhaps) in Japan for this rare accomplishment. Women are frustrated by their lack of opportunities, as seen in the following comment by a twenty-eight-year-old postal worker:

> We are not treated fairly, we are not treated equally in the kinds of jobs we do and the responsibility we are given. Even though we want to do something worthwhile, they won't let us do that. They just want us to smile prettily and serve tea, just be nice and pleasant. This may be all right while you are young, but now I'm frustrated. Very few women are promoted. It's really impossible for us to even consider it. In terms of enjoying my work, I find it is really a struggle to satisfy myself. . . . We get some pay raises, but in order to get a big increase, you have to get promoted and there's little chance for

a woman to get promoted. . . . Most of the women have given up. Those in their late thirties or forties don't even complain any longer. They realize that is the way it is, and they have given up. . . . I would really like to get married, but I have no one to marry. I used to think that age didn't matter. Until I became twenty-four or twenty-five I didn't think about my age. But after that people around me started to react when they found out that I am single. This makes me think I'm not stable. I don't have this foundation in my life. Whenever I think about it, I can't help feeling insecure and scared.[21]

Women also face discrimination because it is perceived that men cannot handle the shame of having women coworkers achieve more success than themselves. Therefore raises, bonuses, and promotions are doled out in a manner that will not deflate male morale. One female administrator reported that

usually 2.5 months' salary is an average bonus. The one who gets a good appraisal can get a little bit more, one with a poor one gets a little less. Placing people in these ranks is very delicate. [In some departments or sections] the percentage who can get the A rank is limited, so the chief clerk can't give everyone the A rank. Usually men are very concerned about promotions, so he would rather give the men A ranks. He cannot afford to give women workers A ranks. The best I can get is a B rating because I am a woman.[22]

As mentioned earlier, another barrier is women's domestic burden. They must do the chores, educate the children, find proper child care, and suffer the guilt of not fulfilling these tasks optimally if they choose a career. This is a situation not unlike that of the American "super-mom"; however, in Japan, the pressure is even more intense. Men also strongly dislike being subordinate to women, not only because of their sexist socialization, but because they know that having been mentored by a woman will be a detrimental mark on their records.

The male bonding that is widely practiced in Japanese corporations presents yet another obstacle for women. Even if women have the freedom from domestic duties to participate in the evening and week-end social events necessary for advancement, they find it difficult, if not impossible, to fit in. Evenings include not only heavy drinking but a variety of sexually oriented entertainment. Japanese professional women claim that they do not advance because men see them solely as sexual objects. The men find it very difficult to have the traditionally close corporate relationship with female employees because of sexual tensions and/or rampant rumors.

Women Themselves as a Barrier

It seems that most Japanese women are reluctant feminists. One report suggests that women are somewhat responsible for their lack of inequality, stating that "the prospects for real advances remain slim until both men and women begin to recognize that women are more than a supplemental source of labor in Japan."[23] Women usually accept discriminatory practices without question. In one poll, 55 percent of Japanese women said they were not treated equally in the workplace; however, only 26 percent felt the need for a women's movement. The relatively docile and accepting manner of Japanese women on this issue perhaps reflects their history of oppression based on religious tenets, their subservient socialization as women, and the overall Japanese cultural standard of nonconfrontation. In general, the Japanese make decisions in an indirect, consensus manner, and they do not like to challenge authority. None of this breeds a very fertile atmosphere for a growing women's movement.

Many Japanese women are often content to be housewives. The majority feel that taking care of home and family is a woman's priority, and they also find the long hours and evenings of carousing that fall to men's lot to be unattractive. Many more young women are attracted to the role of the housewife because it has a very positive image. Even so, there are poor Japanese women who must work.

The trailblazing women in corporate Japan are disappointed with the apathy of the women who have followed them. They feel that most Japanese women only persist in their jobs if the situation is sufficiently comfortable. Japanese women on the career track are not only treated as oddities by men but women as well. Tomoko Ueguri, who runs time management seminars, says her old school friends do not understand why she is still working at the ripe old age of twenty-six. A high school teacher in her late thirties had a similar complaint:

When we have a meeting among the graduates from my university or a senior high school reunion, I don't like to go. My friends will be very surprised to find me still single: 'You are very strange. You haven't married yet, you must have bad health or personality problems.' Students have said that to me even. I was very shocked. Both male and female students say these things, and the male teachers don't stop them.[24]

JAFE president Nakamura gives advice to young executive women that sounds anything but progressive, saying that a woman should stick out a job for at least ten years no matter how tedious or discriminatory and that she should serve tea if asked. She must do this to prove herself to be the ultimately devoted and hardworking employee. Nakamura also says that women must "tread softly" and "try to be easy for the men to accept" so as not to upset the very conservative men still running the establishment.[25]

Even women in positions of power can perpetuate discrimination against other women. One woman who owns a company says she cannot give higher salaries to women who outperform men, because of opposition by her male managers. She reports that the women would be poorly treated and pressured by the men if they made more money, and that she alternatively endeavors to reward them through bonuses. "I'd like to change the system," she says, "but I have to do it little by little."[26] Some Japanese women who have been successful report that they would prefer a male supervisor to a female one.

Like many American working women, women in Japan who pursue careers are subject to much guilt; despite progressive beliefs, years of socialization are hard to erase. One "feminine activist" admitted that she feels guilty when she cannot make it home to prepare her husband's meals. Another woman, an architect, feels that in order to improve the status of women, children must become victims of neglect; therefore, her feelings about working for female equality are mixed.

Women's attitudes may hurt them in many ways. Some see their increasing equality as detrimental to society. Others feel that their lack of opportunities are their own fault because they cannot be trusted to remain employed or show sufficient motivation. Still others are content in their traditional roles, as they have been frightened by the perceived difficulty and male-centered culture of corporate/administrative careers. Of course, many women do work in tedious jobs at low pay with poor benefits. This underclass of women clearly does not have the time or money to enjoy the fun, tennis-playing fantasy of a housewife's life-style and surely would welcome a more equitable employment scenario.

Changes Are Happening, But Slowly

Earlier in this chapter, the story of Chief Cabinet Secretary Moriyama trying to present a sumo trophy was used as an example of the barriers women face in Japan. The full story, though, illustrates how far Japanese women have come. In 1978, Moriyama, then a government bureaucrat, championed without success the case of a girl who wished to participate in a children's sumo contest. When the request was refused, Moriyama asked if the Japanese Sumo Association would deny a woman the right to award a sumo trophy in the event that a woman was appointed chief cabinet secretary. They replied that her question was ridiculous, since "such an eventuality was impossible and unthinkable in Japan." Over a decade later, Moriyama proved them wrong by becoming the first woman to assume that position.[27]

Regardless of all the negative information previously detailed, positive change *is* happening for women. Two major trends account for this—one being gradual, the other a more recent and urgent phenomenon. First, over the last decade or so more women have been entering the work force in all occupations, obtaining higher education and working longer years. The sheer volume of their numbers will produce change; in 1990, a record 2.44 million women entered the work force.[28] Second, Japan has begun to experience a chronic labor shortage (interrupted by the 1990s worldwide recession) that will only worsen as its birthrate continues to decrease, its population ages, and it emerges from recession. Women will be needed to fill this void.

Female labor force participation increased from 45.7 percent of all women in 1975 to 50.1 percent in 1990. In 1975 there were 12 million women in full-time jobs; in 1991 that number was 19.8 million, or 38.3 percent of the work force. More than half of all women held jobs, and of those with jobs nearly two-thirds were married.[29] The greatest growth in female employment has occurred among those aged twenty-five to thirty-four, with an increase from 43.2 percent in 1975 to 52.2 percent in 1985 and 55.6 percent in 1991. The number of women in management positions increased 50 percent from 1982 to 1989. These numbers indicate that women are opting to remain in the work force continuously, interrupting their careers for marriage and children less often.[30]

For women with college degrees, the numbers have also improved. Only 10.6 percent of female graduates entered the work force in 1960,

compared to 23.2 percent in 1985. These numbers pale when compared to the numbers for men: 89.4 percent in 1960 and 76.8 percent
in 1985. (Women only represented 25 percent of all college graduates
in 1985.) By 1989, however, change had occurred so rapidly that 78.5
percent of female graduates found employment, an all-time high (the
number for men was 80.1 percent, making women nearly equal).[31]
The number of all women graduates (in both two- and four-year programs) was 243,000 in 1989, surpassing the number of male graduates
(231,000) for the first time since the current educational system was instituted in 1950. Another positive sign was that nearly half of all female
graduates were employed into the more prestigious service sector
(45.6 percent).[32] Also, in 1990 more than one-third of Japanese college-
aged women were enrolled in two- or four-year programs, as compared
to 17 percent in 1970. Despite this good news, in 1990 women accounted for only 2.2 percent of the section chief positions of management, and only 0.7 percent of the director-or-higher class in the more
prestigious areas of management, government service, and sales.[33]

But what is it that has caused the numbers of women being educated
and employed to skyrocket in recent years? It is not the sudden enlightened realization by male-oriented Japanese society that women
are equal. Rather, it is what has fueled change in Japan for decades
(and most other countries as well): economic need. With the labor
shortage of the 1980s, Japanese unemployment levels were less than
3 percent, and even with the recession they have remained below 3
percent. The long-term value of a shrinking labor pool will increasingly
force employers to look at heretofore ignored worker populations—
like women—to fill jobs. Companies must now try to attract and retain
women. Even such dinosaurs as Sumitomo Bank (cited earlier in this
chapter for making women wear uniforms and forcing retirement upon
them) are getting into the act: of 864 new hires in spring 1991, 250
were women, and these 250 women were college graduates being put
on the career track.[34] Out of 900 new hires at Asahi Breweries, 110
were women who will be sent out to sell Asahi products to liquor
stores—an until now exclusively male-dominated field.

Working Mothers

Corporations are trying to make work more attractive for women by
improving child care and family care policies and services. Naomi

Watanabe, an insurance agent at Saison Group, received one year of maternity leave and now takes her son with her to work, leaving him at the company day care center in the same building where she works. The needs of working mothers were the top item on the agenda for the 1991 spring *shunto* (labor/management bargaining session). The unions were demanding one-year leave for all new parents (either the mother or the father); at that time, a mere 20 percent of companies were providing any type of leave.

The first successful child care law was passed in 1991 with the support of the Liberal Democratic Party, which formerly opposed such laws at the behest of its corporate constituency. The law guarantees unpaid leave of up to twelve months for a mother or father.[35] The government is finally realizing that they can improve the birthrate not by discouraging the education of women but by making the workplace more accommodating to working mothers. The government is also considering giving tax breaks for children and raising the level of nontaxable part-time income to make life easier on such mothers. Current child leave policies generally give women six weeks of maternity leave before childbirth and eight weeks after, six weeks out of the 14 weeks which are compulsory but only sometimes paid (health care will cover 60 percent of mother's salary during leave).

Now that Japanese mothers have more free time because of modern conveniences, they are fleeing their cramped homes for part-time employment. In 1990, 35.8 percent of mothers with preschool children and 65 percent of those with grade-school children were working (either full- or part-time), with the rate increasing further for mothers with children of middle or high school age.[36] These numbers still do not match the U.S. rates: 58.4 percent of American mothers with preschool children and 72.6 percent with elementary school children work full- or part-time.[37] Unfortunately, the percentage of women workers who are part-time workers is on the increase (2.2 percent in 1975 to 17.4 percent in 1989). This is bad news because part-time workers, although often performing the same tasks as full-time workers, are not as well protected by labor laws, have poorer working conditions, are not paid as well (86 percent of the hourly full-time rate, with only 20 percent of the bonuses), and rarely have a retirement allowance system.[38]

The divorce rate in Japan, although the lowest among advanced nations in the world, has been steadily increasing; it was 1.26 per

1,000 marriages in 1990, compared to 4.8 in the United States and 2.89 in the United Kingdom.[39] Some reasons for the increase include the growing intolerance of young Japanese women for traditional marriage, the growing economic autonomy of housewives with part-time jobs, and the increased life expectancy of Japanese women (older Japanese women find it difficult to share their domain with their demanding retired spouses, with whom they have spent little previous leisure time). In any case, the trend is sending more mothers back to work sooner than expected. Mothers get custody of children 80 percent of the time. When fathers are awarded custody it is usually of older children; therefore, mothers are left with small children, small earning power, and little or no child care facilities. Instead of alimony there is generally a lump-sum settlement. Child support is negligible, and the vast majority of fathers are remiss in their payments. The growing reality of divorce will have to be addressed by better child care facilities, better divorce laws, improved alimony and child support policies, and more equitable pay for women.

Now that women, in response to the 1986 law, have been hired into career-track positions in greater numbers, their rise to management would be inevitable if the Japanese system of seniority was applied equally to women. As noted in the previous chapter, however, the traditional policies of Japanese management are changing as Japanese companies work to become more competitive. For once the traditional system, if equitably applied, would be working for rather than against Japanese women. Women's attitudes are also growing more aggressive. Increasingly young career-track women are ready and willing to drink with the boys and have dreams of being among Japan's salarymen and not its housewives.

Women are also proving themselves to be assets beyond filling in the gaps in market segmentation. Dentsu, the largest advertising agency in Japan, realized that no one knew how to sell to office ladies (with their 100 percent disposable income) and housewives (who control the family budgets) as *women*. Office ladies have virtually no expenses, as they live with their parents, and husbands hand wives their paychecks weekly to budget as necessary. Dentsu has started a women's subsidiary to court these powerful demographic groups.

The Mating Game

Women are growing more assertive and independent; single women are enjoying their freedom and increased earning power. Apparently there are 462,900 more marriageable men than women in Japan, leaving women the luxury of picking and choosing. Consequently they are in no hurry to marry, and the average marrying age for women rose in the 1980s to 25.9 from 24.4 years for women and to 28.4 from 27.2 years for men. Women complain that men are "self-centered, boorish, boring and predictable." Many men are very anxious to marry—it is a necessary step for career advancement—and companies that throw matchmaking parties have sprung up to help them find mates. Many Japanese men, however, complain that the now choosier women are not being cooperative.[40] Experts agree that this trend is at least partially responsible for the shinking birthrate.

Sexual Harassment

Another positive sign of change for Japanese women came in spring 1992, when a landmark ruling was made on a sexual harassment case. Although for years sexual harassment has not been taken seriously in Japan, the case of a writer at book publisher Kyu Kikaku may change all that. When an unnamed woman filed a complaint against her editor/boss for "lewd remarks and spreading rumors that she was promiscuous and an alcoholic," she was told not to bother returning to work again. Kyu Kikaku was forced to pay her $12,400 in damages (a small settlement, but an "epoch-making decision" nonetheless). Two days after the court decision, ten thousand copies of a government pamphlet on sexual harassment were scooped up. Several other Japanese companies now face suits in Japan, including Hitachi, which is being sued for $437,000 for paying men 10 to 74 percent more than women doing the same work. Even so, the fact that 43 percent of Japanese women in management positions claim sexual harassment—despite their submissive cultural socialization—indicates the widespread nature of the problem, and very few companies have set up in-house procedures for sexual harassment claims.[41]

A Concluding Story

We will end the chapter with the story of Takako Doi to illustrate how far women in Japan have come and how far they still have to go. In 1989 Doi, then a sixty-year-old former law professor, became the first woman to lead a major political party in Japan. She was chairperson of the Socialist party, the largest opponent to the ruling Liberal Democratic party, which has had a stranglehold on power since the 1950s. She was known as a direct, tough, and exciting public speaker, which even in Japanese male politicians is found to be shocking. Doi and her party rode to popularity as a breath of fresh air after the disillusionment with the ruling party that followed repeated scandals and the passage of an unpopular 3 percent consumption tax.[42]

Doi's gender was often perceived as her greatest asset. Her successor lacked the advantage of Doi's "instant recognizability in a political world . . . almost entirely dominated by elderly men."[43] It is clear that her own party was trying to use her gender to its advantage in attracting the often-overlooked vote of women. In fact, the Socialist party started to promote many local and national female candidates in an effort to capitalize on Doi's popularity, a plan that became known as the "madonna strategy." And after her departure from her post, a major concern of Doi's successor was "to build on Miss Doi's popularity among women at the polls."

Japan soon grew disillusioned with Doi and her party, however, when they were not able to unite their many factions or to develop mainstream policies. Ultimately, the Socialist party remained too Marxist for the average Japanese voter.[44] Doi was quickly abandoned by the party, which reportedly had chosen her as leader solely because she was "a fresh face"; she was never perceived as having control of the party and did not belong to any of its major factions.

On the positive side, Doi's plight reveals that Japanese government is becoming aware of the power of the female vote and is openly courting it. This may lead to more legislation benefiting women in order to capture them as a constituency. The Japanese also have shown that they can handle the idea of a woman in a top position of power— and an outspoken and aggressive woman at that. Doi's failure, however, lies in the fact that her party was exploiting her gender and not her other assets. She was never given real control, probably because she had no major faction to claim her and back her up. If more women existed in positions of power in government and business with the necessary education, training, and management skills, they would be more likely to succeed in their appointed positions. And a larger pool of well-trained women would lead not only to the selection of better, more successful female leaders, but also to a more competitive Japanese economy, both domestically and internationally.

Japanese Ethnocentrism and Racism

Except during brief periods, Japan had minimal contact with its Asian neighbors and extremely little with Europeans until the middle of the nineteenth century. Portuguese missionaries and merchants first appeared in Japan in the 1540s. This began a limited amount of trade with Europeans; however, concern about the potential threat of Western influences and religion (Christianity was outlawed in 1614, and tens of thousands of Japanese Christians were executed) led the rulers of Japan to close their borders to the rest of the world from 1638 until 1853. In 1853 Commodore Matthew Perry, with a large U.S. naval armada, forced the Japanese to open their country to foreigners. Several years later the presence of the British and United States navies forced the Japanese to sign trade treaties to open their borders.

The culture of Japan has been built around its sense of racial superiority and uniqueness. In the early nineteenth century, in order to keep out the Western influences that they believed had helped make the Chinese empire a semicolonized possession of Europe, the Meiji dynasty (1868–1912) and its successors reinforced the feeling among Japanese that they were superior to others.[1] In the early twentieth century, Japan's successes in Asia, based in large part on the Meiji dynasty's decision to move rapidly into industrialization and modernization to be able to oppose Western powers, reinforced the Japanese feeling of superiority. This sense of superiority grew sufficiently that Japan in 1941 thought it could start and win a war with the United States.

Nationalism in Japan is again rising. In 1989 the Ministry of Education ordered that all high schools raise the Japanese flag and sing the national anthem on all special occasions. Cabinet members are now making frequent visits to war memorials; in the past such activities were avoided as Japan tried to live down its former warmonger image. Such incidents as one Japanese top executive saying, "America [is] like Rome. It [is] finished," are becoming fairly common.

The historically documented distrust of foreigners has made it nearly impossible for such outsiders to become members of the inner circles of Japanese business. Ryutaro Komiya, a Japanese executive, wrote that the Japanese maintain strong nationalistic characteristics and have difficulty bending to the local culture. Komiya says that Japanese enterprises are far from being globally mature and able to deal effectively with diverse populations.

Discrimination Against Ethnic Japanese

Not only does Japan have a class-oriented society, both socially and economically, but it is also a caste society based on the Indian model. In India there are "untouchables"; in Japan there are the *burakumins*. The burakumins (who number approximately three million) are ethnically Japanese; however, even today many Japanese believe they are a distinct and different race. They were originally put in an outcast status because work they did conflicted with a key tenet of Shintoism, the former national religion of Japan. Shintoism, a form of Buddhism, states that human and animal corpses are dirty and impure, and that anyone who works with or disposes of these corpses is similarly unclean. Burakumins killed and butchered animals, tanned their hides, and made leather products from the hides, tasks "regarded as filthy and despicable under the tenets of Buddhism."[2] From 1603 to 1868, during the Tokugawa era, a rigid caste system was formalized: samurai were on top, followed by; farmers, artisans, merchants and (on the bottom) the burakumin. The burakumins faced discrimination in all aspects of their lives, from marriage to home buying; the Japanese even established separate places for them to eat, drink, bathe, and gather. Those who would associate with them were discriminated against as well. Civil and criminal justice for the burakumin was nil.

Discrimination against the burakumins was legally ended in 1871, prompting violent reactions in which thousands of burakumin homes were burnt and scores were killed. Even today they face both overt and covert discrimination in all aspects of their lives. For example, records are kept on the burakumins, and they are tracked as they change residences. (The existence of these records was not revealed until the 1970s.) Japanese corporations use these data to discriminate against burakumins; currently they are restricted primarily to recycling and selling used goods. Many are still in the leather-tanning business. A great many live in poor areas and slums, have poor health, and are less well educated than other Japanese.

In order to try to correct the burakumin situation the Japanese government has implemented a series of strategies called *dowa,* meaning assimilation. Despite limited successes in correcting centuries of discrimination, however, the Japanese government abandoned its efforts in 1992 because it believed it had done all it could do and had fulfilled its obligations. Thus the burakumins, a Japanese people, are still discriminated against in a most blatant manner.

Discrimination Against Foreign Residents in Japan

Besides having a caste system, the Japanese have strong elements of racism in their society. Racism is considered a taboo subject of discussion; the controversy regarding sumo wrestler Saleeva Atisanoe was shocking to Japanese society not for its allegations of racism but rather because the subject was spoken about openly. Despite meeting all requirements, Atisanoe, a Hawaiian, for months was not promoted to the highest level of the sport (grand champion) because he was not Japanese. His accusation of racism created a furor in Japan, but it did result in Atisanoe receiving his well-deserved grand championship.

Since World War II the Japanese have not lost their strong racial superiority complex toward Koreans, especially toward the 700,000 Korean immigrants in Japan. Many of the latter have had family living in Japan for several generations; however, it was not until 1965 that Japan gave these "visitors" permanent resident status. In addition, it was not until the 1980s that Koreans were granted full social welfare benefits. Koreans living in Japan are faced with discrimination in jobs, housing, and marriage and have only since the 1980s felt fairly comfortable using their Korean names. Until 1989 the Japanese still required persons of Korean descent living in Japan to carry identification cards, and many are denied citizenship despite generations of residence in Japan.

In addition to the Koreans who live in Japan as permanent residents, there are a small but increasing number of Indians and Pakistanis who work as skilled or semiskilled laborers. In the city of Kawguchi, which is dependent on foreign labor to run its small factories, the local police issued a report suggesting that these subcontinental Asians were dirty, smelly, diseased, fast tempered, and deceitful. The same city barred a Pakistani from teaching because "there are a lot of communicable diseases and crime among Pakistanis," and the mayor complained that "Japanese people could bump into Pakistanis at night because of their dark skin." Racism against Pakistanis is not isolated; the national police agency wrote and distributed to regional police offices a 179-page report full of racist slurs and stereotypes about Pakistanis (for example, that detention and interrogation rooms would stink because of the Pakistanis' unique body odor, and that officers should wash their hands after questioning or detaining them because they have contagious diseases.)[3]

Japanese perceptions of African Americans in Japan are no better than their perceptions of Pakistanis or Koreans.[4] Americans must remember that many of these attitudes about African Americans were formed during the U.S. occupation after World War II, when black and white Americans served in a segregated army. It was not very difficult for the Japanese to adopt American stereotypes of and racism toward African Americans. When a Japanese girl on a subway train pointed at a black woman and asked, "Daddy, what's that?" the father referred to a popular fable in which the hero is Songoku, a monkey. The woman whose appearance provoked the question had been in Japan for a year teaching English. She stated, "It's the same whether they're three or twenty years old; they stare and point. Japanese are all children when it comes to dealing with other races."[5]

The toy company Sanrio, after considerable external pressures, had to withdraw one of its leading new items, the "Little Black Sambo" collection. Sambo caricatures, however, can still be found throughout advertising and on T-shirts. The Japanese find the character with its thick lips and distorted features cute, not offensive; meanwhile, African Americans living in Japan face considerable discrimination in housing, employment, and social activities.[6] Because of increased interracial dating between African-American men and Japanese women, a number of Japanese leaders have openly worried about whether the offspring from these relationships are the future of Japan.[7] The prestigious Bungil Prize, given to new and emerging Japanese writers, and the Naoki Prize for literature were both given to Eimi Yamoda's novel *Bedroom Eyes,* which describes the black lover of a Japanese woman as dirty, smelly, and inferior.

Considering Japanese views about African Americans, it is not surprising that Japan filled the trading gap with South Africa after the imposition of UN sanctions. Japanese companies or subsidiaries supplied photographic equipment and material, data processing equipment, and light and heavy motor vehicles—state-of-the-art technology used to prop up the apartheid regime. Japan also increased its investments in South Africa, building more or expanding existing car assembly plants, extending favorable loans, and monopolizing the electronics market in the country.

Leading Japanese officials have often made racist remarks. For example, former prime minister Yasuhiro Nakasone commented in 1988 that blacks and minorities had low intelligence levels; Michio Watanabe, the former finance and trade minister, commented that blacks spend irresponsibly; and former justice minister Seiroku Kajiyama in 1990 opined that American blacks, like prostitutes, destroy neighborhoods.

Such statements color the views of ordinary Japanese regarding the United States and its melting-pot culture. In a *Business Week* Harris poll, 42 percent of Japanese thought that "too many minorities" was the major problem in the United States. The Japanese tend to think that the homogeneity of their society accounts for their success and, therefore, that the diversity in America contributes to our problems. Yuji Aida, a specialist in European Renaissance history and a professor emeritus at the University of Kyoto, wrote an article in 1991 describing the problems America will face because of its diversity. Aida claimed that much like the former Soviet Union, the United States would soon be faced with battling ethnic groups demanding "autonomy and even political independence" and that this would lead to "industrial America's undoing" and a nation that was "ungovernable."

Aida pointed to the fact that white Americans would be a minority within the next fifty years as something to be feared, as it would mean widespread illiteracy and a nation where most people do not speak standard English. He suggested that Americans should concentrate on being an agrarian giant (as well as continuing to pursue those high-tech areas where it already has an advantage), as blacks and Hispanics even in forty years' time would not be able "to run a complex industrial society like the United States." He pointed to the fact that European colonizers were unable to create industrial economies in either Africa or Latin America. Although he denied calling these people racially inferior, Aida wrote that "Iberian and African cultural traits seem to impede industrialization" and that he doubted "that many African or Latin American countries, for instance, will become high-tech societies in the foreseeable future." He criticized "idealistic" Americans and Japanese intellectuals (whom he said were afraid of being labeled racists) because they espoused the idea that education and improved living standards would properly prepare people of color for the impending challenge. Aida contended that the past five hundred years of world history left "little room for hope."[8]

Racist Attitudes Toward Americans

Japan has provoked many negative feelings with the very conspicuous airs of superiority revealed in its recent spate of America-bashing regardless of the Americans' color. In February 1992, Prime Minister Miyazawa himself insulted Americans by saying, "I have felt that the ethic of working by the sweat of one's brow has seemed to be lacking" in U.S. workers in recent years. The speaker of the Japanese House of Representatives, Yoshio Sakurauchi, angered Americans with his statement that U.S. workers were lazy and illiterate; he also called America "Japan's subcontractor." Politician and author Shintaro Ishihara, further rubbing salt into the wounds, argued that workers were not at fault because "U.S. management is no good. I guess it is the cultural difference." Ishihara also said that "the White House and the U.S. Congress are unable to understand Japan, as well as their own country."[9]

These negative comments about Americans are not just held by a small number of politicians and authors. One-third of the Japanese in a 1990 *Newsweek* Gallup poll responded that they had less respect for Americans now than they did five years earlier.[10] Meanwhile, a highly rated Japanese morning news show features what could very well be called "Stupid American Tricks." On this show, the actual name of which is "Daybreak," clips (mostly provided by CNN) show slices of American life that portray U.S. citizens as stupid and/or crazy. Some sample features are as follows.

A man in Louisiana who turned a room of his house into a shrine honoring a roll of toilet paper he stole from Graceland, the Elvis Presley museum in Memphis. A contest in Texas where men reach into a basket of rattlesnakes to see who can pick up the most without being bitten. Women in Florida arguing for their constitutional right to reveal bare buttocks on the beach. A "pierce boom" in California, where some teenagers have pierced not only ears, but also noses, navals, nipples, chins and fingers, to wear jewelry.[11]

One Japanese political scientist states that the popularity of the show feeds on the Japanese perception that America is a country in decline. With the rise of Japanese nationalism, Japan is seen as a country on the rise while America sinks in crime, drugs, corruption, and greed. Indeed, the Japanese media often focus on such negative American issues as crime, racial tension, AIDS, and other social problems.

George Friedman and Meredith LeBard explain Japanese ethnocentric and racial attitudes by writing that the Japanese are a proud but very confused people. Still smarting over their defeat in World War II, they relish what they view as the decline of America, despite any gratitude they feel for American-sponsored reconstruction after the war.[12]

Perceptions of Jews

In addition to racism toward different people of color, in recent years there has been an increase in the popularity of anti-Semitic books suggesting that Jews are behind world problems.[13] These books accuse Jews of anti-Japanese sentiment. One writer, Masami Uno, in his book *If You Understand the Jews, You Will Understand the World,* charged that Jews were in control of such American companies as General Motors, IBM, and Exxon, and that they were out to dominate the world. Within several months of the Persian Gulf War, more than one hundred new books with anti-Semitic titles and tones appeared. The prestigious Akutagawa prize for literature was given to a Japanese woman whose book *Passover* claimed, among other things, that the Jews were responsible for Chernobyl as part of a financial conspiracy. Another popular book in Japan is *Confessions of the Jews,* which was written by U.S. right-wing extremist Lyndon LaRouche's followers. It argues that the Anti-Defamation League of B'nai B'rith controls drugs and crime in order to gain control of legitimate corporations.

A final popular theme in books about Jews (which sell very well in Japan) is that the Holocaust never happened and that the main goal of Germany and Arab groups is to stop the Jewish conspiracy for world domination. The Anti-Defamation League noted that

> Anti-Semitism in Japan is not endemic, but it is a problem. Jews, particularly American Jews, are today being cast by some Japanese writers in the age-old role of scapegoats for the ills in a society. The phenomenon has displayed itself in a proliferation of anti-Jewish literature in Japan which blames the country's current economic problems on American Jews. These economic problems include the rising value of the yen against the American dollar, which has made Japanese exports more costly and less competitive. They include a growing conflict with the United States over trade, and U.S. sanctions imposed on Japan for the "dumping" (selling below cost) of certain products. They include a decline in investments and profits in Japanese industries, and rising unemployment.[14]

It is important to remember there are only about one thousand Jews in Japan. The astounding ability of Japanese to deny their anti-Semitism in the face of contradictory evidence is demonstrated by the comments of Takeshi Muromatsu, a literary critic who is on the board of the Japanese-Israel Friendship Association. He reported that more than 80 percent of the Japanese were estimated to "accept this Nazi-style stereotype that Jews control the world's finances"; however, he said, "in Japan, there is no anti-Semitism."[15] The irony is that the same negative words and terms used by the Japanese to describe Jews are used by many other nations to describe the powerful Japanese world economic position. A leading Japanese government official was quoted as saying, "Japanese are geniuses in the factory and morons outside."[16]

Discrimination Against Foreign Workers in Japanese Companies

These racist attitudes greatly influence the treatment of non-Japanese residents working for Japanese companies. The number of foreign illegal immigrants in Japan is officially stated to be one hundred thousand, but as is the case with the United States, some experts believe the accurate figure is four or five times as large. Of the five hundred thousand or so, two hundred thousand to three hundred thousand are unlawfully working in Japan today.

Although Japan enjoys a closer economic relationship with Asian countries than Western countries, "it has been standoffish, or even hostile, to permitting other Asians to live [in Japan]. And those who do come often complain of discrimination."[17] A Japanese lawyers' committee also reports that other Asians are treated unfairly not only in jobs, housing, and social events, but also in Japanese courts. Japan's foreign workers complain that one cannot rise within the system unless one is Japanese because all the business practices are thoroughly steeped in Japanese culture, thus creating communications problems and inefficiencies when dealing with outsiders. In India and Malaysia, workers and union officials resent the fact that Japanese managers expect them to sacrifice their personal lives for the good of the company. The superior attitudes of the Japanese and their distrust of foreigners have excluded long-term foreign employees from really learning and understanding the businesses they work in. For example, a Malaysian who worked for a cable plant for seventeen years was barred from entering one of its plants in Japan because he was a foreigner: "The plant was working on optic fibers. And I was told that it was top secret even for someone like me, who had been with the company for so many years!"[18] Ironically, Japan is successful in its own country because of trust, which creates an atmosphere that involves workers in improvement and decision making; however, foreign workers are culturally excluded and not fully utilized. Therefore, Japan's foreign operations will ultimately not be as successful as the United States and the European community become more competitive. In addition, its home-based operations will be hampered as the need for foreign workers increases in the coming years as a result of the low birthrate and aging population.

As Japan goes through its recession, foreign workers who came to fill jobs shunned by Japanese workers face a grim fate. The illegal immigrants, the first to go, (about 40 percent are unemployed) have no real recourse except to survive the best way they can. Another abused group are the estimated two hundred thousand Latin American workers of Japanese descent. In 1991 these workers were making $2,460 per month in factories; now they make $820. They were strongly recruited in 1990 and 1991 to replace foreign workers from Pakistan, Bangladesh, Iran and the Philippines (who were forced to leave after their work permits expired). Japan believed it was much better to have Lain American Japanese than non-Japanese foreigners in their country, but despite their Japanese background, the Latin American workers are discriminated against in many aspects of their living and working conditions.

Discrimination Against American Workers

By the year 2000, the four hundred thousand Americans who currently work for about two thousand Japanese companies' U.S. subsidiaries will grow to one million. Antipathy toward the Japanese was formerly a blue-collar phenomenon caused by the loss of automaking jobs. When Japanese auto plants were built in America, however, blue-collar workers related better to the Japanese because their management style emphasized teams and empowering employees through quality procedures. They responded more readily to the egalitarian notions of the Japanese management style than the hierarchial, autocratic notion of many American car factory managers. With increased Japanese production in the United States, however, bad feelings are increasing among American workers, especially white-collar workers.[19]

One reason that American white-collar workers in Japanese companies are unhappy is because of differences in cultural style. The long-term, all-for-the-good-of-the-company attitude, the lack of formal performance appraisals and feedback, and the slow consensus decision process do not conform with American values of individualism, short-term goals, and regular individual performance feedback. Many white-collar workers are also unhappy because of shadow managers— Japanese executives who have the real power while Americans have the titles. An American vice president in a Japanese bank said that all his recommendations are second-guessed and that any transactions of any size must be approved by Japanese managers, many of whom are located in Tokyo.

Americans are also becoming increasingly concerned about Japanese companies' recruitment policies. For example, Recruit, a California corporation, operates an employment referral service primarily for Japanese companies. Interplace, which is also incorporated in California, recruits prospective employees for American and foreign companies operating in the United States. On April 26, 1989, and May 2, 1989, the *San Francisco Chronicle* published articles revealing allegedly discriminatory hiring practices engaged in by these two companies. The first article, which focused on Interplace, described an internal coding system used to sift prospective employees in accordance with the client's age, racial, ethnic, and sexual preferences (see Table 5–1).

For example, if a client is looking for a person who is preferably (1) Caucasian or Japanese and (2) male, but will also accept someone who is Hispanic, then the job order would read (after inputting the other requirements):

1. Talk to Mary or Mariko
2. See Adam
3. Also meet with Maria

It may be better to number them in order of importance or preference. Please note that these phrases are only to be used when a job order calls for a strict restriction on certain age, sex, or race. If a client, for example, says that he/she definitely DOES NOT want to hire nor interview a Japanese person, then "DO NOT TALK TO MARIKO" would be included on the job order. Additionally, if a client ONLY

TABLE 5–1
Interplace's Discriminatory Coding System

JOB ORDER DESCRIPTIONS

SUITE 20 THROUGH 35 OR SUITE 20-35: ages 20 to 35

FLOOR 40: person in his/her 40s

TALK TO MARIA or SEE MARIA or MEET WITH MARIA: prefer/will accept Hispanics

TALK TO MARY or SEE MARY or MEET WITH MARY: prefer/will accept Caucasians

TALK TO MARIKO or SEE MARIKO or MEET WITH MARIKO: prefer/will accept Japanese

TALK TO ADAM or SEE ADAM or MEET WITH ADAM: prefer/must be male

TALK TO EVE or SEE EVE or MEET WITH EVE: prefer/must be female

TALK TO MARYANNE or SEE MARYANNE or MEET WITH MARYANNE: prefer/will accept blacks wants a Caucasian person between the ages of 30 and 40, the description would read, TALK TO MARY; SUITE 30-40.''

Another key reason Americans are unhappy is because of what they perceive as a lack of advancement opportunities. Japanese companies are not known to heavily promote locals. Just one out of three senior management positions at Japanese U.S. subsidiaries is filled by an American, and only one out of five CEO positions; in contrast, 80 percent of the top jobs of American companies in Japan are filled by Japanese. For example, Kao, a top Japanese package goods company, has sixty Japanese managers and technical people running an overseas work force of two thousand. Its American counterpart, Procter & Gamble, has half the number of American managers and technicians in an overseas business that is twenty times larger. All top Kao overseas management personnel are Japanese, while only five of forty-four Procter & Gamble overseas managers are American. NEC Corporation of Japan has only one American out of its top seven executives, and only one out of one hundred seventy middle managers is a minority (a Hispanic male). Finally, Hitachi, after locating in this country thirty-two years ago, 22 percent of the middle managers are Japanese, while only 1 percent of the work force is Japanese.

Several Japanese companies—including Quasar, Honda, and Toyota—have been found guilty of discrimination charges and have paid tens of millions of dollars to those who were discriminated against. (It should be noted that very few cases go to trial; Japanese prefer to settle out of court.) Quasar had to pay $4.8 million for discrimination against Americans during a reduction in force from eighty Americans and nine Japanese to twenty-three Americans and nine Japanese. The company had tried to argue that Americans were let go rather than Japanese because speaking Japanese was necessary to do certain jobs. Honda in 1988 had to pay 370 African Americans and women $6 million in back pay, and Mitsubishi in 1991 settled a claim of $2.5 million in a bias suit. One hundred and thirty people, including many in sales and marketing, successfully brought a discrimination suit against the Japanese trading company Sumitomo Corp. of America. This case went all the way to the Supreme Court, which held that a wholly owned American subsidiary of a Japanese company is technically a U.S. corporation and thus subject to U.S. laws. Sumitomo agreed to a $2.8 million training program for women, $1 million in payment to past and current women employees, and a number of other proactive steps.

Not only does discrimination occur against women and people of color but there is increasing evidence that the Japanese discriminate against white males in favor of Japanese employees. For example, charges have been leveled against NGK Spark Plug that there is a two-tier reward system, with the one for Japanese being much higher than the one for Americans. Two senior American executives have filed suit against NEC Electronics for anti-American bias, as well as for retaliating against them because they expressed concerns about Japanese employment practices that they felt violated U.S. law. We should note that Japanese companies are not taking this laying down; they are punishing employees who speak up and have hired large teams of American lawyers to frustrate civil rights enforcement. Yoshi Tsurumi, a professor of International Business at Baruch College, noting that no official numbers exist, believes that there are at least one or two bias suits pending against many large Japanese firms.

It should not be a surprise that Japanese companies who locate plants in the United States avoid areas where there are large African-American and Hispanic populations. And even when these companies do locate in areas with significant numbers of African Americans and Hispanics, the latter are not hired in representative numbers. In the Marysville, Ohio, Honda plant, one would expect 10.5 percent of the employees to be African American based on the local population, but only about 3 percent are. Nissan's plant in Smyrna, Tennessee, has only 14 percent of its work force who are African Americans, yet they make up 19.3 percent of the local population. The Mazda plant in Flat Rock, Michigan, has less than 50 percent of parity with the African-American population (plant employment 14.1 percent, population 29 percent).

In fact, the Japan External Trade Organization helps companies examine data to locate plants, with one set of data being race. It suggested that companies should locate in California because its large Asian population would make good workers. This suggestion was taken wholeheartedly by the Japanese company Consumer Products of America, located in Compton, California. Its employee work force was made up of 50 percent Asians and 25 percent blacks; in the immediate area, the black population was 75 percent and the Asian population only 1.7 percent. We should note that the General Motors–

Toyota joint venture in Fremont, California, which has a great reputation for quality and productivity, has 23 percent black and 28 percent
Hispanic workers, well above the minority population in the immediate area. This, though, is due in greater part to the UAW's and
General Motors' commitment to diversity than to Toyota's enlightenment. Because of the increasing numbers of discrimination complaints against Japanese-based American companies, the House of
Representatives Government Operations Subcommittee on Employment and Housing held hearings on the subject in August 1991.

While there are many complaints about Japanese companies, the
Japanese have their own concerns about their American operations.
The Japanese managers reportedly feel that local workers should raise
company loyalty above family, as they themselves do. Japanese managers complain as well about the lack of performance of American-
based units that they believe are contributing little to the Japanese
parent companies. *Business Week* noted that 60 percent of 264 Japanese executives rated small earnings of U.S. subsidiaries as their main
concern, and only one out of five said their U.S. operations were paying
off. Both Japanese and American managers attribute much of this lack
of performance to cultural conflicts and communications problems
based on different language values and norms.

Even though Japan is aging more rapidly than any major industrialized power, it has had a shortage of workers (and demographics indicate a greater shortage will occur in future economic upturns), and
72 percent of Japanese executives believe that the shortage of labor
and aging of the labor force will be the most important factor holding
back Japan's economic growth in the 1990s and beyond, the Japanese
are unwilling to let foreign workers come into their country. In the
first half of 1990, 51 companies had to fold because they could not
find qualified workers, double the number for the same period from
the previous year. In addition, 268 firms told the Ministry of Labor
that they could not recruit 25 percent of the skilled workers they
needed.

The Japanese (and, as the reader shall see, the European) response
to demographic problems has instead been to tighten immigration
laws. The law passed in 1989 was the first significant change in Japanese law since 1952. The key reasons for the law were the increase
in foreign travel to Japan (2.4 times larger in 1988 than 1978) and
the increased concern about illegal immigrants. The Japanese now limit

immigration only to those with certain professional skills, such as engineers, legal service providers, accountants, entertainers, and sport figures. The law also holds businesses liable if they hire illegal immigrants. As a result of the restrictions, Japanese companies increasingly are seeking to hire Japanese-origin citizens living in foreign countries, which is legally permitted. In the past five years, the number of foreigners forced to leave Japan has doubled.

Japanese fear that their culture will be overwhelmed if immigration is not carefully monitored. Some feel that immigrants should be subjected to blood tests, intelligence tests, and criminal investigations before being issued visas. This attitude persists even though, according to the owner of a cast-iron company, Japanese businessmen are "finding that foreigners do work of very high quality."

Attitudes Toward Koreans

A more detailed look at the Japanese relationship with Koreans will help bring together in a concise picture Japanese racist and xenophobic attitudes. Korea, like many of its neighbors, fears Japanese domination—economic or otherwise. The United States is reducing its military forces in the region, and Korea (like China) fears Japan may wish to fill that gap or take advantage of the situation in the future. Korea's trade deficit with Japan has grown to $9 billion, and Korean industry is losing ground both economically and technologically to Japan. Very much like the United States, Korea has received admonishments from Japanese leaders to work harder and improve quality. The Koreans are also angered that the Japanese, despite their immense trade surplus, maintain high tariffs on all Korean imports. Said one Korean restaurant worker, "The Japanese are our neighbors, but they behave as if they are better than us. . . . So when Japanese customers come in here, I don't feel like treating them very well."[20]

Animosity due to Japanese World War II atrocities still exists throughout the Pacific Rim nations. During former Prime Minister Kaifu's tour of the Far Eastern nations of Singapore, Malaysia, Brunei, the Philippines, and Thailand, he apologized for Japanese actions during the war. The apologies were quickly accepted in Singapore and Malaysia. The bitter feelings held by Japan's neighbors, however, will prohibit Japan from taking on the leadership role its current economic power would otherwise assure. It seems that many Asians are angry over what they perceive as Japan's whitewashing of wartime atrocities; for example, the Japanese Ministry of Education has prohibited any full accounts of the war's events in Japanese textbooks.

The Koreans suffered the greatest at the hands of the Japanese. The Japanese occupied Korea from 1910 until the end of World War II. Their rule is often described as brutal, entailing the forced expatriation of Koreans to labor camps in Japan and throughout their Asian military acquisitions. Korean property was seized, and a systematic effort was made to destroy Korean culture. Koreans were also forced to adopt Japanese names. Only after nearly fifty years did the Japanese issue a full apology, and then only under great pressure from their Asian neighbors. Emperor Akihito was quoted as apologizing in the following terms: "I think of the sufferings your people underwent during this unfortunate period, which was brought about by my country, and cannot but feel the deepest regret." The phrasing formerly used to describe the events of the war by Akihito's father, Hirohito, was milder and did not acknowledge any responsibility by the Japanese.

The emperor's remarks were echoed soon after by former Prime Minister Kaifu, who stated the Japanese "inflicted unbearable suffering and sorrow on the people of the Korean peninsula." These apologies came during the visit of President Roh Tae Woo of South Korea, who readily accepted in an effort to put "the mistakes of the past truly behind us." Incidentally, the visit by Roh culminated in new economic accords that signaled a loosening of Korea's strict boycott of all things Japanese. It would seem that good Japanese business sense has been the catalyst to this recent round of diplomatic concessions and apologies. Roh's trip, however, was marked by various marches and riots in South Korea caused by years of resentment and anger resulting from Japan's years of mistreatment and perceived lack of remorse.

Certainly one of the most divisive incidents between Korea and Japan was the revelation in January 1992 of documents proving that the Japanese government forced tens of thousands of Korean teenage women into prostitution in China during World War II. (Considering that Japan had a history of treating its women in a subservient manner and sold women as commodities until the early part of the twentieth century, perhaps one should not be surprised.) The Japanese put the women on trains with promises of manufacturing jobs, but in fact imprisoned them in barracks described as "filthy" and forced them to service between twenty and fifty Japanese soldiers per day at fifteen-minute intervals. Many of the women were no more than twelve years old; those who contracted venereal diseases (which were rampant) were left untreated to die or were shot. Said one victim, "The Japanese treat their dogs better than they treated us."

The number of "comfort girls" is estimated as between sixty thousand and two hundred thousand. The women reportedly were often brutally beaten and killed; ironically, a government document from the camp era declared that the camps existed to prevent the Japanese troops from raping local women. The surviving women have had to live with the shame, as well as the physical and emotional scars. Many were shunned by Korean society and their families after the occupation because their loss of virginity resulted in unmarriageability.

The revival of these atrocities was devastating to Japan's image in Korea. Only after a Japanese professor, working independently, handed documented proof of the government's involvement to one of Japan's leading newspapers did the government finally apologize. Previously it had not even acknowledged its responsibility, saying that private enterprise had created the camps. A further source of embarrassment was the revelation that the documents were actually easily available since 1958 and that many scholars and government personnel must have been aware of them.[21] The Japanese government has aggravated the situation by resisting demands for restitution and issuing apologies that have been perceived as half-hearted. Japanese officials are denying restitution for these crimes for fear that this action would bring a flood of new suits and nullify the 1965 treaty with Korea that was meant to cover compensation of all wartime atrocities by Japan.

Understandably, this issue brought tension between the two nations to its worst in years. South Korean protesters burned an effigy of Japan's Emperor Akihito soon after the revelations, and during Prime Minister Miyazawa's visit to Korea, one former comfort girl was quoted as saying, "I wanted to hurt him physically. He's just like all Japanese. He wants us all to die so there will be no one left to tell the truth."

Overall, Japan must acknowledge its bad image with South Korea. When Koreans were asked, "What do you think of when you hear the word *Japan?*" six of the eight most common answers were negative; the most positive response of "friendly image" ranked sixth overall with a meager 5 percent. The top response was "colonial rule, historical suffering" with 33 percent, followed by "economic expansion (technological advantages)" (16 percent), "selfish, acts in its own interest" (14 percent), "Hostility, anti-Japanese sentiment," (10 percent), and "war (aggression)" (8 percent).

Furthermore, when asked whether relations between Japan and South Korea would improve, 56 percent of Japanese thought so, while only 35 percent of Koreans were of that opinion. Fifty-one percent of Koreans believed that relations would not change, outnumbering the 34 percent of Japanese who felt that way. Interestingly, only a very small percentage of either group thought relations would worsen (2 percent of Japanese; 5 percent of Koreans), perhaps signaling a positive atmosphere for future relations. This survey was taken in 1990, however, before the turmoil over comfort girls arose.[22]

The Koreans have a right to be angry not only because of Japan's attitudes toward Koreans in Korea but also, as noted earlier, because of the treatment of those living in Japan. Until the late 1980s Koreans who have lived in Japan for generations paid taxes but were denied benefits under the Japanese national pension plan. In addition, William H. Lash, an expert on Japan, noted that "Japanese employees and prospective in-laws support a virtual industry of hundreds of investigators who check into the ethnic backgrounds of applicants and potential spouses to ascertain the existence of any Korean ancestry."

Japan's Success in Asia

It is no surprise that Japan saw the economic potential of the Far East long ago and is already reaping the benefits of early involvement and investment in the region. Economically, it is clear that Japan has created a latter-day version of the Greater East Asian Co-Prosperity Sphere. If Japan's war goals were wealth, military security, international respect, and economic domination of its Asian neighbors, then it has achieved through industry what it had sought through military might. Also, Japan's domination economically does give it great influence over the ideas and cultures of its neighbors. In this light, Asian fears of dominance seem more credible and Japan's presence more threatening.

Once a hotly contested battleground in World War II, the Pacific island of Saipan is now overrun with Japanese hotels, restaurants, and tourists. The Indonesian oil fields that Japan seized during the war are now producing for Japan once again under long-term contracts. In addition, Japan is weaving together an economic structure that links a number of countries together. Production of raw materials, manufacture of parts, assembly, and final use of a product may all occur in different countries, coordinated and controlled by Japan.

A key reason for Japan's success is its heavy investment in terms of loans and economic aid to Asian countries ($3.3 billion from the Japanese as compared to $414 million from the United States in 1990). Geography is on Japan's side as well; salespeople and executives can fly from Tokyo to other Asian countries much more rapidly and cost-effectively than their counterparts from Europe and the United States. Finally, cultural proximity helps—although Japan's culture surely differs from those of its neighbors, it much more closely approximates their beliefs and values than any Western culture.

Asian Fears and Concerns

There does exist a major obstacle to Japanese economic expansion in Asia: the lingering memories of World War II, when Japan sought to annex East Asia to its empire and caused great suffering through the death, imprisonment, and torture of many East Asians. Despite their need for and appreciation of Japan's financial aid and investment, the area's countries are wary of Japanese dominance of their economies. Many already feel it is too late to stem the tide of Japan expansion. Although experts do not predict a reoccurrence of such reactions to Japan's economic domination as the violent protest in Thailand in the 1970s, the issue is a very serious one.

Many countries feel that they have no choice in dealing with Japan because their lack of some advanced technologies puts them at a competitive disadvantage in producing quality, sophisticated goods at a reasonable cost. Japan's trade surplus with the Asian countries has continued to rise even during hard times, and the widening gap could cause a reemergence of ill feelings between these nations and Japan. Even where Japan is not the leading trade partner, it plays a dominating role; for example, Malaysia depends on Japan as its largest investor, and South Korea is dependent on Japan for technology transfers.

Karen Cornelius, executive vice president of our company, Advanced Research Management Consultants, after several trips to Asia concluded that many Asians are increasingly upset about the restrictive role the Japanese place on them in terms of management positions and skills learning. In addition, they believe the Japanese do not transfer technology that will assist the recipients in becoming less reliant on Japan. She noted that some Asian countries like Thailand complain not only of being taken over by Japanese businesses but also of being saturated with Japanese products and Japanese pop culture.

What is happening in Thailand succinctly illustrates Japan's relationship with its Asian neighbors. Thai factory workers can make salaries beyond what they ever dreamed, but rarely do they receive the management, technical, or engineering jobs held by Japanese. (American companies, by contrast, keep few Americans on staff.) Thai partners with Japanese firms also complain that the Japanese do not willingly share their technology. In 1991, National Thai, a parts manufacturing company, sent its first Thai employee to Japan on assignment since its inception in 1961, but many Thais say this process of amelioration is very slow, and one referred to the efforts as "window dressing." For their part, the Japanese are bothered by Thai individualism (as evidenced in frequent job hopping by professional workers) and see Thais as not being loyal to the companies. One Japanese executive even worried that rising economic well-being will make Thais "lazy."

The fear of Asian countries is that greater prosperity will also bring a loss of self-determination. The Japanese revolutionized—or, rather, created—the Malaysian automobile industry by the manufacture of the Proton model. A joint venture with the Malaysian government, the company that makes the vehicle is nevertheless still run by Japanese managers. The Japanese have achieved their dual purpose in Malaysia: making themselves indispensable to one of the world's fastest-growing industrial nations, and progressing in their mission to create an East Asia trading group "in which different Southeast Asian nations specialize in technologies that will feed Japan's biggest industrial giants."[23] The assumed role of cog in Japan's economic machine is one that most Asian nations resent but have thus far had to accept reluctantly. The question is how long can the Japanese maintain these relationships with its neighbors before animosity surfaces.

Japan has worked to improve its image and assuage the fears of its neighbors (and other allies) through actions such as its new foreign-aid-for-peace policy. Japan refuses to aid countries who produce and export too many weapons or who do not allocate a certain portion of their budgets to economic and social, rather than military, concerns. (Japan provides approximately $10 billion a year in aid to other countries.) The policy is believed to be a direct result of criticism leveled at Japan during the Persian Gulf War; Japan is making an effort to convince its allies of its commitment to promote peace.

Japan also is working toward success in Asia by keeping a low profile. "We try to solve problems in the spirit of cooperation and compromise," says Japan's ambassador to Seoul, Kenichi Yanagi.[24] The recent events in Korea, however, illustrate that Japan's past actions cannot be overcome merely by promoting a positive image or keeping a low profile. Japan will have to acknowledge its past fully to assure itself of a bright future. Also, Japan must convince its neighbors that its intentions are nonaggressive and that it is as concerned with overall Asian welfare as with Japanese success. This task will prove formidable, if not impossible.

Conclusion

The Japanese view the homogeneity of their society as a key to their success and see any threat to that homogeneous state as negative. This attitude leads to racist and ethnocentric policies that exclude and discriminate against foreigners and minorities on Japanese soil, as well as discriminate against non-Japanese employees in Japanese companies throughout the world. The Japanese even blame the problems of other countries, such as the United States, on the diversity of their populations.

As the United States, the European Community, and other economic entities learn to compete more effectively with Japan, however, the inefficient utilization of foreign workers will have an extremely negative impact on the Japanese ability to remain a top worldwide competitor. Japanese demographic trends dictate that Japan must utilize foreigners to keep its economic machine running. The continuous alliances, mergers, and takeovers that will increase in a global marketplace dictate that Japan learn to understand and appreciate diverse people. Despite the problems that were discussed, Japanese are slowly but surely trying to adapt to the American and other cultures (more so American, because of our laws against discrimination). For example, Fujitsu USA has only 2 percent Japanese (mostly engineers) in its employee body of five thousand, and Nissan put Americans in true control of its Sonyina, Tennessee, plant. Honda and Toyota are moving in this direction, but at a slower pace. This chapter illustrates that in order to achieve success in the globalization process, the Japanese will have to abandon their long-held beliefs in the superiority of homogeneity and embrace and fully utilize diversity.

6

European Community Structures, Business, and Labor

In this chapter we shall provide the reader with some general information about the European Community, its structure, and its general business and labor practices. This will assist the reader in understanding what the EC is attempting to accomplish and lay a foundation for how the diversity issues of race, ethnicity, and gender will influence its ability to evolve into the largest economic world power.

Many European, Japanese, and U.S. business leaders were jolted just as hard as local politicians were by Denmark's unexpected rejection of the Maastricht treaty for European unity. The fact that all other nations, except England, have now approved the treaty suggest that the EC will survive; however, the Dutch vote, the narrow approval vote in France (51 percent to 49 percent), and the strong English opposition to certain aspects of the EC (monetary and political union, and the free movement of people) has made the EC modify its schedule of implementation of the more controversial aspects of the treaty.

Until the Danish vote, a great deal had been made of the potential economic power of the European common market, the newly born twelve-country unit comprising Belgium, Denmark, France, Germany, Greece, Ireland, Italy, Luxembourg, the Netherlands, Portugal, Spain, and the United Kingdom. The formation of this community consists of key initiatives such as the removal of all tariffs, capital fund barriers, and obstacles to the movement of people among member nations. More specifically, the EC has passed directives and legislation to accomplish, among other things, the following:[1]

- Citizens can set up businesses in any of the other countries just like they can in their own.
- A free flow of people, goods, capital, and services among the nations.
- U.S. and other non-EC citizens need only pass through customs once, even if they visit all twelve countries.
- A mutual recognition of university degrees.
- Citizens of one EC nation will be able to deposit money in the others.
- Banks can become partners and fund projects outside of their native country.
- Companies can bid for government contracts in other countries.
- Companies can compete as freely in any country as in their own.
- There will be safety and quality standards set for products considered "vital to create a uniform continental market."
- Key environmental standards on water and air must be followed by all members, along with safety standards for nuclear energy plants.

The EC will create the largest trading bloc in the industrialized world and number at least 340 million people, compared to about 255 million for the United States and 127 million for Japan. The EC seems so formidable that Austria, Sweden, Finland, and Norway are extremely interested, and some eastern European countries are afraid that they might be left behind.

The main reason for its formation is not the Europeans' love for each other but rather the well-founded fear that unless Europe unites, the United States and Japan will dominate the separate European nations. Because its management and labor relations systems, capital markets, technological orientation, and government policies did not change to meet the new realities of the global postindustrial economy, Europe as a whole performed poorly. During the 1970s, western Europe was faced with stagnation, double-digit inflation, and unemployment. In addition, Europe recognized that it had a high-technology gap with Japan and the United States. Despite significant improvement over the 1970s, the 1980s did not see Europe's overall economic competitiveness increase.

Even though Europe outspent Japan in research and development

(R & D), the lack of collaboration between scientific institutions and industry—together with the presence of different national standards throughout Europe—made success hard to achieve. The lack of an EC-wide market also imposed real constraints. The fixed costs of R & D in developing telecommunications products, for example, required a large market with common standards. But the "uncommon market," in which each nation sought to advance its own "national champions," precluded the emergence of companies with genuinely European strategies.

The vast majority of firms in almost all EC countries are small or medium-sized and operate within a single country only. This is a distinct disadvantage for Europe as a whole, as economies of scale in production, marketing, sales, and R & D expenses can be better absorbed by larger firms. In comparison, the average firm is bigger in both the United States and Japan: In the United States because the market is considerably larger than the individual markets of the EC countries, and in Japan because of the essentially global outlook that firms adopt (often visualizing the entire world as a single market). In addition, while European industries were struggling because of many of the above factors, big U.S. companies such as IBM and Ford were enjoying success because they approached Europe as a single large market, which provided them with numerous economies of scale (for example, IBM makes one product at each of its thirteen European plants and distributes them throughout Europe). In the face of Japanese and American successes, it became increasingly clear to European governments and businesses that they had no real choice but to move forward as a European community. Because of the rejection of the Maastricht treaty by Denmark, however, at least two Danish companies have delayed or halted expansion plans: plastic building-block maker Lego AS has stopped plans to spend an estimated 250 to 300 million krones ($40.2 to $48.2 million) to expand one domestic factory and build another, and the electronics company FL Smidt AS is limiting its foreign investment in the EC only to plants and factories that it already owns.

In 1988 the European Community Commission published "The Costs of Non-Europe," widely known as the Cecchini report. It reports the findings of a study (by a group of experts chaired by Paolo Cecchini) of the potential benefits of an internal common market. The report noted that as an integrated market the EC would achieve the following types of cost savings and benefits:

- Fewer costly "barriers such as customs formalities, protective public procurement, divergent national standards, and restrictions on services and manufacturing that hinder trade, limit competition, and sustain excess costs and overpricing."
- Reduced "costs through increased economies of scale in production and business organization. This would be accompanied by a more cost-effective supply of labor, capital, plant, and components for industrial production, and improved allocation among firms, sectors, and countries."
- Higher profit margins for individual companies based on cost savings, the ability to take on foreign competition in global markets, and a structural increase in European demand. Despite the downward impact on prices, increased operating efficiencies would reduce many companies' overhead by 10 percent or more.
- Increased innovation, resulting in the creation of new businesses and products. Larger markets and the restructuring of Europe's productive potential would enable many firms to finance and undertake R & D projects previously considered too costly and risky.

The report claims that these and other developments would result in a 5 percent growth in the EC's gross national product, a 6 percent reduction in prices, and two million new jobs. It has since become clear that these estimates are likely to be achieved only after the EC countries are able to deal more effectively with the recession, their strong nationalistic feelings, the unification of Germany, the collapse of communism in eastern Europe and the Soviet Union, and issues about immigration and women. The evidence suggests this will not happen for a very considerable time.

After a long period of strong growth in the middle and late 1980s, the economic results and outlook for the EC in the early 1990s has been unfavorable. In fact, the separate national economies have slipped further into recession along with the rest of the world. Employment growth, as a result, has slowed considerably; the overall EC rate of unemployment rose from 8.3 percent in 1990 to 8.7 percent in 1991 and to 9.7 percent in 1992. The unemployment situation has not improved in 1993. Philips, Europe's largest electronics company, intends to eliminate about forty-five thousand jobs (one-sixth of its work force), many in Europe. Car sales for the three largest German automakers shrank by about 15 percent in 1992; this fact, combined with a need to improve productivity as Japan enters the European market, means job cuts. BMW laid off about three thousand employees in 1992 and Volkswagen will let go of ten thousand by 1994.[2] Mercedes Benz cut between eight thousand and ten thousand jobs in 1992 and will reduce its work force overall by twenty thousand in the coming years, mostly in its German plants.[3] In addition, because of the high cost of German labor, BMW and Mercedes Benz have decided to locate production plants in the United States, thus causing a further loss of jobs for Germans. Although the unification of Europe was meant to strengthen job security and create jobs, a period of cutbacks seems necessary, especially with a recession from which even the powerful Germans have not been immune.

In the remainder of this chapter and the next three chapters, we will discuss the European Community in more detail and suggest why we believe that it will have difficulty achieving the dominant economic position so many have predicted. The EC's problems will occur not because it has been or will be unable to deal effectively with the "hard" issues of the economy, trade, and the environment, but because of trouble in dealing with the "soft" issues: race, ethnicity, religion, language, culture, gender, and national pride. As they begin to understand the potential impact of the EC on national sovereignty, many citizens have developed anti-EC sentiments. In addition, when both citizens and immigrants begin to make use of the new freedoms granted by the EC, there will be tremendous potential for conflict based on such issues as ethnicity and language. There are significant and increasing racist, ethnic, linguistic, and religious conflicts occurring in most EC countries following the influx of large numbers of immigrants from the Third World and recently from eastern European countries. Add to these the historical conflicts among and within European nations over ethnicity, religion, and language, and one can begin to imagine the potentially severe problems the EC will have regarding the issues of human diversity.

European nations have gone through two major world wars in this century and numerous other wars in the previous centuries. The animosities associated with these wars are still seething just under the surface; we believe they will rear their ugly heads more openly as the EC becomes a reality. Yugoslavia's ethnic and religious wars are a prime example. Another illustration is the firing of Nicholas Ridley, Britain's secretary of trade and industry, for publicly stating views that have been expressed privately by many in Britain. In discussing the possibility of monetary union, Ridley referred to the Germans as "uppity" and said giving up monetary rights would be like giving in to Adolf Hitler. Although Ridley was punished for these comments, an internal British government report essentially said the same thing, and a survey of British citizens found 33 percent who agreed with him.

Demographic Problems and Economic Implications

Because of advances in medicine, the European population expanded rapidly during the eighteenth and nineteenth centuries. As a result, many people left their native lands to colonize the Americas and other parts of the world, and many more emigrated during periods of famines and poor economic conditions. In the late twentieth century the European population is rapidly aging, birthrates are very low, and population growth has slowed; these trends will accelerate during the first half of the twenty-first century.[4] Since the mid-1970s many EC countries' birthrates have fallen below the population replacement rate of 2.1: in 1990 the birthrate among all EC countries was 1.58, down from 2.63 in 1960 (see Table 6–1 for the breakdown of birthrates for individual EC countries).[5] Moreover, the notion that western Europe can obtain the required numbers of workers from other European countries is not viable, because their birthrates are also below 2.1 with the exceptions of Albania (3.0) and Moldava (2.3). Although the EC population will grow from 327,136,500 people in 1990 to 333,873,900 in the year 2000, it is expected to decline to 319,623,000 by the year 2020.

Not only is the birthrate low, but Europe is aging at a rapid rate. The percentages for the population sixty years of age and older in 1990 were as follows: Spain, 17.3 percent; France, 18.5 percent; West Germany, 20.5 percent; and Britain, 20.6 percent. By 2010, the percentages in this age group will be Spain, 20.5 percent; France, 22.6 percent; West Germany, 26.9 percent; and Britain, 22.2 percent.

TABLE 6–1
Birthrate Percentages in EC Countries, 1990

Ireland	2.11
Britain	1.85
France	1.81
Denmark	1.62
Belgium	1.58
Netherlands	1.55
Luxembourg	1.52
Greece	1.50
Portugal	1.50
West Germany	1.39
Spain	1.30
Italy	1.29

Though the United States has and will have large numbers of illegal and legal immigrants to replenish its aging population, the Europeans, like the Japanese, have had little immigration and are implementing strict laws that will severely limit any further immigration. In addition, there are movements, particularly in France and Germany to send foreigners (especially North Africans and Turkish people) back to their home countries. The demographics of an aging and declining population, combined with the hostile attitudes toward immigrants and not very progressive attitudes toward women, have the potential of seriously damaging the EC's economic growth and possession of the requisite skills to run the national and global companies of the 1990s and beyond.

Surveys have suggested that with the exception of Ireland and Denmark, difficulties in the recruitment of appropriately trained workers increased throughout the EC before the worldwide recession of the early 1990s. The biggest shortages occurred in the United Kingdom, France, Germany, Belgium, and the Netherlands and took place especially over the second half of the 1980s. In general, because the degree of capacity utilization increased only to a minor extent, it could be deduced that skill shortages were becoming a bigger problem throughout most of northern Europe during the 1980s.

While there are significant skills shortages in key segments of manufacturing, recruitment difficulties have not been confined to this sector. Studies in the United Kingdom and Ireland have reported various kinds of skill shortages in the financial services sector. In western Greece, small and medium-sized firms in the high-technology sectors report severe shortages of clerical, marketing, and skilled manual personnel. Italian studies have shown skill shortages in such traditional sectors as clothing and food. Studies in Spain and other southern European countries have shown skill shortages in other service areas, such as tourism. Shortages of certain occupations (for example, nurses) are commonplace throughout the community.

All of these shortages have come about despite the commitment most EC countries have to training. In Germany, the so-called dual system of initial vocational training (which combines practical experience with theoretical instruction) provides a broad range of skills for most school-leavers and ensures their early integration into the labor market. This reduces the need for training later in working life, compared with countries like the United Kingdom where many young people have in the past entered the labor market without such broadly based vocational training. France has long-established and widely developed government regulations for the training of employed adults. Under a 1971 law, all French firms with more than ten employees are required to commit a part of their wage bill (currently 1.2 percent) to further training, either by spending it directly for their own employees or through mutual training funds established on a sectoral or regional basis. Where firms fall short of the required training expenditure, the deficit is collected by the state in the form of a training tax. Ireland has a similar compulsory levy-grant scheme covering certain industries, including most of manufacturing. It requires enterprises to spend between 1 percent and 1.25 percent of their payroll either for training or for levies that are collected by the labor market authority and spent on the promotion of enterprise training. The United Kingdom had such a scheme to promote basic vocational training in the early 1970s, but it was later abolished.

In brief, the EC's economic successes will be greatly hindered because of demographic changes. As the reader will see, the EC's skilled labor shortage is also a result of discrimination against EC women and restrictive immigration laws. When the recession ceases, when the work needed to rebuild eastern Europe becomes more evident, and as shifting demographics begin to have a more profound impact on the labor supply, the shortage of necessary talent to make the EC a top economic power will become severe unless the EC changes its racist, sexist, ethnocentric, and xenophobic attitudes and behaviors.

Government and Business in the EC

If leaders in both government and business in the EC countries come to recognize that their future successes will be based on the ability to develop diverse high-performance teams in both their own countries and their international operations, the close ties between government and business developed in those countries over the years could allow them to make quantum leaps in employing diverse employees. To understand why we conclude thus, it is necessary to understand EC government-business relationships.[6]

There are some significant differences between the market systems of the United States and the EC, as well as among those of the separate EC countries. Overall, the United States has a much freer and more competitive market system than any EC country, whereas large segments of the EC economies have been directed primarily by an elite group of national bureaucracies staffed by technocrats. More specifically, European governments play much more intrusive and controlling roles than the U.S. government concerning their respective economies. There are a large number of government-owned companies, and many industries (for example, airlines, agriculture, transportation, textiles, steel, telephones, and banks) are highly regulated, fending off even internal competition from other national producers. In addition, most industries have been characterized by oligopolistic competition or "gentlemen's agreements" in fixing prices or restricting operations to certain geographical locations. Government spending related to business in European countries is substantially higher than the United States. Finally, there is much more of a "protect your industries," "welfare for your people" mentally in Europe than in the United States. One can trace this centralized control by government to the remnants of the feudal system.

Over time, reduced competition has made business executives feel secure. This has further impaired the ability of their companies to utilize diverse workers effectively and to compete with outsiders, making them even more vulnerable and dependent upon additional legislation or other measures to protect them from imports. Firms continue to exist in Europe that are as bureaucratic, inefficient, and unable to adapt to the changing environment as the governments that strive to protect them from outside competition. For example, the former West German Bundespost takes six weeks (three months if street work is involved) and two separate appointments with different technicians to install a phone line and hook it up to one's wall. In Germany, "money transfers take two weeks, [and] trains and planes are canceled without notice on holidays. Grocery stores close during lunch hour, on weekends and before many people get off work."[7] German ideas about perfectionism and efficiency have actually resulted in inefficiency and increased bureaucracy.

In addition to the government financial support for businesses, there is an array of legal, technical, and cultural barriers to keep foreign companies at bay that a number of experts believe is as effective as the Japanese protectionist machinery. Even though there have been no custom duties on exports among EC countries for the past several years, there have been barriers to free trade in the form of technical standards and regulations, administrative rules, and fragmented local markets. Non-EC-member companies that wish to locate in EC countries face even more barriers. The case of Toys R Us is a lesson of how business is done in EC countries. Toys R Us hired a German managing director to start its entrance into that country's market. Despite a wealth of experience in German retailing and being a board member of one of the biggest department store chains, he had an uphill battle. German toy manufacturers ran a public relations campaign condemning the "dangerous toys" the company sold and the self-service warehouse concept of Toys R Us. Several leading toy manufacturers said that they would not allow Toys R Us to sell their products because it would cheapen their image. German officials politely rejected proposals, claiming that space in Germany was limited and that the huge warehouse concept was impractical. With persistence, financing, and marketing, however, Toys R Us has overcome these obstacles.

Some writers have noted that protectionism in Germany has been less open and pervasive than in Japan; however, it is deeply rooted and very effective. It is present not only in legal requirements at the local, state, and federal levels, technical barriers, and extensive government subsidies, but also in cultural barriers that are at times personally determined by the numerous bureaucrats at various levels.

Many of Germany's neighbors are concerned about the threat of German domination of their markets while finding penetration of the German market impossible (Germany has eighty million people and represents the world's third largest economy). This illustrates how difficult it will be as economics dictate that firms throughout the EC merge and attempt to penetrate markets outside their small national boundaries. Cultural conflict, nationalism, ethnocentrism, and xenophobia will have very negative impacts on the EC's ability to develop into a competitive economic power.

Labor and Management in EC Countries

As increasing numbers of American companies try to expand to Europe and/or as mergers take place between American and European companies, it is important for American executives to have some understanding about the labor/management practices in Europe, which differ considerably from American practices.[8] If applied equitably and fairly to all employees in EC countries, many of the EC labor practices (such as contract and termination procedures) could benefit women and foreign employees. Many of the practices that contribute to excessive wages, low productivity, and other inefficiencies, however, must be changed to make the EC truly competitive with the United States and Japan.

Somehow American workers have gotten the reputation of being lazy and overpaid in comparison to European and Japanese workers, but the fact of the matter is that U.S. workers have fewer days of vacation, work longer hours and get paid less than many Europeans. For example, in France more than 50 percent of the workers take August off, and in Germany most workers have six week vacations; British workers get twenty-seven days off, Japanese eleven days, and Americans only twelve days. In addition, per week, Germans work about 37.7 hours, British 38.8 hours, Americans 40 hours, and Japanese 42 hours. American manufacturing labor is cheaper in comparison to European and Japanese labor; Germans receive $21.89 per hour, British $14.28, Japanese $14.94, and Americans $13.97. The main reasons for the extremely high cost of German labor are nonwage costs for social security, workers' compensation, and unemployment insurance. Labor unions have a key role in the high cost.

Hirings, Firings, and Layoffs

Prior to the formation of the EC, only Greece, the Netherlands, and Spain had no substantial formal hiring procedures. In Ireland employees could request a written statement; in Denmark the contract was usually oral; and in all other countries (Belgium, France, Germany, Italy, Luxembourg, Portugal, and the United Kingdom), some form of written contract was required.

Firings, layoffs, and other terminations in member countries were also highly regulated even prior to the formation of the EC. As of 1989, all EC countries with the exception of Greece had minimum standards for notice to be given by employers for layoffs and termination. There was quite a range of standards, with Ireland giving as little as one to eight weeks and the UK giving one to thirteen weeks. In France employees must receive one month of notice after six months of employment, and two months after two years of work. In some countries, such as Italy and Portugal, companies can only dismiss workers for "just cause" or redundancy. Most nations have payments for unfair dismissal or severance payments, and some (such as Germany and the Netherlands) require that terminations be approved by work councils or labor offices. Firing an employee thus is very costly, because the employee must be compensated. The cost of terminating a $50,000-per-year-middle-level manager with twenty years of service in 1992 ranged from highs of $130,000 in Italy and $125,000 in Spain to $19,000 in France and Britain and $13,000 in Ireland.[9,10] Although EC countries are not known to provide lifetime employment in the same manner as the Japanese, in reality it exists for many European employees. Companies' abilities to restructure, downsize, or close plants to meet economic necessities is very difficult because of government regulations and unions. In addition, because of the 1990s' recession and resulting high unemployment, some European governments must be consulted and agree to terminations.

These laws and practices, however, do not protect all workers. Cheap labor has been flooding western Europe from the east as a result of political shakeups in formerly communist nations. As state-run industries have crumbled, eastern Europeans have replaced the Turks, North Africans, and Italians of thirty years ago as the grunt workers of northern Europe, filling the occupations shunned by the locals (such as road and factory work). Their desperation is exploited: they are paid mostly under the table for very low wages (and therefore have no legal rights), work long hours, and live in crowded quarters. Many observers complain that the illegal labor traffic is costing law-abiding companies while offenders get unfair cost breaks, that it robs governments of tax revenues, and that it is hurting efforts to standardize the European labor market. It also delays modernization efforts by creating artificially low costs and, therefore, injures future competitiveness.[11]

Employee Representation

Belgium, Germany, France, Luxembourg, and the Netherlands have official work councils to provide employee participation in the decisions that affect them and their companies. Some of these countries (Luxembourg and France) also have employee or union representation on the council.[12] Other countries with some form of employee or union representation in the decision-making process are Denmark, Greece, Portugal, and Spain; Italy, Ireland and the United Kingdom have no formal requirements.[13]

The right of workers or their representatives to information and consultation is guaranteed in Spanish labor legislation. Under the terms of the Spanish Workers' Statute, works councils have the right to information and consultation regarding company finances, restructurings and layoffs, plant transfers, training, new methods and technologies, merger, takeovers, and job evaluations insofar as such matters affect employment. In the Netherlands, information rights apply to "all Dutch undertakings, including those belonging to a concern or group with subsidiaries outside the Netherlands." (This deviates from some other EC nations' policies; in Italy, for example, firms are only made to comply if located in the national territory.)

Although the British government represents itself as "firmly committed" to employee information, consultation, and involvement, it is opposed to prescriptive legislation on the matter as it would be against the UK's traditional industrial relations, which is based on the notion of volunteerism. The government does want to encourage (although not by law) voluntary employee involvement by promoting good company practices; specialist, business, and professional organizations; government-sponsored and -supported research work on employee involvement; and financial participation.

There are a number of different European models of employee representation on boards of directors; however, we will focus on Germany in order to provide an illustration. Employee representation on company boards of directors differs greatly between the United States and Germany and is responsible in part for the higher wages and benefits received by German workers. In the United States, employee representation exists on very few boards of directors, and only then because of union pressure or employee stock ownership plans. In Germany, three models of employee board representation are guaranteed by law: one for coal and steel industries, one for companies with two thousand or more employees, and one for companies with five hundred to two thousand employees. All guarantee from one third to one half employee representation on the board. The last category has only one-third representation, and therefore employee representatives sometimes find themselves bypassed or slighted; even this, however, is far more of a share than U.S. representatives receive. Chief operating officers are not on the board of German companies, as is the case in the United States. In Germany, union officials work with and on the board; however, in the United States they are seen as neutral or friendly only by employee representatives on the board. U.S. board members also like to keep collective bargaining operations separate from the board. German employee representation ensures that the interest of employees is served in terms of programs for displaced employees, early retirement, severance, and retraining.[14]

Unions: The Right to Strike, Freedom of Association, and Collective Bargaining

France is representative of EC union policy.[15] Its constitution allows for the right to strike to "be exercised within the framework of the laws governing it," a framework that has very rarely been invoked. In the public sector however, since there is more need for continuity of service, limitations on striking are more often imposed. Belgian law does not recognize or define strikes, but striking is allowed as long as "the freedom and rights of other persons and the legal provisions and regulations which may restrict the exercising of this freedom are respected." Denmark has no legislation preventing employers from joining employer's organizations or preventing employees from joining unions, whereas other countries (like Greece) actively encourage employees to join unions.

As noted earlier, the power of unions helps explain the high cost and low productivity of many European workers. For example, a key problem Europeans have in the auto industry in being competitive with the Japanese is in regard to management policies, which are controlled in part by strong unions. Because of the unions there are many employees in the shop who add no real value to the production of the goods; in fact, these excessive workers are there to correct the mistakes others make. Absenteeism is often high and productivity low, since workers know that they cannot easily be fired. Indeed, even if they are, the social security system is such that the economic benefits of unemployment compensation may even work as a disincentive to finding alternative employment.

MIT researchers say that European automakers will have to cut their work force in half. Data show that European automobile plants and auto-component manufacturers are judged to be, on average, less productive than Japanese plants. A recent study by MIT concluded that European-owned car producers in 1989 had an average productivity of thirty-five hours per vehicle, compared with seventeen hours for Japanese-owned firms based in Japan, twenty-one hours for Japanese firms in North America, and 25 hours for U.S. firms in North America. Quality, measured by the number of defects per one hundred vehicles, showed similar relative performance.

Even Bernard Espel, leader of the Confédération Française Democratique du Travail union, said that "we have a huge amount of changes to make in our working systems if we're to compete with the Japanese." Though many companies are radically changing their production methods to compete with the Japanese, they have yet to realize the necessity to make changes in labor relations. Such fragile but highly effective Japanese methods as the "just-in-time" production system require tranquil labor relations in order to work, and European workers are seen as too contentious. Of course, within the EC, different cultures are seen as more contentious than others, with the French being the most difficult and the Germans adapting most easily to new production and labor methods. Although Greece (887) and Spain (647) have the most days lost per thousand employees, compared to Germany (5) and the Netherlands (8), the French generally cause the most disruptive and costly strikes, as demonstrated by the trucking strike in the spring of 1992, which paralyzed much of the EC.[16]

Despite the anticompetitive nature of union contracts, the EC in early 1992 intended to solidify union rights as a result of concessions given to corporations. Rather than have a company incorporate in every country and be subjected to numerous codes of law under the European Company Statutes, the companies would have been subjected to only one law code for taxes and labor laws (but not accounting procedures). For these concessions, companies agreed to select one of the following models of employee participation:

1. *German model (Mitbestimmung)*—Worker representatives would have a seat on the supervisory board (similar to the board of directors in a U.S. company).
2. *French model*—There would be a separate system of independent internal employee councils, but workers would not have a seat on the board of directors.
3. *Scandinavian model*—Collective bargaining would determine the form of worker representation, but a member state would be free to disallow a representation option it did not like.

In December 1992, under tremendous pressure from some countries (such as England) and major corporations, the EC postponed any implementation of this agreement.

Thus, a major challenge for EC firms (and governments) will be to check growth in wages, salaries, and fringe benefits, as they are at a disadvantage vis-à-vis U.S. and Japanese companies (which make considerably lower social security contributions and fringe benefit payments). Unless EC firms can cut their costs, they will remain at a competitive disadvantage, with higher labor costs and productivity well below that of the United States or Japan. Labor unions and labor strife will increase as the EC countries face uncertain economic times and workers become concerned about the impact of the EC on their way of life. In 1992, the numbers of strikes caused by EC membership requirements increased tremendously. Another factor that has increased the labor strife in the EC is the economic recession and all the raise of nationalism to protect one nation's economy against the others.

1989 Community Charter

In December 1989, 11 heads of state of European Community nations (excluding the British) approved the Community Charter of the Fundamental Social Rights of Workers (see Appendix A for details).[17] The commission responsible for the charter also created a program for the rapid implementation of the rights guaranteed in it. The charter covers a number of important areas to protect workers. The key components are stated as follows: "All workers, women and men, have the right to work in any EC country and to be treated fairly and equally in access to employment, wages, rights to join or not join unions, vocational training, working conditions, health, safety, social protection and adequate retirement resources."

While most member states agree about general rights in the areas of workers' health, safety, the transfer of private pension rights across borders, and the mutual recognition of technical qualifications, there are several problem areas (for example, workweek hours and some issues concerning child labor). With the exception of Britain, all the EC nations (particularly Germany and France) were eagerly in favor of endorsing the charter; however, the United Kingdom felt that the EC should not have jurisdiction over social concerns. Some of the prime areas of concern covered by the charter are

> the freedom to stay and work in any member state, the regulation of the working day, the right to holidays, hygiene and safety standards at the work place, the right to fair pay, the freedom to join a union, the opportunity for workers to be informed and consulted about their company's practices and plans, access to professional training to adapt to changing technology, the protection of young workers and, for all, adequate social protection. Provisions in the charter range from such items as a "decent wage" to worker participation in management decisions.[18]

As the reader will see in the coming chapters, this charter will have to be strengthened in order to give women and immigrants fair and equal opportunities for employment in EC countries.

Conclusion

Although the EC has come far in setting up the necessary structures to achieve unity, there are a number of business and union relationships and practices that must be redefined in order for it to become the world economic power it hopes to be. Unions and businesses are resisting acceptance of the necessary hardships—reduced wages, longer working hours, and shorter vacations—that they must adopt to become more competitive with the United States and Japan. Nationalistic protection of industries, many of which are owned or subsidized by governments, will be a crucial problem to overcome. In addition, the birthrate and aging populations of the EC countries will increasingly become crucial problems to resolve.

As the European Community looks to its future, it sees a declining and aging population that will lead not only to a labor shortage but also a decreased customer base. Thus, it must look to global markets for economic growth and to women and immigrants to fill jobs. Another major problem the EC will face on an ongoing basis, if it is successful, is the eventual addition of other members. For example, the EC is showing some of its racial, ethnic, and religious biases as it considers the admission of Turkey, a poor, relatively uneducated Moslem country. In the next three chapters we shall focus on the issues of race, ethnicity, religion, and gender to understand the potential of the EC to utilize its increasingly diverse population in becoming the leading economic power in the 1990s and beyond.

European Women

Though most European nations maintain a multitude of highly progressive family-oriented programs in comparison to the United States, Europe lags far behind the United States in providing equal employment opportunities to women.[1] A unique combination of social, historical, and economic conflicts have enabled European countries to institute advanced family policies. This may also explain why equitable employment policies such as those initiated in the United States were not developed throughout Europe, as there seemed to be no pressing need for them. European policies have, however, introduced large numbers of women into the work force, not necessarily due to a changing perception of women's roles (as occurred in the United States), but rather as a function of historical and economic reasons. Sweden's historically socialist philosophy is grounded in the concept of providing citizens with the tools that will enable them to act as productive members of society. France and Germany, though they differ philosophically from Sweden, were pushed into more aggressive and comprehensive family care programs as a result of a labor shortage following World War II; they chose to assist women in entering the work force rather than import large numbers of foreigners in order to revitalize their economies.

As the need for female workers to augment the labor force began to subside in the years following World War II, labor laws and attitudes continued to reflect inequities toward women. Some discriminatory laws have only recently been repealed. For example, it was not until 1977 that West Germany repealed a law granting husbands the right to prevent their wives from working outside the home. Inequitable laws outside of the workplace were called into question as well: the German Federal Constitutional Court ruled in the 1980s that forcing a woman to adopt her husband's name was contrary to the principle of equal treatment for men and women.[2] In 1992 it ruled that women wage earners could be employed at night, bringing to an end a one-hundred-year-old night-shift ban on female blue-collar workers. The ban was based on the prejudice that women's constitution made them less able than men to withstand the rigors of nighttime work.

Discriminatory French laws are being struck down as well. Janie Chouvac, chairperson of the Women's Committee of the Center for Political and Social Studies (CEPS) of the Louise Michel Club, has for several years studied marital law in order to pinpoint changes that should be made in divorce proceedings so that discrimination against women could be circumvented. French law dicates that in the case of divorce after six years of de facto separation, income taxes and other costs related to the couple's joint property must be borne by the abandoned spouse (usually the woman) even if the latter's sole income is a monthly allowance ordered by the judge. In addition, the fees and other expenses of the proceedings are borne in practice by the abandoned spouse. Given these injustices, Chouvac demands that mutual insurance company premiums be borne by husbands seeking divorce, that monthly alimony payments no longer be taxed, and that court fees for dividing property be paid by the spouse who is seeking the divorce.[3]

That there are still mixed views about women in the EC can be demonstrated by the fact that only in Ireland (78 percent) and Great Britain (79 percent) did a significant majority of those polled believe women should have more freedom to do what they want; at the low end of the range were Portugal (38 percent), Belgium (47 percent), and Italy (48 percent). As A. B. Antal and C. Krebsbach-Gnath wrote about German female managers:

> The sociopsychological barriers faced by women in management in Germany probably do not differ significantly from those faced by women in comparable Western industrialized cultures. They have to deal with the same kinds of prejudice based on stereotypes, misinformation, fears, and insecurity. Women are not hired or promoted because it is believed that they are not capable of making difficult decisions, or it is argued that the organization's investment will not pay off since it is expected that women will leave after marriage, when children are born, or when their husbands move for business

reasons. The mobility of women is automatically assumed to be less than that of men. It is presumed that women are not career oriented, just task oriented. These unspoken beliefs play a subtle role in decision-making processes concerning hiring and promoting women.[4]

Women in Education

The number of women in the EC labor force is increasing in proportion to the growing number of women obtaining postsecondary educations. Within EC nations, the number of women pursuing such education increased from 1.3 million in the 1970–71 academic year to 3.4 million in the 1989–90 academic year.[5] Nevertheless, most of the degrees they pursue remain in traditionally female areas. For example, approximately half of all Italian university students are women, but a continued imbalance is apparent in the choice of subjects studied: 80 percent of the female students opt for literary subjects, while 83 percent of male students choose engineering. More Italian women, however, are moving into business-oriented fields. Women represent 40 percent of the students working toward degrees in economics, and professional training for women has risen from 29 percent to 42 percent. Even so, it will take about ten more years for a genuine balance to be achieved.

Analysis of Germany reveals that continuous progress is not assured. The proportion of women in universities there has fallen from 40.4 percent to 39.2 percent, despite the fact that as many women completed secondary school as men.[6] Heike Wipperfurth, a reporter from Germany, told us that the decrease occurred in part because of the economic slowdown and the more conservative social trends occurring in Germany. Once German women obtain a degree, they have great disadvantages in comparison with men. Although 77.3 percent of female university graduates feel the need to continue their education, only half of them have the opportunity to do so. According to the respondents, employers tend to send men rather than women for advanced courses. The Association of Women Graduates therefore proposes that the government provide more subsidies to firms that practice affirmative action.[7]

The assumption that the higher one's level of education, the less likely one is to be unemployed does not apply to men and women in the same manner. The work of the European experts on female employment have found that the advantage conferred by higher education seems to favor men.[8] For example, while only 25 percent of the German working population are women with university degrees, they represent 45 percent of the unemployed college graduates.

Women tend to be poorly represented among those employed in European universities. Although almost equivalent numbers of women and men study in Flemish universities, this near equality disappears when one examines the teaching and support staff, in which men account for an average of 80 percent of the total. And the higher the employee rank, the rarer the presence of women: women account for 34 percent of the temporary scientific staff, 17 percent of the tenured scientific staff, 8 percent of the lecturers, 6 percent of the professors, and only 2.9 percent of the tenured professors.[9]

Women in Politics

Women represent only one out of five elected members of the European Parliament, but the number of women who practice politics throughout the EC countries varies greatly. For example, the conservative government of Denmark retains only four female ministers out of a total of nineteen, despite the fact that one-third of Denmark's Parliament is composed of women. Currently, 9 percent of the members of the Belgian Parliament are women. In the Senate, they occupy 10 percent of the seats, and they make up one-fourth of the Regional Council of Brussels. Only four women out of a possible sixty, however, hold the title of secretary of state or executive.

In the Irish public services, very few women occupy positions at the decision-making level. Of the members of the state boards, 15 percent are women, which represents a growth of 3 percent since 1985; at this rate, it will take until the year 2060 to realize an equal distribution.[10] In England, the Hansard Society's Commission on Women at the Top notes that seventy years after women won the right to vote, few women make it to the top of the major institutions of the United Kingdom.[11]

In Germany, only 24.5 percent of Social Democratic party members are women, and they are even less well represented within party institutions. Women fill only 15 percent of the seats on the National Policy Committee and 7.2 percent of those on the National Council. They account for only 6.8 percent of the party's members of Parliament

(MPs).[12] The current German government includes four women ministers out of nineteen, and four women secretaries of state out of thirty-one.

EC nations are beginning to address the issue of disproportionate representation. British Tory MP Teresa Gorman introduced a bill in January 1992 that would mandate an equal number of male and female MPs. As a result, new voting systems would be implemented in order to ensure equality and proportional representation throughout all British political parties. The initiative has predictably met with much virulent opposition, including the objections voiced by Sally Hamwee, Liberal Democratic party leader on the Planning Advisory Committee, who has argued that quotas would have the effect of marginalizing women. Political leaders continue to battle over an effective policy to ensure equality of representation.[13]

While British women remain in the minority in the political arena, they are in fact a majority of the electorate. Furthermore, recent studies reveal that women do maintain a distinct political agenda, although no party appears to be in a principal position in respect to appealing to women's concerns. Women who were interviewed reported concerns ranging from increased investment in health services and child care issues to further commitment to policies ensuring the safety of urban women. Both men and women in Britain responded favorably to the proposal of a separate ministry or a reserved cabinet seat for women.[14]

There have been a few women who have made it to the top. Margaret Thatcher is the best known; another is Mary Robinson, Ireland's first female head of state, a former lawyer and senator who expresses special concern for the powerless and disadvantaged social groups. In France, Edith Cresson, the former prime minister, appointed two women to her cabinet, including Martine Aubry, as labor minister. In the Netherlands, Yvonne van Rooy, a lawyer, has become minister for foreign trade. Simone Veil, a French survivor of a German concentration camp, was elected the first president of the European Parliament in 1979. Rita Klimova was the first Czechoslovakian ambassador to represent the newly democratic nation in the United States, and Vasseo Papandreou from Greece was one of only two women to have been appointed EC commissioner.

Women in the EC Work Force

Despite the fact that the employment rate of EC women aged fourteen to sixty-four is rapidly increasing, European nations still have considerable discrimination against women.[15] There are significant differences in employment of women in EC countries, as is shown in Table 7–1.[16] Denmark, for example employs 76.2 percent of its female population outside of the home. The next highest percentage was in England (62.7 percent), and the lowest percentage was in Spain (38.1 percent). In Denmark, 90 percent of married women aged twenty-five to forty-four are working outside of the home; Spain (40 percent) and Ireland (38 percent) are least likely to employ women in the same group. There is no direct correlation between the fertility rate (number of children per woman of childbearing age) and activity rate outside the home. This is due in large part to the significant differences among EC countries in providing child care facilities.

Despite the impressive numbers of EC women who work, there are wide disparities among countries in regard to women working full- or part-time. Part-time work remains much more a characteristic of

TABLE 7–1

Percentage of the Work Force That Is Female, 1990

Country	Female
Belgium	33.7
Denmark	44.6
East Germany	45.5
France	39.9
Greece	26.7
Ireland	29.4
Italy	31.9
Luxembourg	31.6
Netherlands	30.9
Portugal	36.7
Spain	24.4
United Kingdom	38.6
West Germany	37.2

women in northern Europe than southern Europe. For example, the percentages of part-time workers in the total female active population are 60 percent in the Netherlands and 44 percent in England, compared to 8 percent in Greece and 10 percent in Portugal. The overwhelming majority of part-time women workers are in the services—those in which women are already heavily concentrated and in which the levels of skills and wages are low (waitresses, sales, cleaning, and so forth). In speaking about such jobs, the Belgian Women's Employment Council points out that "some jobs are so onerous that they are designed to be carried out only a few hours a day, i.e., on the part-time basis. This is typically the case for cleaning."[17]

Such observations are a far cry from the picture of part-time work being a deliberate choice allowing women to combine family obligations and work, even though this choice does exist for women in different branches of the service sector. The fact that entire swatches of economic activity have been invaded by part-time work seems to indicate that companies are as instrumental in creating part-time jobs as the demand voiced by women themselves.

As one might expect, the rate of unemployment among women is higher than that for men in all EC member states except for the United Kingdom (in Ireland and the United Kingdom, the only two member states where women compose significantly less than half of the members unemployed, the proportion is 35 percent to 40 percent). In Greece, the percentage of unemployed women is nearly three times as great as that of unemployed men. Although the differences tend to be smaller in northern countries, unemployment of women is still more than 75 percent higher than that of men in France, Germany (excluding the former East Germany), and the Netherlands. In September 1992, the unemployment rate for women in the EC was 12 percent. These differentials in unemployment rates mean that even though the number of women employed within the EC is considerably less than the number of men—only about one-third as many, on average—women now constitute more than half the total of unemployed individuals within the EC.

Actual unemployment rates of women may, in fact, be higher than these figures suggest. In several EC countries, unemployed women may receive benefits not specifically appropriated as unemployment insurance. In particular, in the United Kingdom, Ireland, the Netherlands, France, and Germany, lone parents (usually mothers) supporting dependent children are eligible for income maintenance and are also exempt from the requirement to register at employment offices. Though such mothers are in actuality unemployed and may be seeking a job, they may not be officially registered as such.

High unemployment of women is, in part, a function of the types of jobs available to women. Women fill a majority of temporary, part-time, and subcontracted positions, which often require little skill and offer low pay. As a result, especially during economic downturns, women are more likely than men to become unemployed, and it is often more difficult for them to find new work. This issue is one of the many addressed in recent EC initiatives to develop a more egalitarian work force.

Another form of discrimination is the fact that when they are unemployed, women are less likely than men to receive unemployment compensation. For the whole of the European Community, 26 percent of female and 34 percent of male job seekers received compensation, whether in the form of unemployment benefits or welfare. This is in part because many women work part-time; therefore, they find it more difficult to fulfill the contribution requirement during the working period to receive benefits. In addition, means testing for married women has negative consequences because of the husband's income.

The need for reforms addresssing women's rights within the workplace is urgent, as the number of female-headed households has risen along with the number of divorces, not only driving more women into the work force but creating a necessity for addressing the special concerns of working women and mothers. The Geneva Labor Organization conducted a symposium addressing the rights of men and women in the work force in November 1990, from which it concluded that while "in quantitative terms, women's progression in the labor market has been remarkable in the past two decades, in qualitative terms the achievement has been less impressive."[18]

The situation in the former East Germany shows the desperate situation of some European women. Women make up two-thirds of the unemployment rolls in the formerly communist region, and the closing of state-run day care centers, kindergartens, and youth clubs has hit working mothers especially hard. Sybille Richter, the women's commissioner in the town of Stendal, says, "We are aware of several cases of nineteen- to twenty-one-year-old women who have had themselves sterilized out of fear of unemployment. Then they submit the official confirmation of their sterilization to the employer." A hospital in the town of Magdeburg reported that it sterilized twelve hundred women in 1991, compared to eight in 1989. Doctors and women's advocates have said that many East German women, accustomed to free contraceptives, full and guaranteed employment, and free all-day child care, report great difficulty in adjusting to Western ways.

Types of Jobs

Despite recent initiatives, European working women continue to be frequently channeled into traditional female occupations, and few of them are in key line management positions; if they are in such positions, it is usually at lower levels. As in the United States and Japan, most European women are in service industries characterized by high percentages of part-time work. Seventy-one percent of employed French women hold jobs in the service sector, while 16.7 percent are employed in industry and 5.8 percent in agriculture.[19] Women account for 36 percent of the radio and TV work force; 52 percent of all women in broadcasting are in the administrative area, but only 2 percent of the top managerial levels in administration. Overall, men are seven times more likely to find their way into top positions.

A recent study in the Netherlands demonstrates the psychological consequences of historical gender discrimination. According to the study, when an advertisement for employment is placed, women account for only 20 to 45 percent of the ad respondents. If the advertisement indicates that the position being offered is particularly well suited to women, however, the female response rate jumps to 77 percent. In Germany where there is a law against gender-related advertisement publications, companies still project male-dominated images. This message that it is a man's world discourages women from applying; thus, not only are jobs often initially segregated for men and women, but socialization processes increase segregation through self-selection.

Job Levels

Although women make up 40 percent of the French work force, only a handful of corporate CEOs are female. Korstadt, a major German retail chain, has an employee work base that is 65 percent female, but women make up only 2 percent of its senior managers. Boyr Chemicals and Pharmaceuticals has about 62,000 employees, of whom 18 percent are women; however, women represent only 3.9 percent of senior managers. Of the top one hundred companies in Britain, there are no women CEOs, and only nine out of more than a thousand directors of these companies are women (several are on the boards only because of their family ties). According to the Italian Confederation of Executives, only 4,765 of the total of 144,576 Italian managers are women. Even in the firms where women constitute 30 percent of the personnel, only 3.3 percent of them fill key positions, and their salaries are at least 10 percent lower than those of males in the same or similar jobs. Spain employs 39.5 percent of its female population, but only 6 percent of working women hold middle-level positions, senior management positions, or higher-skilled jobs, in comparison to the 14 percent of working men who hold middle-level positions.

The EC itself, which is intended to champion women's rights, also has a dismal record. At this time, only one in ten people employed by the EC is a woman, and the EC Commission acknowledges a significant problem in the number of women promoted to top-level positions. Only two divisions—personnel and communications—are presently headed by women. Germans have the highest percentage of women among their top EC positions, at 15 percent. Luxembourg, France, Denmark, and the Netherlands maintain a representation of 11 percent to 13 percent each, and the United Kingdom maintains a representation of 10 percent.

Beatt Hesse, a writer on women's issues, observes that "Even in fields where women provide a large percentage of the labor force, such as the textile and clothing industry or in the health services, they are still found in positions of dependence rather than in positions at the top end of the scale, which are predominantly filled by men. The fact is that women still clearly have fewer opportunities to promote their careers than men, despite improved levels of education."

The most comprehensive survey about working women, based on a sample of fifteen hundred women and eight hundred men, found widespread prejudice. Some typical comments were as follows:

With massive unemployment, we don't need to encourage women into the workplace when they already have a role as a mother.

In general, women do not make good managers—although they have much to offer in the workplace.

Successful management requires commitment with no outside worries. For women to succeed they must therefore be single or have adult children.[20]

These attitudes lead to widespread discrimination. Table 7–2 shows the responses from women about their perceptions of discrimination.

Despite the fact that a majority of female employees throughout the EC are concentrated in clerical, service, sales, and middle-level professional positions, a growing number of women occupy "nontraditional" positions, including administrative and managerial occupations. In fact, the increase of women filling these positions is greater than the rise in total employment. Recently, organizations have been developed within many countries in order to attract women into new occupations; one such effort was made by the Confederation of Employers/Federation of Employers in the Metal Industry. In addition, many EC countries currently provide financial incentives to employers who hire women to fill nontraditional positions.[21]

TABLE 7–2
Career Barriers Encountered by Women, by Percentage

"Mens' club" network	43
Prejudice of colleagues	35
Lack of career guidance	28
Sexual discrimination/harassment	23
Lack of training provision	18
Lack of personal motivation/confidence	18
Family commitments	17
Inflexible working patterns	12
Social pressures (e.g. friends, parents)	12
Lack of adequate child care	9
Insufficient education	7
No barriers	19
Other	9

Salary

Most EC countries enacted equal pay policies in the 1970s. Italy, however, started in the 1960s with the first such policy, an agreement on wage parity reached by parties to the collective bargaining process. It was not until the 1980s that Spain, Germany, and Greece passed such laws.[22] Despite these laws, women in EC countries tend to earn lower salaries than men who perform similiar job duties. In 1991, female employees earned, on average, only 72 percent of the average salary of their male colleagues.[23] By examining earnings within specific industries, one can better discern sources of inequities. In the Portuguese hotel and tourist industry, women earn at least 17 percent less than men performing the same work.[24] Spanish women earn 19 percent less, on average, than men employed in the same positions within the same company. In Northern Ireland, women's salaries average about 73.5 percent of those of males in identical positions.

Some countries have actually regressed in their provision of equitable salaries. Danish women employed as unskilled laborers in 1977 earned 92 percent of what their male counterparts earned; in 1987 they earned only 89 percent.[25] The gap between male and female salaries is also widening in such countries as Italy and Great Britain. In Italy it is explained as a result of the goverment's wage policy to establish wage hike ceilings and inflation adjustments. In Great Britain the general economic policies of the 1980s are blamed; people in high salary brackets received large wage increases, while the wages of lower-income and hourly rate workers (including most women) remained the same or fell. Women tend to be among the low wage earners in all countries, and therefore they are more subject to economic fluctuations and fall outside of many social policies to deal with unemployment crises. We believe however, that pay disparities are largely due to sexual stereotypes about women that lead to discrimination. The British Equal Opportunities Commission, which examines the country's merit pay system, found that stereotypes about women greatly influenced evaluations, especially in areas where the measures were qualitative rather than quantitative. The reasons women are not catching up with men are because (1) typical female jobs are in poorly paid sectors such as textiles, cleaning, and apparel; (2) vertical segregation prevents women from reaching the occupational hierarchy at the rates men do;

(3) the valuing and rewarding of traditionally male skills and traits are greater compared to those of female skills and traits; and (4) women are more often part-timers who do not receive bonuses or work in sectors with no bonus pay schemes.

Women and Unions

Women face discrimination not only in employment but also within the unions that represent them in the labor force. The participation of Greek women in the decision-making process within labor unions is actually decreasing, despite the 1990 establishment of a secretariat for women within the nation's General Confederation of Workers (GCW). Although the GCW maintains a 25 percent female membership, a recent request by the secretariat for women to make representation within the union's administrative bodies more equitable was rejected. As a result, the number of women within administrative bodies of the GCW has decreased from 7 percent to 2 percent.[26] In Italy, the election of new officers of the GCIL's Confederal Secretariat was marked by a long-awaited novelty—the election of three women officers. The secretariat now consists of fifteen members.[27]

Despite its position on the forefront of equal employment laws, England's trade unions have made little progress in achieving equality. In 1991 elections, the Trade Union Congress (TUC) elected fifteen women to its fifty-four-member ruling general council. While progress is being made, it must be noted that one-third of the TUC's members are women, and according to projections, women will outnumber men in the union by the year 2000. In addition to the inequity in numbers, debates at the TUC annual conference further concerned several female trade unionists, as women's issues were given low priority. Nevertheless, the TUC continues to make overtures at addressing inequities and is currently urging trade unions to nominate increasing numbers of women (as well as blacks) as delegates to its annual congress. They declare that by 1994 the number of women in each union's delegation should be proportionate to their numbers in the union.[28]

Unions currently dominated by women also lack equality. In Ireland, for example, the primary schoolteacher's union has ordered a study to ascertain why women hold none of the senior posts in that organization. Although 80 percent of the rank-and-file members are women, the executive central committee of the union has only one female member.

As regards collective agreements, the EC has directed that parties to such agreements must be careful to avoid promulgating any type of discrimination. Authorities are generally hesitant to move even discriminatory portions of agreements, however, although they may be null and void. In the Netherlands, the minister of social affairs maintains the power to pull out clauses in collective agreements that are contrary to the policy of equal pay, yet this has *never* been done. Furthermore, European labor inspection services in charge of investigating wage agreements are severely lacking in staff, training, and resources.[29]

Progress is, however, slowly being made in the creation of more equitable collective agreements. Many countries, for instance, have become sensitive to the discriminatory nature of computing wages based on job classifications. Spain has recently eliminated its classification structure for footwear industry employees. Even so, it continues to fall under criticism in this area because it has replaced the classifications system with equally discriminatory grading systems. In order to prevent recurrence of this problem, the EC has dictated that any agreement that excludes part-time workers (in which women constitute a majority of the work force) from benefits is a purveyor of gender discrimination. The only exclusions allowed for are those that can be justified by unique subjective factors.[30]

EC Laws to Prevent Gender Discrimination

As is well known, EC countries are much more progressive than the United States when it comes to maternity and parental policies. It was not until 1993 that the U.S. government provided national maternity leave law; all twelve EC countries have done so for years. Table 7–3 shows country policies. Regarding parental leave, seven of the twelve EC countries have such laws or policies (see Table 7–4). Of the five without parental leave provisions, the Netherlands has made a proposal for such part-time leave and Belgium has leave for personal and family reasons.[31]

When it comes to antidiscrimination laws, the United States is far more advanced than the EC. As a result of strong EC Commission pressures, most of the EC nations have put into effect laws, policies,

TABLE 7–3

EC Maternity Leave Laws/Policies

Germany	6 weeks before birth, 8 weeks after (12 for multiple births). 100% of earnings.
France	6 weeks before birth, 10 weeks after (longer for 3rd plus and multiple births). 84% of earnings.
Italy	2 months before birth, 3 months after. 80% of earnings.
Belgium	14 weeks altogether; 8 weeks must be taken after birth, the other 6 weeks can be taken before or after. 75% of earnings (82% for first month).
Netherlands	16 weeks altogether; 4–6 weeks can be taken before birth, 10–12 weeks after. 100% of earnings.
Luxembourg	6 weeks before birth, 8 weeks after (12 for multiple births). 100% of earnings.
United Kingdom	11 weeks before birth, 29 weeks after. 90% of earnings for 6 weeks, low flat-rate payment for 12 weeks, no payment for remaining weeks.
Ireland	14 weeks altogether; 4 weeks must be taken before birth, 4 weeks must be taken after and the other 6 weeks can be taken before or after. 70% of earnings (tax free). Mothers can request additional 4 weeks unpaid leave.
Denmark	4 weeks before birth, 14 weeks after. 90% of earnings (up to maximum level).
Greece	16 weeks, to be taken before or after birth. 100% of earnings.
Portugal	90 days altogether; 60 days must be taken after birth and the other 30 days can be taken before or after. 100% of earnings.
Spain	16 weeks altogether; 10 weeks must be taken after birth and the other 6 weeks can be taken before or after. 75% of earnings.

and statutes with regard to equal treatment of women and men. Denmark, the pioneer of this type of legislation, first enacted such a statute in 1921. England's Sex Discrimination Act, passed in 1975, provides that a woman has been a victim of discrimination if she is treated less favorably than a man would be treated in the same situation. Further-

TABLE 7–4
Parental Leave

Germany	18 months; low flat-rate payment for 6 months; payment then depends on family income, so higher income family gets less
France	Until child is 3; no payment unless 3 or more children; then low, flat-rate payment
Italy	6 months, 30% of wages
Denmark	10 weeks, 90% of earnings (up to a maximum level)
Greece	3 months per parent, unpaid
Portugal	24 months, unpaid
Spain	12 months, unpaid

more, the law stipulates that it is unlawful for an employer to discriminate against a female employee by "dismissing her or subjecting her to any other detriment." The 1983 French law provides that no wage earner can be penalized or dismissed because of his or her sex; that no one may "refuse to recruit a person, make a change, revoke or refuse to renew a contract of labor of a wage earner on the grounds of sex"; and that no one may "take any measure in consideration of sex, particularly as regards remuneration, training, posting, qualifications, classification, professional promotion or transfer."

Sexist attitudes and behaviors continue to exist despite two significant initiatives by the EC and numerous directives and laws such as those mentioned above. In Belgium, the National Council of Belgian Women (CNFB) celebrated the tenth anniversary of the Convention on the Elimination of All Forms of Discrimination Against Women by examining Belgium's enforcement of this convention. Their conclusion was that men continued to monopolize many sectors in education, labor unions, management organizations, and corporations, and that unequal treatment persisted. The CNFB called on associations, individuals, the media, and public powers to become more familiar with the convention and to improve its enforcement.

Throughout the European Community, the issue of equality in the work force is gaining prominence, and legislation attesting to the importance of this issue is increasingly being implemented. The key reason for the lack of progress in EC countries is that the laws and initiatives do not have sufficiently strong "teeth" to enforce them. It was not until the late 1980s and early 1990s that any teeth (albeit small) were put into them.

Despite commitments to the elimination of inequality, a lack of material and organizational resources is causing enforcement of equality policies to be quite difficult. Additional problems result from the administrative procedures necessary in filing a complaint. Individuals are often solely responsible for bringing an action in a discrimination case, as well as in presenting their case and defending their rights. The burden of proof is usually on the plaintiff in such cases, and access to necessary records can be difficult or impossible to obtain. A comparative study by the EC Commission revealed that as a result of the difficulty involved in bringing forth a complaint under current discrimination laws, many workers (primarily women) do not even embark on this process. Courts' lack of understanding, coupled with preexisting sexist attitudes, is further discouraging.

Denmark is indicative of problems with enforcement. Despite laws (implemented in 1978) assuring equal treatment, fair opportunities, and equal pay for women, a recent report concluded that Danish women face higher unemployment rates, job segregation, lack of advancement opportunities, and lower salaries than men. This is in large part because employers were not bound to comply with the equal treatment laws unless the men and women involved worked at the same establishment. The EC Commission had to serve several formal notices to the Danish government before it eventually complied by extending the scope of the directive, although it still did not give the directive any general authority. A scant four equal pay cases were filed in Denmark in ten years.

Even in Northern Ireland, which is in the forefront of gender discrimination legislation, penalties are often negligible. An Irish woman brought a lawsuit against her company after being fired subsequent to informing her supervisor that she was pregnant and needed information on maternity pay. Her reward was only $2,026.50 to compensate her for loss of earnings, maternity benefits, and "injury to feelings." Another woman was required to wait six years before she was informed that she was to be victorious in a wage discrimination suit she had brought; she was paid $6,000.

The International Labor Organization, convening in Geneva in November 1990, addressed the aforementioned issues. It declared that in order to create more effective remedies, nations should combine fines and/or imprisonment with such compensation as provided in the United States and Canada (including restoring the victim to her or his rightful position), as well as assure against reoccurrence of the situation in question.

Attention to enforcement of antidiscrimination policies is crucial. A recent British study revealed that in 46 percent of cases, those who had been victims of discrimination experienced difficulty or delay in collecting payments from employers after it had been ordered.[32] One of the most serious flaws of the European laws is that the processes necessary to enforce the laws are lacking, as filing complaints and getting them resolved in courts is a long and arduous process. The degree of penalties for discrimination are minimal, if they exist at all.

Sexual Harassment Laws

Despite recent attention to the issue, sexual harassment in the workplace is not clearly defined by specific laws in most EC countries.[33] The EC Commission developed a code of conduct for the workplace in July 1991, in addition to a resolution committed to "protecting the dignity of men and women at work" that was adopted in May 1990. This resolution goes on to recommend the development of information campaigns and a concerted effort by men and women to eliminate such behavior from the workplace.

In some cases where the words *sexual harassment* do not appear in legislation, it is often assumed that this reference can be interpreted. This is particularly evident in Ireland, where court precedents assure this interpretation. As most EC countries do not maintain their own precedents in similar cases, however, EC directives recommend that sexual harassment be referred to expressly, lest the law be ineffectual in dealing with these cases. For example, Italian experts suggest that a victim of sexual harassment might be able to obtain redress through an article in the country's civil code that renders the employer responsible for the employee's moral and physical integrity. These experts further believe that it may be possible to argue that harassment is a moral and physical injury for which the employer is vicariously liable. Another Italian law states that acts related to the employment relationship that are detrimental to women because of their sex are illegal.

The United Kingdom Sex Discrimination Act of 1975 declares that sexual harassment is unlawful, and it extends to particular portrayals of women in advertisements. Though the sexual harassment laws do hold employers accountable for employees' actions, a severe weakness exists in the British system. Employers are permitted to produce evidence as to what the complainant had told her colleagues about her sexual attitudes and behavior for the purpose of determining the degree of injury to feelings she may have suffered as a result of alleged sexual harassment, because it is "pertinent to enquire whether the complainant is . . . unlikely to be very upset by a degree of familiarity with a sexual connotation." This view that a woman's private and consensual sexual behavior affects the degree of outrage and distress she experiences as a result of unwanted sexual advances by her superior at work is not only objectionable but archaic in its assumptions. In addition, penalties in England are limited by law to $16,000; however, a woman employed by the London fire brigade recently won about $40,000 in damages because of verbal and sexual abuse.

In addition to the vagueness of the laws regarding sexual harassment and the severe weaknesses in the legal procedures, the remedies available to those who have suffered sexual harassment are minimal. An Italian parliamentary committee grappling with this issue is currently drafting a private bill condemning sexual harassment and "blackmail." The penalties provided for are imprisonment from three months to one year, and a fine of up to three million lira. These penalties are doubled if the perpetrator of the offense is a hierarchical superior.[34] In May 1992 legislation was proposed to the French Parliament that would render sexual harassment in the workplace an offense punishable by up to twelve months' imprisonment and fines ranging from $360 to $3,600. Yvette Rowdy, a Socialist lawmaker, proposed an amendment that would increase the maximum fine to $18,000. Finally, in the latter part of 1992, France passed a law with a maximum penalty of one year in jail and a $2,000 fine. A drastic shortcoming of the law is that it only applies if the woman's harasser is her superior in the workplace. Although Germany retains laws opposing sexual harassment, controversy is rampant over the issue of whether a woman who resigns because of sexual harassment by a superior or a colleague should be subjected to a waiting period for unemployment benefits on grounds that she intentionally or negligently caused her own unemployment.

Obviously, EC nations have much work ahead of them eliminating the problems of sexual harassment. That they are increasingly addressing the problem is important, but efforts must be greatly augmented to abolish this often ignored form of discrimination.

Perceptions of Sexual Harassment

Perceptions of sexual harassment often vary among Europeans and Americans, perhaps augmenting the problem of developing uniform and effective sexual harassment laws. Veroniqu Neietz, French secretary of state in charge of women's rights (and sponsor of a sexual harassment bill), said she wants to avoid what she called the excesses of sexual politics in America, "where the slightest wink can be misinterpreted. . . . I am not saying that there is no sexual harassment among colleagues. But where there is no question of power or of economic dependence, women or men who are molested can defend themselves."

With these views in mind, the following findings of a recent French survey are not surprising. French women are less sensitive than American women to some forms of harassment. Responding to a series of questions concerning hypothetical situations, 20 percent of the women surveyed said they would not consider themselves harassed if they were asked to undress during a job interview. In another scenario, a male manager suggests that a woman employee spend a weekend with him to discuss her request for a promotion. Forty-five percent of females and 51 percent of males did not believe this situation to be a form of sexual harassment.

A recent Irish survey defining five forms of harassment queried women as to whether they had personally experienced any of these behaviors in the workplace, and if so, whether they were offended by it. Forty-five percent had "heard comments about [their] own figure or appearance" (20 percent were offended, and 75 percent were not), and 14 percent had experienced "bottom pinching, slapping or things like that" (31 percent were offended, and 60 percent were not). The article's authors conclude that "it's hard to understand the women who said they weren't offended by unwanted sexual advances (which presumably could cover the most serious aspect of sexual harassment, linking job promotion with willingness to fool around). It suggests that some women are still being fooled by men into thinking that they are prudes if they are sensitive about matters sexual."

With the unclear understanding of what is sexual harassment, it is not surprising that there is a great deal of harassment of women in EC companies. In a study of working West Yorkshire women conducted by the Leeds Trade Union and Community Resource and Information Centre, 96 percent of the women surveyed who were employed in "nontraditional" women's occupations reported that they had experienced harassment. A union survey of teachers in Birmingham secondary schools found that 72 percent of women had experienced instances of sexual harassment. Most of the victims reported that they felt "extremely anxious, frustrated, distressed and angry"; however, only 16 percent actually had reported the incident, primarily because "the view of the women [was] that they would not be taken seriously, and the matter would not be handled sensitively or seriously."

There exists widespread reluctance on the part of Spanish women to complain about sexual harassment or to even discuss it among female members of their family as a significant problem. Social pressures in the workplace and society stop even serious cases of sexual harassment from being reported. A recent study revealed that approximately 10 percent of Spanish women surveyed had suffered sexual harassment that had direct repercussions on their work situation. Ninety percent of recently employed respondents had experienced harassment in its wider sense, including verbal insinuations.

Another survey revealed that there was a clear tendency for separated, divorced, and widowed women to be harassed more frequently than married women. This was attributed to the fact that these women not only are considered more free, but also appear more vulnerable. In addition, the survey revealed that women under the age of thirty are at particular risk, in part because of their lack of experience in dealing with sexual harassment issues. Interestingly, the survey classified the women interviewed into four grades of attractiveness: very attractive, attractive, slightly attractive, and unattractive. It found a striking tendency for women defined as very attractive to be harassed more at all levels, and particularly at the most serious level of harassment. Whereas 13 percent of very attractive women experienced heavy physical contact, only 2 percent of slightly attractive women and 1 percent of unattractive women were subjected to this form of harassment.

Sexual Harassment Progress?

While perhaps slow in acknowledging the illegality of sexual harassment, European courts are gradually addressing the provocative issue and requiring compensation for the victims. In 1985 the first judicial decision related to sexual harassment in Ireland was reached. After hearing the case, which involved a minor (employed by a garage) who had been subjected to persistent verbal advances, sexually explicit derogatory statements, and actual physical sexual abuse, the labor court declared that "freedom from sexual harassment is a condition of work which an employee of either sex is entitled to expect." Compensation of about $1,700 was awarded to the employee, who had resigned because of the employer's conduct and had been held to have been constructively dismissed.

An industrial court in Northern Ireland in 1991 fined an employer $5,440 for sexually harassing an employee. The seventeen-year-old victim had been forced to leave her first job after only two weeks in order to escape improper advances. The Equal Opportunities Commission of Northern Ireland applauded the decision, in which the court deemed that the plaintiff had sustained serious injury because of her employer's behavior.[35] In 1990, for the first time in Italian history, a court charged and found guilty an on-duty police officer who had sexually harassed a woman working at a military airport. A 1990 Dutch decision awarded an executive secretary $14,000 in "moral damages" for the years of sexual harassment she had endured from her supervisor. The company was also required to supplement the woman's unemployment benefits to no less than 100 percent of her former salary. This was the first ruling to award such high damages in a case of sexual harassment in the workplace.

Despite its historical lack of sexual harassment laws, for the first time in French history a sexual harasser was sentenced to imprisonment in 1992. This supervisor was to be imprisoned for three months after fondling his twenty-one-year-old telephone operator/subordinate. Though his sentence was suspended, it is apparent that problems of sexual harassment are beginning to be recognized.

Positive Action Plans

Sexual harassment is not the only problem of gender discrimination that EC nations are putting renewed energies into eliminating. Recent legislation and directives address issues of mobility, comparable worth, and other areas requiring equal treatment.[36] In the 1980s and 1990s, affirmative action plans calling for the hiring and promotion of women in both the public and private sectors have been implemented. Most EC countries maintain councils, commissions, and/or agencies to research and enforce policies of equality. France offers financial aid to small and midsize firms so they can comply, and the Netherlands provide subsidies to implement programs for women. Most EC corporations are sanctioned by penalties and compensation should they not comply with equality statutes.[37]

Emphasizing that no individual is to be discriminated against on the basis of sex or marital status, EC countries offer some very progressive programs urging integration of increasing numbers of women into the work force. Greece and Belgium specifically address recruitment of those individuals, particularly women, who have worked very little or not at all during their lifetimes, and they encourage workers to reenter the labor force after a period of caring for a child, spouse, or parent. Spanish law has made strides toward gender equality by offering improved health care for all females, especially those at risk, as well as augmenting social protection of groups of women in need of assistance.[38]

Recent EC measures designed to promote women and their interests are referred to as "positive action" measures and adopt the concept of affirmative action as a basis. These measures include a multitude of commitments that are worth reviewing briefly. They recommend that employers eliminate prejudices and stereotypes aimed at women; improve recruitment, placement, and training of women; adapt working conditions to meet women's needs; encourage men and women to more equitably share work/family responsibilities; promote women into decision-making positions; publicize measures being taken both within the workplace and among the general public; and encourage adoption of these initiatives in every nation.[39]

The International Labour Office, which developed the aforementioned directives, points out that despite noteworthy attempts at eliminating discriminatory practices and policies, many women continue to suffer from indirect discrimination, including a lower wage rate than men, carrying the double burden of work and family responsibilities, and running up against a "glass ceiling" that keeps them from being promoted into managerial positions. Furthermore, the EC Commission points out that as a majority of part-time and temporary work is awarded to women, and because traditional labor statutes were designed to meet the needs of full-time and permanent employees, particular attention must be paid to discrimination in this area. The commission concludes that "the current feminization of employment may have beneficial effects for all men, as well as women, and help to focus issues on human issues at work."[40] Emphasizing a commitment to equal treatment, the progressive policies of EC nations, especially in regard to treatment of work and family issues, have resulted in innovative and egalitarian policies superior to those of any other industrialized nations.

Immigrant and Ethnic Women

Gross inequities continue to exist within the EC despite the initiatives discussed above. Many of these problems are expected to become more intense with regard to particular social groups, especially ethnic minority women. A 1990 British study conducted on behalf of the Women's Rights Committee pinpointed problems that women, especially blacks and ethnic minorities, were likely to experience as a result of the creation of a single European market. These individuals are subject to triple discrimination as women, members of ethnic minorities, and people more likely to hail from communities that are poorer and more disadvantaged than average. This study revealed that the benefits of an increasingly mobile work force, which will be experienced by most Europeans, will likely be lost on black and ethnic women, who will remain largely immobile. As they represent a large number of laborers in industries exhibiting a variety of vulnerabilities, they will be particularly disadvantaged in competitive new markets and probably will remain without access to needed training and career advice.[41]

Even when there are laws to protect the women, such as in Britain, discrimination is still very prevalent. In a recent case, an Afro-Caribbean woman was summarily fired after the cleaning organization she worked for hired all whites to replace the black workers; she received about $800.00 for "injury to feelings." The London Living

Standard survey noted a significant gap between the earnings of white women and black women who were working full-time—160.10 pounds and 124.50 pounds, respectively. In addition, black women earn only 63 percent of what black men earn, while white women earn 72 percent of white men's earnings.

Large numbers of immigrants and illegal aliens currently reside in EC nations, calling attention to the gravity of addressing issues of their rights and responsibilities. According to a study by sociologist Antonio Izquierdo conducted for the Commission of the European Communities, between 72,000 and 124,000 illegal aliens were present in Spain in the first months of 1990. The study also reveals that up to 89 percent of the illegal aliens from the Dominican Republic, 76 percent of those from Cape Verde, and 59 percent of those from Guinea are female. The primary reason for this mass influx of women is a need for employees who will perform domestic duties. According to one survey, the 600,000 women employed in domestic service in Spain are victims of pay discrimination, lack of legal protection, and insecurity of employment.[42]

Four hundred thousand immigrant women reside in Belgium, and the Belgian population often holds unflattering images of these women: women cloistered in their homes, mothers of large families, illiterate women who speak only their mother tongue, and so forth. The most recent female immigrants to Belgium are primarily Moroccans and Turks; thirty years subsequent to their arrival, they remain on the outskirts of Belgian society due to the lack of policy designed to aid families in adjusting to new environments. This phenomenon primarily affects first-generation immigrants who have access to the unskilled jobs disdained by Belgian nationals. These immigrants, however, retain several advantages that help them to cope with their uncomfortable situation, such as relational networks designed to allow the exchange of tools and services. Immigrant women remain the unfortunate victims of much discrimination, despite the large number of them (38 percent) employed in the work force. This figure is probably much higher because many are employed in the hidden economy.

Although in most countries women immigrants primarily came to live with their spouses, in Italy many women came first because they were able to find employment in domestic employment. Female immigrants to Italy come primarily from the Philippines, the Cape Verde Islands, Sri Lanka, Eritrea, Somalia, and Nigeria. Their presence in

Italy did not provoke the negative attitudes that black men who have followed have provoked, partially because of the paternalistic attitude of Italians, their perceptions of these women being erotic, and the fact that the women were "hidden" in domestic employment. Many of these women were Catholic domestics, whereas the men were more likely to be Islamic and self-employed peddlers. Thus, the women immigrants are not seen to be as great a threat as men; however, their working conditions as domestics and in the lowest end of female-dominated jobs in the economic hierarchy has left them in vulnerable positions with little protection. Employers generally refuse to give them (or foreign men) contracts so they can obtain residence permits.[43] It should be noted that many of these women are highly educated, but obviously very underutilized. In addition, Italians prefer Polish and Filipino women over African; thus, these discriminations against immigrant women are based not only on gender, but on their color and ethnic or racial origins.

The European Women's Rights Committee is particularly alarmed, as the EC is being publicized as a solely white community. The committee points out that 5.2 percent of Germany's population, 3.9 percent of France's population, and 2.9 percent of Britain's population are composed of minorities, many of which have decades-old roots in these countries. Furthermore, groups of migrants, refugees, students, and individuals of mixed race augment this minority population. Also troubling is the fact that these minority groups, in EC jargon, are referred to as "third country migrants," robbing them of their permanent, established, and valuable status within Europe. Minority women, largely ignored in EC research and planning efforts, particularly suffer from this lack of acknowledgement. The committee notes that they simply "do not feature in the male economists' vision of Europe."[44]

These women, often the sole support of entire families, contribute immensely to European business, as well as to the arts, education, and media, yet acknowledging their accomplishments and providing resources to this largely exploited segment of society have not enjoyed priority status in European countries. These women are particularly in need of attention and assistance, as they tend to be among the poorest segment of European society, are discriminated against in a multitude of areas, and bear excessive workloads (including housework and care for children, the sick, and elderly). They are often victims of inadequate education, limited opportunities to learn English, poor health care, and domestic violence. A resurgence of religious fundamentalism has augmented the sexist attitudes through which they are victimized, both within their own communities and throughout Europe.

As previously discussed, these women have little legal protection, as antidiscrimination legislation is often ineffectual. Ethnic women are overrepresented in industries subject to relocation and are recipients of inadequate salaries, problems that will increase when European nations realize more flexible and mobile markets. These women, who are already forced to accept jobs that no one else wants, will find this problem worsening. Britain, in particular, with its reputation as a low-wage economy, will be a prime site of these troubles. Furthermore, special measures introduced by the EC Commission will attempt to tighten restrictions on immigration. This is problematic, as the group discussing the policy (the TREVI group of ministers of the interior of member states) indiscriminately lumps together legal immigrants with those termed "undesirable aliens" without any acknowledgement of public opposition to this policy.

Groups sensitive to the problems experienced by ethnic women fear that this will "mean that all who do not conform to the stereotyped image of the European citizen will be under suspicion and open to increased discrimination, harassment, and attack."[45] Further problems are apparent when one notes that while immigration policies may tighten, the number of foreign servants an employer is permitted to bring into each country remains unlimited. The policy, which already leads to exploitation of many Filipino and North African women, allows for no protection from physical, mental, and sexual abuse. Currently, the United Kingdom is the only EC nation that maintains a race relations act, and women's and minority groups urge all EC countries to take action, fearing that the new Europe will benefit only white male EC citizens.

Progressive attempts are being made, however, to obliterate such discrimination. The Social Action Fund for Immigrant Workers and Their Families (FAS) has been heartily encouraging the social and professional integration of female immigrants residing in Belgium. As a prelude to the advancing status of these immigrants, the secretary of state for women's rights and the FAS in 1988 signed an agreement to act jointly to further the integration of women immigrants. Expressions Magrehebines au Feminin, an association of North African women, has pledged to fight "negative preconceptions about immigration: delinquency, failure at school, [and] unemployment."

Conclusion

In part because of the evidence that European women are stereotypically assigned to much more traditional female roles than are American women, the EC must take many significant steps in coming to value properly the diversity exhibited by its work force. Addressing issues of equality for women, particularly women of color and immigrants, is crucial in utilizing and profiting from the many benefits of such a diverse work force.

On a positive note, women are increasing their economic participation—they are entering the ranks of the employed in Europe in droves. This rise in activity coincides with a rise in education and training, and women are gaining more jobs in typically male sectors. There still remains, however, much occupational inequality and segregation of fields. Women are also the first to suffer pay cuts, layoffs, and diminished opportunities in times of economic crisis. Fortunately, unions are increasingly beginning to support women's efforts. Some are urging their governments to include within federal law on the protection of women a clause to encourage government employment of women. These unions favor setting aside a minimum number of civil service jobs for women.

Discriminatory collective agreements are being called into question as well. The European Court of Justice in 1991 declared the illegality of an agreement that discriminated against women working less than full-time hours in Hamburg, Germany. Also, after a five-year court battle, six women pensioners in 1991 won the legal right to compensation for being forced to retire at age sixty from jobs with British Gas. The House of Lords ruled that the company must compensate the women under EC law because men in the company do not have to retire until they are sixty-five. The case went all the way to the European Court of Justice before returning to the House of Lords.[46]

North Rhine-Westphalia's civil service will no longer be a male reserve. The state has adopted the first affirmative action law on hiring in Germany. This law gives women priority over men with equal qualifications as long as the former remain underrepresented (below the quota of 50 percent). Ilse Ridder-Melchers, secretary of state for male/female equality, has stated that more action of this type would soon restore the balance between male and female workers.

In announcing a contest set up to encourage companies to conduct policies to help women (such as flexible schedules, aid for returners, and training), Birgit Bruel, finance minister for the state of Lower Saxony, said, "The companies that act to encourage women will be singled out and rewarded, and these examples will lead to others. The winners will be rewarded in March 1990 with the sum of $7,500 [each]."

Volkswagen has had a policy to assist its female personnel for several years. It consists of a parental leave of up to three years with guaranteed rehiring, improved possibilities of promotions in the company, flexible work schedules, and increased female participation in training courses. Women make up 13.3 percent of the company's total personnel in Germany. The company directors also have a "Women's Advancement" division, established on February 1, 1990; the aim of this division is to increase the number and quality of jobs held by women.

Opportunity 2000, a campaign launched by Prime Minister John Major of the United Kingdom, seems to be producing much more effective results, although the program's long-term effects have yet to be ascertained. Initiated in October 1991, the program was developed to aid companies in setting hiring and promotion targets for female employees. More than sixty organizations committed to the program at its inception, and since then three hundred fifty others have expressed interest in adopting more egalitarian hiring and promotion standards.[47]

Two classifications of these organizations emerged through a recent study—those companies who have previously demonstrated commitment to an equalitarian work force and intend to augment existing policies, and those who must embark on a more fundamental development of policy. Many companies reported that in addition to prior commitment to providing opportunities for women, they were further focused and motivated by the strategic approach of Opportunity 2000. All companies involved in the project have taken some type of action to encourage recruitment and promotion of women, and to advocate greater sensitivity to the work and family concerns that both men and women experience. Several companies report the beginnings of cultural change in the behavior of both men and women.

Countries within the EC, however, have much work ahead of them in addressing historical inequities rooted in gender-specific discriminatory beliefs and practices. Although great strides are being made throughout Europe to address workplace discrimination and sexual harassment, a great deal of inequity remains. EC countries must heed the great successes of their progressive, family-oriented dependent care systems and develop comparable policies in all aspects of their work forces. Only by acknowledging and appreciating its diverse work force can an integrated Europe compete successfully within the global marketplace.

Business Impact of European Culture Clashes

Despite similarities in economies, governments, and religions and constant contact over the years as a result of both geographic proximity and trading partnerships, the European Community has many different cultures, not only among but also within certain countries. More specifically, European nations are prisoners of their cultures and racial/ethnic identities. While marital and reproductive practices have, throughout the past several centuries, created a blending of many European cultures, each European nation retains a distinct culture based in large part on its language. The community has at least forty languages, ranging from Catalan to Luxembourgish and Sardinian to Frisian. Unlike the United States, no European country has had large numbers of racial minorities or ethnic groups who were welcomed as immigrants, nor have European countries been as tolerant as the United States in accepting religious differences. The numerous European wars of previous centuries, the two world wars, and the current conflicts in Northern Ireland, Yugoslavia, and Czechoslovakia all illustrate the disputes and tensions in Europe.

A 1990 study asked EC member state citizens to indicate, on a scale of 1 (low) to 4 (high), the degree of trust they had for citizens from other EC states. It was clear that the people most distrusted by those in other EC countries were Spaniards, who received the lowest marks from all countries except Greece and Italy; the range was 2.13 to 2.64. Denmark received the highest rating of trust from five EC countries, with scores ranging from 2.70 to 3.16. That the highest marks any EC country received from another was 3.16 on a scale of 1 to 4 suggests considerable mistrust among EC citizens. Other examples of distrust are the 31 percent of British poll respondents who agreed that giving up British sovereignty to the EC would be like giving it up to Adolf Hitler. Only 54 percent of the British trust German leaders and 66 percent German people. Only 41 percent trust French leaders and 50 percent French people. In 1989, 32 percent of Dutch residents saw a united Germany as a great danger or potential danger; in 1990 the figure was 46 percent. Thus it is not surprising that the EC's plan to allow people to travel among the twelve nations without even showing a passport has been quietly postponed. Denmark and England strongly oppose removing passport checks at their borders. Of the other ten members, nine seem to be ready to move ahead by late 1994, but recent immigration problems are causing Germany to have second thoughts.

The ongoing cross-Channel squabbles between the French and British are further testimony to "soft" problems the EC will face. During a 1992 official visit to England, French President Francois Mitterand was invited to dinner by Queen Elizabeth. Three high-quality French wines were served, as well as an English wine. The next day the French press declared that the English wine was OK, but without depth. So far, the protectionistic French wine lobby has not given any medal to English wines; the English, meanwhile, are trying to overcome the common prejudice that English wines are like the supposed oxymorons of German humor or Italian efficiency. When the British took over the EC presidency in July 1992, they said that they would serve wines from their own country. This did not sit too well with the French, who threatened to serve pastis and cognac at EC cocktail parties instead of British whiskey and gin.

EC countries' nationalism and past histories hinder their leaders from being able to come together on such important issues as the 1992 Earth Summit in Rio de Janeiro, the wars in the former Yugoslavian republics, and the size of the EC. The Italian environmental minister, Carlo Ripa di Meana (who did not participate in the Earth Summit in order to protest the EC countries' discord on almost every issue), lamented that the member states had agreed that an environmental agency was important but could not come to terms on the place where it should be set up; the British did not want Brussels to make decisions on environmental planning, Spain was afraid that Brussels would veto the building of hotels and recreation centers in the nature preserve of

Coto de Donanza, Germany that the EC was too strict on nitrate in drinking water, and French hunters were upset over the EC's strict ruling on bird protection.

Similarly, it was almost impossible for the EC foreign ministers to come up with a common plan on the civil war in Yugoslavia. While the Germans and Italians wanted to declare the Serbs guilty, France and Great Britain could not join Croatia so easily: France had fought with Serbia in World War I, and Great Britain had given aid to the Tito regime. The British were especially against military intervention, with Foreign minister Douglas Hurd saying that England had learned in Northern Ireland that it is much easier to send troops into a country than it is to withdraw them.

Another problem the EC has to face that shows nationalistic interest is how big Europe itself is. Does it end at the eastern border of Poland? Does it include Estonia or the Ukraine? How many states should be part of the EC? Could Turkey be the only Islamic member? Are thirty-five member states possible for an efficiently working EC? Most of the present twelve member states answer these questions primarily based on their own nationalistic advantages. France and Spain want to wait until new members are admitted. Germany, so far the main subsidizer of the EC, does not mind new members, especially when they are from the East, because this would increase its own power in the EC. Great Britain wants more members because it would make a power transfer from London to Brussels harder. Thus it is becoming increasingly clear that contrary interests and national willfulness are blocking European progress.

EC Languages

There exist nine official languages within the European Community and, as noted earlier, a total of 40 distinct regional languages. Despite conventional wisdom, the vast majority of Europeans speak only the language of their own country. For example, three-quarters of the people of Ireland, Britain, and Portugal speak only their native language. Luxembourg, Denmark, and the Netherlands, however, retain large bilingual percentages of the population (99 percent, 60 percent, and 28 percent, respectively). Presently, the EC employs twenty-seven translators. What will happen if more countries join? Translation costs may eat up a large part of the budget, while time-consuming translations of speeches and referendums will prolong votes and regulations unnecessarily.

Currently, most meetings are held in either English or French. An uproar ensued when German, a language spoken by eighty million EC members and ten million potential members in Austria and Switzerland, was proposed as the third language used in meetings. English newspapers mocked the German language as those "horrible guttural sounds," and many EC member states secretly agreed. Another facet of the language problem was made public recently. It was long after midnight when the foreign ministers of nine EC countries took off their translation headphones to continue a deadlocked discussion on Croatia in English. French foreign minister Roland Dumas, who speaks English very well, continued to speak in French.

EC Religions

Currently, two primary religious groups exist in the EC, both of them Christian. Approximately 65 percent of Europeans are Catholic, and 35 percent are Protestant. With the exception of Ireland, most northern EC countries are predominantly Protestant, whereas the southern countries are predominantly Catholic. The violent history (predated by hundreds of years of conflict) of the Northern Irish Catholics and Protestants suggests that even among those religions which are quite similar, bitter religious conflicts can erupt. Greek Orthodox, the national church of Greece, is a third Christian religion; however, it is quite minor compared to the two dominant versions. While still relatively small, the Muslim religion is continually expanding in its number of members, and it is one of the greatest causes of potential religious concern to many Europeans. France and Germany retain the largest percentages of Muslims: German Muslims are primarily from Turkey, while the French Muslims hail primarily from North Africa. More specifically, France (5.3%), Germany (3.5%), England (2.6%), Belgium (2.5%) and the Netherlands (2.0%) have the highest percentage of Muslims in their populations. Many EC citizens find it difficult relating to some of the tenants of Islam that are contrary to Christian and European democratic values. For example, EC countries essentially believe in the separation of church and state, which is anathema in

Islam. In addition, they are concerned about the very strong attachment of significant majorities of Muslims to their homeland cultures and the transfer of political conflicts in those homelands to the EC. As Muslim populations grow in Europe, how will the EC deal with a restive Muslim population that wants to retain its culture and possibly impose it on others?

On a recent visit to Europe one of the authors spoke to people who described the terrible conditions many of the 3.5 million Muslims living in France have to endure. In Marseilles, where only half of the population of 800,000 pays taxes because of the depressed economic conditions, about 110,000 Muslims live in housing projects in the north of the city. About 40 percent to 70 percent of young Muslim men in Marseilles are out of work. Eighty thousand Jews, who are refugees from North Africa and who speak Arabic like the Muslims, also live in Marseilles. Many of the Muslims want to earn money and return home, but upheavals in Algeria make this difficult, so they continue living in the slums of Marseilles. That Muslims represent one out of five world citizens, and that Europe is very dependent on raw materials from Muslim countries in the Middle East, Africa, and Asia clearly suggests that the EC's treatment of Muslims living in it borders can influence future relations not only within the EC but across the world.

The genocidal practices of Nazi Germany, including the deaths of millions of European Jews and gypsies in concentration camps, has left the numbers of those of the Jewish faith relatively small in EC countries. The greatest number of western European Jews reside in France (740,000). The history of those practicing Judaism in Europe has been stormy. Five hundred years ago, Spain expelled all Jews from its borders, and two hundred years later France was gripped by the Dreyfus affair, in which a Jewish army captain was unjustly convicted of treason. A frightening amount of hateful, anti-Semitic attitudes currently persists; in fact, the contemporary politics of the European far right are primarily based on racism and anti-Semitism. Jean-Marie Le Pen, leader of the French ultraconservative faction, dismisses the Holocaust as "a detail of history." In Germany (and especially former East Germany) anti-Semitism is reemerging, as chillingly demonstrated by the recent march of neo-Nazis through the Dresden streets, giving straight-arm salutes to shouts of "Sieg heil!" in commemoration of the 102nd anniversary of Adolf Hitler's birth.

Ethnic Group Conflicts

The EC's success will depend a great deal on its economic growth and stability, its ability to build strong economies in all twelve nations, and its attainment of a fairly even distribution of economic success in all regions of each country. Should the EC be unable to accomplish these tasks, we predict that a number of historical conflicts (many of which have existed for centuries) will become even more pronounced with the appearance of economic downturns and economic imbalances. Cultural, ethnic, and religious groups will become increasingly enmeshed in conflict. Below we shall review various conflicts among citizens in the nations of Belgium, Spain, France, Italy, and Germany. These countries were selected to give the reader information about diverse EC countries in terms of size, heterogeneity, religion and language.[1]

Belgium

Formed by major European powers as a neutral state in 1831, Belgium was the site of intense religious-political (Catholic-Protestant) wars. Despite its neutrality, major European powers have historically coveted or attempted to influence Belgium because of its strategic geographical position. As a result, there have been numerous conflicts in and around its land, primarily between the Dutch and French, whose influences have left Belgium divided into two linguistic zones. Dutch is the official language of the north (or *Flanders*), which maintains 57 percent of the population. This farming region has historically been considered inferior to the southern regions of Belgium. French is the official language of southern Belgium (or *Wallonia*), with 42 percent of the population, including the nation's government and its elite. Due to German occupation of Belgium during both world wars, there is a small German-speaking region along the Belgian-German border consisting of approximately 1 percent of Belgium's population.

This split between the French and Dutch languages has shaped Belgium's politics, as well as its structures of government. Each region retains its own executive and legislative bodies, which maintain considerable jurisdiction over issues such as education. Major political parties and union federation memberships are based on languages; for example, the Flemish primarily belong to the conservative Christian

Social party and the nationalist Volksunie, and the French-speaking people belong predominantly to socialist parties. Historically, there have been considerable battles between these groups, so much so that in 1986 the Belgian government collapsed. In recent decades, the traditional industries of the south that brought it prosperity early in this century have declined, while the undeveloped, agrarian north has gained new industry and prosperity. This transposal has only increased animosity between the Dutch-speaking north and the French-speaking south.

In the latter part of 1992, stronger divisions have appeared in Belgium. Belgium's center-left coalition government has agreed on a package giving Brussels the same regional status as Flanders and Wallonia. The regional parliaments, directly elected by the people, will have control of everything except for finance, foreign policy, and defense. As a result, Belgium's embassies will have such structures as three separate commercial attachés. The country also will have three ministers of agriculture, one for each region. The financially strong, Flemish-speaking Flanders region is pushing for this greater move toward separation, because it claims to be tired of subsidizing the French-speaking Wallonians.

Spain

When most Americans think of Spain, they think of a homogeneous country; however, Spain has had long-standing and strong separatist movements among the Basques and (known to few Americans prior to the 1992 Olympics) in Catalonia. In the first months of 1992, terrorist groups had already killed five people in Barcelona. In 1991, two Spanish policemen were sentenced to more than one hundred years in prison for killing several Basques in southern France during the mid-1980s. The judge avoided proving their membership in the Grupos Antiterroristas de Liberacion (GAC), a terrorist group formed as a reaction to Basque terrorism, and ascribed "personal motives of hate" as the cause despite the fact that both men had received money from the GAC and lived far above their own means. During the Franco regime, French Basque country had taken in many Basques from Spain; this changed under the French presidency of Jacques Chirac, who returned the refugees to Spain, and violence has since escalated. Despite the grave concerns of the Spanish government, the threat that Basque terrorists would disrupt the 1992 Olympics (held in Catalonia) never materialized. The government had trained more than 10,500 police, civil guards, and other security officers to deal with potential terrorist attacks. The Basque Homeland and Freedom group, responsible for more than seven hundred deaths since the late 1960s, is committed to continuing, in intensity and scope, its terrorist attacks, according to Spanish police who have intercepted critical Basque documents. Despite this, it is generally felt that Basque separatist factions are not growing, as they realize the counterproductiveness of their activities.

The Catalan independence movement is not as well publicized, because it has not been nearly as violent as the Basque separatist movement. Catalonians have, however, probably been more successful. Until the death of right-wing dictator Francisco Franco, all notions of separatism and regional languages, customs, and cultures had been oppressed. Those who dared to celebrate their cultural uniqueness openly could face imprisonment. After Franco's demise, the Catalonians began taking control of their region and have since imposed their language and, to the greatest extent possible, their culture on the large numbers of Spanish children whose parents migrated here during the building boom that was initiated in the late 1970s and 1980s. Castilian Spanish has been relegated to a minor role in Catalan public life and public schools, which has caused considerable resentment among the non-Catalonian Spanish. A truck driver who moved to Catalonia in the mid-1970s complains, "My children are getting Catalan pushed up their nose." Despite this, Catalan has now been recognized by the EC as an official community language, and it was one of the four official languages of the 1992 Olympics.

France

Another long-term ethnic conflict based on language disputes is that which has taken place in France since the late eighteenth century concerning the last Celtic language on the continent of Europe—Breton, the sister language of Welsh. Centuries before the French Revolution, people emigrated from England to settle on the northwestern coast of France in the Armorican peninsula, now called Brittany. Although England has tolerated the use of the Welsh language in Welsh schools and on Welsh television and radio channels, the Breton language has been subject to systematic elimination by the French government since the revolution. In 1972, French president Georges Pompidou emphasized that "there is no room for regional languages in France." Attitudes such as this have led to the almost total abolishment of Breton from the news media, schools, and local governments. (Note that at the time of the French Revolution, less than 50 percent of the population living in France spoke French.) In response to the systematic oppression of the Breton language and culture, the "International Committee for Safeguarding the Breton Language" was formed (by a non-Breton). Now fifteen years old, the organization is represented in twenty countries.

In acknowledging the difficulties experienced in maintaining the anatomy of the language of Breton over the past two centuries, many supporters say it is a miracle that the language still continues to exist. Alan Riding, a *New York Times* reporter who has written extensively on these subjects, noted that "the Breton language may be steadily losing ground to French, the Brittany Liberation Front and its protest bombs have long been forgotten and only a handful of intellectuals still advocate separatism. But Breton cultural nationalism is probably running stronger today than at any other time this century." And, we might add, so is there an increase of cultural nationalism in other countries of the European Community.

Italy

Since Roman times, the Italian north and south have had hardly anything in common. While the north is considered "the paradise of the rich," the south is called "the poorhouse of Italy." The *terroni* or "dirt-eaters" live here, subsidized by millions of lira from the north. A July 27, 1992, article in *Der Spiegel,* a prominent German magazine, called "Democracy Only as a Facade," said that the political parties in Rome transferred millions of lira into the south not to develop the economy but to build up a base of voters, often with the help of the Mafia. Whereas the 44 percent of the population in the north creates 55 percent of the country's gross national income, the 37 percent of Italy's population in the south creates only 25 percent. Regionalists like Umberto Bossi, who founded the Lega Lombarda party in 1984, want to split up Italy into north, south, and center. In 1992 elections, his party, which uses slogans against the underdeveloped south, received 8 percent of the votes. While he received over 17 percent of the votes in the north, central and southern Italy gave him less than 1 percent; nonetheless, this made his party the nation's fourth largest power (of the other sixteen parties, twelve received less than 6 percent of the votes). Northern Italians like the symbolic animal of Bossi's party: a goose that lays golden eggs in the north, which are stolen by Rome and transferred to the south. These increasingly strong movements to divide Italy up into various pieces follow 122 years of unity.

There are also latent problems in the northern regions of Italy. The province of Alto Adige, which lies in the far north of Italy (next to Austria) is an excellent example of the problems encountered by ethnic minorities annexed through war, and how the situation can change over the decades. For centuries, the province was part of Austria and the Hapsburg Empire. Italy was awarded South Tyrol in 1919 as a result of being on the victorious side after World War I. During the interwar period the Italian government made every effort to Italianize the area, changing place names in particular (thus, South Tyrol became Alto Adige) and encouraging Italian immigration. The latter policy was linked to the industrialization of what had been a largely rural area. As a result of this immigration, nearly 130,000 citizens of Italian origin moved to the territory, which contained 270,000 German-speaking Tyroleans. This Italian population initially enjoyed a higher standard of living than the Tyroleans. Working in industry, they received higher salaries than farmers, which is what many of the traditional ethnic Germans were. This changed during the 1960s, however, when the tertiary sector (tourism, commerce, cottage industries), consisting primarily of ethnic Germans, came to the fore. Currently, the German-speaking population enjoys an equal, if not higher, standard of living than the ethnic Italians.

After World War II the province was annexed by its southern neighbor, the province of Trento, to make up the region of Trentino–Alto Adige. The German-speaking population became a minority in the region, and the reactions were violent. Small groups of terrorists of German descent began to operate in the 1950s and 1960s. Negotiations finally produced peace. In 1972, a new statute was passed in the Italian legislature that decentralized power in favor of the provinces. This statute, called "the package" because of its diversity of provisions, made German an official language on a par with Italian for all inhabitants of Alto Adige. It also provided that a number of posts in the public service be shared proportionally between the linguistic groups, and that all public servants be bilingual (which posed problems for the Italian speakers).

Since 1972, there has only existed a semblance of social peace between the two culturally distinct groups. Although there are more mixed marriages than previously, they remain the exception. Even though they live in peace, the possibility of the groups resuming open hostilities is always present. It is important to note that the ethnic Italians consider themselves to be a minority in Alto Adige, while the ethnic Germans feel they are a minority in Italy.

Germany

Ethnic conflicts between EC member countries, such as Germany and Poland, are a distinct possibility as well. The German and Polish borders have changed constantly over the years as a result of wars, and animosities between the two nations are becoming more evident, as the following illustrates. When Germany lifted visa restrictions for Poles, a small welcoming committee from Germany crossed the Oder river bridge at Frankfurt with such welcoming gifts as flowers and champagne. At the same time, however, about two hundred teenage neo-Nazis gathered, shouting "Sieg heil!" and "Germany for Germans." In addition, they pelted a bus carrying a Polish friendship orchestra with rocks. An elderly Polish woman observing these events said, "These people still have Hitler in their souls." The German chemistry conglomerate Henkel, meanwhile, was surprised by the uproar in Poland when it bought the state-owned chemistry firm Pollena from Poland. Polish people have not forgotten that six million Poles died in concentration camps and during battle in the Nazi era; presently, many Polish are afraid of becoming Germany's colony.

The two major supporters of the EC, Germany and France, still have underlying concerns and hatred brought on by centuries of war. Many French are concerned about the newly unified Germany. It seems that Gaullists, communists, and socialists agree on one thing: a powerful Germany could degrade France to a provincial state. French president Francois Mitterand was a prisoner of war in a German camp, and his country in the early 1990s watched a documentary on television called "The Brown Plague" about young German neo-Nazis. Headlines like "The German Nightmare Shakes Europe" sell French newspapers. Interest in Germany is great all over Europe; when former

West German writer Gunther Grass and former East German writer Stefan Heym came to Brussels to discuss the new Germany, seven hundred seats in the Palais des Beaux Artes were quickly sold out. In Spain, people discuss a new book about Germany called "The Fourth Reich." The publicist, a man in his sixties who remembers World War II, believes that not much has changed in Germany since then. He calls Germany a deeply Hegelian country that demands conformity and allows little differentiation.

In Czechoslovakia, Mercedes-Benz formed a joint venture to manufacture buses and trucks. When Mercedes-Benz proposed to impose custom tariffs to keep out competitors, this suggestion caused an uproar that surprised the German managers. Historically, the Czechs have feelings of unease with their German neighbors; since the seventeenth century, they have wondered whether they should keep separate identities or dissolve into the German nation. Mercedes-Benz management had to learn that not only profit and loss statements but also acknowledgement of Auschwitz and blitzkrieg are part of the deal with their eastern neighbor. Even though Helmut Kohl may be the head of state most convinced about forming a strong European community, Germany's neighbors are watching its actions very carefully.

Cultural Clashes in European Businesses

As the above example suggests, diversity issues play themselves out in many subtle (and not so subtle) ways in the economic system and in particular corporations. Cultural identity, if not properly managed, can lead to corporate misunderstanding, conflicts, and inefficiency.[2]

Most EC companies have been country specific, in contrast to many American companies—including Whirlpool, IBM, Procter & Gamble, Xerox, Ford, and GM—that have been international. In particular, Whirlpool in the past five years has been extremely successful internationally because of its strategy to provide extensive cultural training and systematic movement of its managers across borders and among continents. A key to EC success will be the ability of the country-specific companies to expand, merge with, and take over companies in other EC countries in order to attain the advantages of economies of scale and new markets enjoyed by American and Japanese companies. They will have to learn how to utilize effectively employees not only from the national countries of the companies, but also from other countries.

European managers have a long way to go. For example, such experts as Percy Barnevik, president and CEO of Asea Brown Boveri (ABB), see massive overcapacity and few companies with the critical mass to hold their own against Japanese and U.S. competitors. The European electrical industry is crowded with twenty national competitors. Half of these companies are losing money due to overcapacity of up to 50 percent, high costs, and little cross-border trade. Barnevik wonders why there have been so few cross-border mergers in Europe; instead, there have only been strategic alliances and minority investments. These European alliances are poor substitutes for complete mergers and cross-border internationalization.[3]

Many EC government and business leaders profess to accept the cultural differences of the twelve member nations and view them as a source of strength rather than weakness. In general, however, the cultural, religious, and language differences are divisive forces. Nationalism influences European corporations' decisions about whom to place in management positions. Daniel Goeudevert, an extremely competent executive at Volkswagen, did not get the top slot because shareholders believed the company should be run by a German. Similarly, French stockholders had problems with Stephen Walls, the head of an Anglo-French paper group, Arjo Wiggins Appleton, and he was ousted. Ronald Singer, who controls a paper-products group that controls fifteen companies in twelve European countries, admits that his company, despite much talk of the "Euro-manager," will continue to staff subsidiaries largely with locals. This is the opposite of what the American-based Whirlpool company does.

A top German executive for a major automobile company told one of the authors, "Contrary to the U.S, where pluralism and a multicultural environment have a long tradition, European countries were never interested nor motivated to work or live together, but rather tried to fight and defeat each other." Unfortunately, this tradition of mistrust and lack of understanding persists in the EC despite the tremendous need for mergers, acquisitions, and buyouts for EC businesses to be successful in the new markets.[4] Thus we feel that the following statement is more indicative of European attitudes: the head of a major Dutch retailer has refused to even consider doing business in Germany, not because it is not a lucrative market, but "because we [in the company] don't like Germans."

A significant problem likely to arise from this situation is that of cultural clashes among managers and employees as a result of different values and styles of interaction and each group's belief that its own particular values and styles are superior. Claude Rameau of INSEAD, a business school in France, said his studies show extreme differences still remain among various management systems in Europe. He says that most managers still find it difficult to manage different cultures, no matter how sensitive they are to them.

Some general trends have appeared in various cultural surveys of managers. For example, while many managers from the Netherlands and Denmark feel it is unimportant and undesirable for managers to always have precise answers for their subordinates' questions, the opposite is true in France and Italy. Most managers from Great Britain, Germany, and Belgium fall somewhere between these two extremes. Whereas Germans are not especially likely to believe that the main reason for having a hierarchial structure is merely so that everyone knows who has authority over whom, 75 percent of Italians believe that passing the chain of command is acceptable and will not negatively affect working relationships. Furthermore, almost three times as many Italians (87 to 90 percent) as British (30 percent) believe that most managers seem to be more motivated by obtaining power than by achieving objectives.

Another example of cultural managerial style differences would be instructive. Most German executives believe professional competence, knowledge, and coordination skills are crucial to organizational successes; most British executives believe interpersonal skills, communication skills, the ability to influence others, and negotiating skills are key. The French present another position, believing that the ability to organize, control, and work the system is critical. Finally, as suggested above, the Italians emphasize flexibility in using the bureaucratic structure to gain organizational success. All of these different styles can lead to conflicts and ineffective corporate operations at a time when high-performance competitive teams are crucial to corporate successes.

International consultant Robert J. Brown, in discussing the well-known Italian entrepreneur Carl De Benedetti, documents some of the problems that can occur as a result of latent cultural hostilities when companies do finally converge:

De Benedetti visited Rene Lany, governor of Societé Generale de Beligique (SGB), and advised him that his Paris-based holding company, Cerus, had built up a sizable stake in the Belgian company. The subsequent shock wave upturned the normally discreet facade of courtesy that has characterized European business, and released expressions of latent cultural hostilities. After the meeting Lamy attacked De Benedetti as "an imperial colonizer." A former Belgian high-level diplomat was even more explicit: "We are Belgians and however brilliant this adventurous Italian may be, La Generale must remain Belgian. It is Belgium, Inc. We must fend off all international raiders."

A British and Italian firm that started a joint venture and located its headquarters in Brussels is doing well; however, it is experiencing ongoing clashes based on subtle cultural differences. The concept of what is an effective meeting is an example. In general, many Italians are comfortable with more than one person talking at the same time and having heated direct confrontations on even personal issues. The British manner is in stark contrast to this method of conduct. A noted international business author writes, "the British prefer to do one thing at a time, such as first participating in a meeting, then taking phone calls, then reading the newspapers. Italians can merge these different activities in the same setting without any apparent problem."

Before the massive mergers and takeovers necessary to make EC companies competitive take place, the shortage of good Euro-managers (managers who can operate effectively in different cultural settings) is already here. According to headhunters and personnel managers we interviewed, European business has a problem because there is a shortage of good senior executives. Colgate quizzed all of its top European managers about what kind of executive would work best in the new borderless setting. They were especially interested in a manager who could understand, value, and thus interact well with people from many different backgrounds. Unilever Group, the Anglo-Dutch food and soap giant, decided to avoid bossy executives; instead, they are looking for people who can work in teams and understand the value of cooperation and consensus. In a continent where cultures have clashed for centuries, this is easier said than done. Unilever admits that most executives come from the unit's home country, because it is the natural inclination of a boss to surround himself or herself with people from a similar background, speaking the same language. Some European companies, though, hire American executives because they have always viewed Europe more as one big market than as a series of small nations.

Percy Barnevik provides additional insight into the issues of cultural clashes in corporations.[5] His company is spread over sixty countries and has investments totaling more than $3.6 billion. Barnevik is well aware of the problems facing European business; he knows that mixing nationalities does not just happen. He also advises that cultural differences, such as a Swede thinking that a Swiss is not completely frank and open, should not paralyze a manager. Instead, the Swedish manager has to know that this is a cultural phenomenon because Swiss culture, in oppositon to the Swedish culture, shuns disagreement. According to Barnevik, "a Swiss might say, 'Let's come back to that point later; let me review it with my colleagues.' A Swede, on the other hand, would prefer to confront the issue directly. How do we undo hundreds of years of upbringing and education? We don't, and we shouldn't try to. But we do need to broaden understanding."

As an international manager, Barnevik also stresses the importance of knowing the country of operation. For example, ABB in Switzerland understood the depth of Swiss concern for the environment and was therefore willing to invest heavily to switch freight from polluting trucks to more environmentally friendly trains before it successfully bid on a $3.6 billion order from the Swiss Federal Railway to build locomotives that will move freight through the Alps. He also states that his company has to be a Norwegian company in Norway to work effectively. For example, Norway's oil operations in the North Sea are a matter of great national importance and intense pride; the government would not—and, according to Barnevik, should not—trust some faraway foreign company as a key supplier for those operations.

In order to overcome the cultural hurdles confronting European managers, Barnevik suggests that the simple pattern of surrounding oneself with people like oneself has to be broken. Instead, he feels that managers should be not only encouraged but forced to work in mixed-nationality teams and to create personal alliances across borders.

Cultural Misunderstandings with the United States

Issues of culture and language in the business world have caused and will continue to cause much confusion in terms of product names and advertising campaigns, management, and employees between the

United States and EC countries. English-speaking companies must be careful not to use the word *mist* in a product name when marketing in Germany, because the word means "manure" in German. Chevrolet's Nova translates as *no va* or "it doesn't go" in Spanish. An Electrolux vacuum cleaner ad was once translated from Swedish to English and ran in a Korean magazine reading, "Nothing sucks like Electrolux." And an ad for a laundry soap designed to clean "really dirty parts" was translated into French for a Quebecois audience as a soap for washing private parts.[6] In 1990 the U.S. firm Totes announced the launching of a marketing campaign in Germany of "Totes Deutschland"; Totes received a number of phone calls because the phrase translates to "dead Germany."

According to the German president of one German subsidiary in the United States, most failures of German ventures in this country occur because managers expect the same strategies that have made them successes at home to work in the new market. German managers sometimes even speak German during executive meetings in foreign subsidiaries and make decisions in that language when non-German-speaking fellow managers are in attendance. (This practice in Japanese companies in which Americans and Europeans work is also a problem.) German companies also see mixed nationalities working together as a problem rather than an asset, because "Americans, for example, don't see working here as a long-term venture. They see it only as a step in their career. That tends to create conflict with German employees."[7] German managers also fail to understand that their focus on quality and service is less important than competitive pricing. For example, one high-class washing machine company in Germany could not understand that Americans would prefer cheaper washing machines with three cycles to their expensive forty-cycle model. According to a professor of international management at the Wharton School of Business, European electronics companies coming into America have lost money because arrogant managers have failed to understand the American market and adapt to its competitive pressures.

Advertising is another area where lots of mistakes are made because managers are not aware of cultural differences. Advertising and creating an image is much more important in the United States than in Europe. Many European consumer-good companies fail to gain the necessary market share in the United States because they budget their American advertising by European standards; therefore, the budget is too low. One European advertising company failed to set up an international marketing campaign that included America because it showed people drinking alcoholic beverages. The ad executives had not been aware of the law against the display of alcohol consumption on U.S. television. U.S. firms, conversely, have to learn that comparative advertising is seriously frowned upon in Europe and considered bad taste in Japan.

Since Europe lags behind the United States in accepting women in leading positions, it may be hard for European male managers to deal effectively with American female executives. One multiculturalist in New York who works mainly with German companies said that in America it is the custom that a man opens the door to a restaurant and the woman enters first; in Germany, the man opens the door and enters first while the woman follows. From experience, the multiculturalist stated that German managers who did not know the cultural differences in these customs quickly formed prejudices against female executives who entered a restaurant first, considering them to be unfeminine, very aggressive, and not very educated.

Another cultural difference between U.S. and European culture is in attitudes toward sex and nudity. One European picture book series was a best-seller in Europe but could not be sold in the United States because the artist included images of a boy urinating. The European publisher solved the problem by substituting a fully clothed boy in the American version.

Some other examples of marketing mishaps are as follows. In France, Hallmark cards are bombing, as the French dislike syrupy sentiment and prefer to write their own cards. Coca-Cola had to withdraw its two-liter bottle in Spain after discovering that few Spaniards owned refrigerators with large enough compartments to store it. Tang initially failed in France because it was positioned by General Foods as a substitute for orange juice at breakfast; the French drink little orange juice and almost none at breakfast.

In Germany, Campbell's reportedly lost over $10 million trying to change the soup habits of the German consumer from dehydrated to canned soup concentrate. When surveying the Italian market, Campbell's discovered that a major cultural factor in food marketing is in the attitudes and practice of housewives toward food preparation. Italian housewives were spending approximately four-and-one-half hours per day in food preparation, in contrast to less than one hour spent by U.S. housewives. These differences in time spent reflect not only a cultural pattern but also the different income levels in the two countries. Indeed, Campbell's discovered how strong the feeling against convenience food in Italy was by asking a random sample of Italian housewives the following question: "Would you want your son to marry a canned soup user?" The response to this question was sobering; 99.6 percent of the respondents answered no. In the United States, CPC International faced the same problem in reverse in trying unsuccessfully to penetrate the U.S. soup market, which is 90 percent canned soup, with Knorr dehydrated soup. Knorr, a Swiss company acquired by CPC, has a major share of the European prepared soup market, where bouillon and dehydrated soups account for 80 percent of commercial soup sales.[8]

The importance of knowing and respecting a country's culture and utilizing that knowledge to gain acceptance is apparent in the enthusiastic response elicited by John F. Kennedy from thousands of Germans with his declaration of *Ich bin ein Berliner* ("I am a Berliner") in postwar Berlin. Heinrich Lubke, a German president in the 1960s, on the other hand, is remembered less illustriously for his literal translation of *Gleich geht es los* ("It will start soon") as "Equal it goes loose" when he was talking to the Queen of England during an official visit to Great Britain.

European Attitudes Toward the Japanese

It is clear that for the EC to prosper, it will have to form alliances not only among EC corporations but also with Japanese companies. Despite this reality, though, many Europeans have problems with the Japanese. Many of Europe's problems and attitudes concerning Japan mirror those of the United States. Europeans fear that Japan will invade their markets with high-quality, low-cost products, causing European companies to lose market share and profitability and ultimately resulting in a loss of jobs for Europeans. The EC does not want to become another marketplace for Japan (or the United States) to conquer. With regard to Japan, Europeans see its invasion of the American marketplace as a cautionary tale. Therefore, due to long-standing European policies of protectionism against Japanese products and services, the Japanese presence is not yet as pervasive in Europe as in the United States, and European fears regarding the Japanese are not as violent as those of many Americans. Emotions are becoming more volatile, however, as the EC braces itself for a possible Japanese "invasion" of its newly formed common market.

Former French prime minister Edith Cresson said in the spring of 1991 that the Japanese stay up nights thinking of ways "to screw the West." Cresson made additional comments that pictured Japan as a power-hungry country that now has Europe in its sights. "They are in a position to destroy any industrial target that they decide to destroy," said Cresson in July 1991; on a prime-time television program, Cresson expounded that the Japanese believe "the Japanese market is ours and the rest of the world is for us also." She went on to say, "But we don't want to live like Japanese. . . . I mean, in the small flats, with two hours to go to your job and—we want to keep our social security, our holidays, and we want to live as human beings in the way that we've been always used to living."[9] Her remarks resulted in protesters decapitating her in effigy on Bastille Day in Japan. And the French government, nervous about losing the lucrative Japanese market for its perfumes, fashion, and other exports, obviously told her to tone it down and eventually removed her from her position. Several weeks after the above remarks, Cresson made a point of sitting next to the Japanese ambassador's wife at a fashion show.

But Cresson is not alone. Electronics industry consultant Robert Heikes said that Europe risked becoming a colony of Japan, and the former chairman of Cerus (a French company owned by Italian businessman Carlo De Benedetti) said that Europeans had foolishly trusted Japan to "play by the rules of fair trade" and, therefore, their computer and electronics industries were in jeopardy.[10]

Bill Powell of *Newsweek* writes that European (as well as all Western) Japan-bashing results from "growing Western economic insecurity and some post cold-war realism." Powell says that "Japanophobia" in Europe is very acute presently because Western economies are slow and it is expected that Japan will pick up a large portion of the astronomical cost of rebuilding eastern Europe.[11] Despite the decrease in Japan's economic strength, this is an opportunity ripe for the taking, and Japan still has the sturdiest economy and largest investment capital. Though Europeans long for Japan's capital, they dread surrendering control.

Europe is determined to keep Japan out of full participation in the newly unified EC. Because Japan has allowed very few European companies into its markets, the Europeans are not of a mind to be generous to the Japanese in allowing them full competition privileges in the European market. The Europeans, as noted above, also look at America as a cautionary tale in terms of Japanese expansionism and are determined to avoid the same fate.[12] (While talking of Japan's predatory trade practices, European officials have failed to note that the U.S. automakers virtually surrendered their market by failing to adapt to fuel-, quality-, and cost-conscious U.S., Japanese, and European consumers.)

Japan is not pleased with what it views as Europe's belligerent attitude. After all, Japanese companies are investing billions of dollars in building auto plants in Europe. A Nissan plant in Newcastle, Britain, has a two-hundred-thousand-car assembly capacity, and Toyota and Honda also are building plants in Britain while Mitsubishi plans a joint venture with Volvo. Japan feels that the EC should consider EC-built Japanese cars to be a European product and a plus to their local economies, as they employ domestic labor. Japan, however, is fighting against the racism, nationalism, ethnocentrism, and xenophobia that are part of the current European landscape.

Conclusion

Europe is faced with tremendous historical animosities and nationalistic attitudes. Without maintenance of stable economic growth, eruption of these hostilities is inevitable and will prove devastating. Already much internal trouble is brewing between northern and southern Italy, between the French- and Dutch-speaking Belgian regions, and in separatist movements like those of the Basques and Catalans of Spain. These problems could erupt in violence and widespread destruction, as in the former Yugoslav republics. Even if peace is maintained, such unresolved animosities will simply continue to hamper relations and progress within their respective countries. Much hostility and bad feelings exist as well between such nations as France, England, Germany, and nearly everyone else in Europe due to centuries of wars.

To ensure the survival of many EC companies, corporations must form alliances with other companies inside and/or outside of the EC and among disparate ethnic groups. They must develop the managerial skills to utilize and develop diverse groups of people effectively and to market to diverse customer bases. As noted throughout this chapter, however, hostile nationalistic and ethnocentric attitudes persist and are hurting efforts to build a European challenge to U.S. and Japanese economic dominance.

Europe and Immigration

Despite recent rumblings from both conservative and liberal politicians about too many immigrants, the United States since the 1960s has been light years ahead of the EC on immigration policies.[1] With unification looming and requests for asylum by Third World immigrants booming, French political scientists Remy Leaveau said, "Immigration is the biggest problem facing the whole European community."[2] Fifty percent of Europeans polled by Eurobarometer believe there are too many immigrants in Europe, and fears about illegal immigration are threatening the dream of a free flow of people inside the EC. Besides traditional sources of immigration from Africa and Asia, immigrants are flocking to the European Community as the Soviet Union crumbles and Yugoslavia is torn by war. Two-thirds of Europe's immigrants are now Muslims, a culture that is alien and frightening to many Europeans. Traditionally, the European countries have never accepted large numbers of immigrants from either European or non-European countries. In the past they have reacted with superiority and disdain to American acts of racism (countries like England and France tend to forget the extreme racism they exhibited during their colonial days); however, now they are faced with becoming a more integrated, multiracial, and multicultural society and are reluctantly acknowledging that the United States is better equipped to handle heterogeneity.

The European Community as an economic bloc currently does not have direct provisions outlawing racial discrimination.[3] Five EC countries have no laws against racial discrimination. Some individual EC countries, like Germany, have no antidiscrimination laws specifically to protect the rights of foreign immigrants, while France's laws are rarely enforced; the Netherlands and Great Britain have the best discrimination laws and penalties. Due to this new fear of immigrants, the EC wishes to close itself to non-European nationals, in effect creating a "fortress Europe." This policy is regressive and counterproductive and will cost the European nations in future competitiveness. Europe's continuing inability to deal productively and effectively with its immigration issues is threatening foreign investment, closer political union among EC nations, and the harmonization of EC labor practices.[4] It has also threatened Europe's ability to form constructive, long-term relationships with Third World people.

In the past, when European countries opened their borders to immigrants, it was usually only for a short period of time and for the purpose of meeting specific national needs. Although immigrants arrive in Europe from many sources, the share from developing countries is on the rise.[5] In the 1960s, for example, the Netherlands received only about 10 percent of its 60,000 annual immigrants from Third World countries. By the late 1980s, nearly 50 percent of its immigrants were coming from the Third World. Similar trends are evident in the United Kingdom and Germany, among others. In addition, on a net basis, fewer Third World immigrants tend to leave once they have arrived, and immigrants who become residents tend to have more profound effects on a society. In the 1990s after the dissolution of the communist states, a new phenomenon of eastern European immigrants have become another major concern. Two and a half million immigrants have entered Germany since 1990 began—twice the rate, as a percentage of population, that Ellis Island accepted during its prime years in the early 1900s. France, Italy, and Britain have accepted more than one million asylum seekers since 1990.[6]

Of the 340 million people living in the European Community, however, only 15 million are immigrants or their descendants. Of these 15 million people, 8.5 million are from non-European states. They represent 5.2 percent of the population of the former West Germany, 3.8 percent of that of France, and 3.3 percent of that of Great Britain. In 1990, the former West Germany had about 5 million foreigners; 33 percent were from Turkey, and 13 percent from Yugoslavia. The former East Germany had only 191,200 foreigners (about 1.5 percent of its population); 31 percent were from Vietnam and 27 percent from Poland.[7]

Unlike Germany, whose short-lived colonial history ended with World War I, the British, French, and Dutch have absorbed many people from their former colonies. France has 4.5 million immigrants, mostly from Portugal and North Africa, whereas Britain's 2.5 million immigrants are primarily from India, Pakistan, and the West Indies. Italy has more than 1 million immigrants, primarily from North Africa. Belgium and the Netherlands also have a significant population from their former colonies. Spain has slightly fewer than 1 million foreigners, most of whom are from North Africa and Latin America.

In the EC overall, Turkish people make up the highest percentage of non-EC immigrants, followed by Algerians, Moroccans, Yugoslavians, and other African nationals. Before the collapse of communism, the issue of immigration from the south, especially from Africa, had emerged as a hot topic in the European immigration debate. Whereas the population in Europe is either stable or falling, Africa's population is growing at the rate of 3 percent per year, outstripping its economic growth. North Africa alone, which counted 62 million people in 1950, could grow to 285 million by the year 2025. The poor North African economy combined with the existence of millions of immigrants of North African descent already living in Europe, is enough to make one predict that immigration into the economically more fortunate northern European countries will increase.

As we noted earlier, the dissolution of the former Soviet Union and the eastern bloc nations is another concern for the EC. Since the fall of communism, tens of thousands of Soviets with proof of German ancestry settled in Germany, with millions more expected. This phenomenon promises a glut of foreigners in the EC and a drain of intellect and skills from the new eastern European democracies.

As a result of the increase in immigrants, ultraconservative political parties are gaining at the polls all over Europe. In spring of 1992, the right-wing Die Republikaner party won 11 percent of the vote in Baden-Wurttemberg, Germany's wealthiest state; right-wingers garnered 23 percent of a vote in Austria; and Jean-Marie Le Pen, with his fifty-point plan to "turn immigrants into third-class citizens" gained 14 percent of the national vote in France, with percentages running even higher in southern France. (More than 30 percent of the French electorate supports the policy of immigrant repatriation promoted by Le Pen's National Front.) In the 1993 French elections, President Mitterrand's party lost badly to France's right-wing parties.

In Belgium, the right-wing Vlaams Blok party has grown in strength to twelve seats in the national chamber, nearly one-third the number held by the nation's largest party.[8] It won as much as 25 percent of the vote in certain urban areas in Flanders.[9] In Austria, Sweden, Italy, and Switzerland, rightist parties have gained support by stating that immigrants were second class citizens. In Denmark, the justice minister attempted to push a proposal through the Parliament refusing family reunification rights to Turkish immigrants while allowing it for American and Japanese immigrants. The Netherlands is proposing to link family reunification rights to income level; this would eliminate many Third World applicants.[10]

Yet even as polls show that most Europeans believe that there are too many immigrants in their countries, the fact remains that Europe needs immigrants to do the jobs that its nationals will not do and in the future will need them for many other jobs as the EC population decreases. As we noted, only Ireland, with a 2.11 fertility rate, has a rate above the replacement level of 2.1 children per woman. The former West Germany was expected to shrink by nearly one-quarter over the next four decades; only reunification has changed the German picture (a total of 344,000 East Germans moved to West Germany during the opening of the Berlin Wall alone in 1989). France's population would be nearing decline if it were not for a high birthrate among its immigrant population. Generally, resident aliens in the EC have about one child more than natives; the number is even higher if the resident alien has arrived from a developing country. These statistics work to France's advantage: demographer Herve Le Bras has calculated that France's population would have been 48 million in 1983 if there had been no immigration. With immigration, in 1990 it was about 55 million.

Not only will there not be enough workers without immigration, there will also be serious social dislocation. For example, the German population will diminish from 80 million to 66 million during the next forty years. Meanwhile, the number of foreigners living in Germany will rise from 5.4 million to 8.9 million due to their high birthrates alone. The number of foreigners, however, is not large enough to replace the loss of Germans needed for Germany to maintain its existing social welfare system. According to statistics from the Association of German Pension Funds, today there are three people aged twenty to sixty for every person older than sixty years. Without immigration, in 2040 every person under age sixty who is gainfully employed will have one older person who is reliant on their financial care; the financial responsibility for payments into Germany's social security system could climb to 40 percent of the annual income of the wage earner.

By the year 2010, Germany may need three hundred thousand new immigrants per year in order for German nationals to continue working and living at the same economic level. A caseworker with the French Democratic Confederation of Labor said that "any economist will tell you these people [immigrants] are necessary for the economy. But there are three million unemployed, so they are a scapegoat."[11] A 1990 survey found a wide range of views among EC country populations about whether migrant workers in their country should be sent home. The positive responses ranged from lows of 7 percent in Luxembourg, 12 percent in Ireland, 13 percent in Portugal, and 18 percent in Spain to highs of 41 percent in Denmark, 39 percent in Greece, and 34 percent in both Belgium and Italy; the remaining EC countries ranged from 29 percent to 33 percent.

Overview

Immigration in Europe became significant after World War II, when there was an extreme shortage of men in most EC countries. The industrialized areas of Europe needed workers to rebuild their economies after the destruction caused by the war.[12] For the most part, EC countries (except for England, whose colonial immigrants are British citizens) control their migrant workers strictly through "guest worker" systems. England and France sought workers from their colonies and ex-colonies. The Netherlands sought assistance first from its former colonies and then from southern Europe. Belgium also sought workers from southern Europe.

West Germany attempted to recruit people from eastern Europe; however, the communist countries closed their borders. After the Berlin wall was built, West German firms, especially those in the metal industry and the building trades, needed workers desperately. Ultimately, West Germany went as far as Turkey for its workers. On October 30, 1961, it and Turkey signed a contract that regulated the numbers and the situations in which Turkish citizens were allowed to travel into West Germany and work. West Germany also concluded agreements on the recruitment of foreign labor with Italy, Spain, Greece, Morocco, Portugal, Tunisia, and Yugoslavia. As a result, the foreign labor force increased from 80,000 in mid-1955 to 2.6 million in the fall of 1992, accounting for 11.9 percent of all wage and salary workers. These workers were considered migrant or guest workers who were expected to return, eventually, to their native countries.

The foreign workers were highly productive. They bought German products, and they worked in jobs nobody else would take. By doing so, they helped their German colleagues rise to better positions with more responsibility. Foreigners at first were not considered threatening but somewhat magical and very exotic. By 1964, however, an anti-Turkish image emerged, and Germans were popularizing the stereotype of "Ali, the leech." Resentment and prejudices against Turks have increased since then, leading to violent and even deadly attacks.

These immigrant workers are victims of a fundamental shift in the nature of the European economies and the type of work forces the latter have required. Workers had been recruited to work in the factories and the mines, the heavy industries in the 1950s and 1960s; by the 1970s, though, the imperatives of postindustrial society required that they be retrained, laid off, or—preferably for many Germans—sent back to their countries of origin.

Today, Germany's foreign workers account for more than 14 percent of the work force in nine out of fifty-two sectors; the proportion is even higher in coal mining. Seventeen percent of Britain's industrial workers and 25 percent of those in France and Belgium are foreign immigrants. In fact, immigrants are so important to the smooth functioning of northern European countries, according to the research institute of the Federation of German Industries, that some areas of German life (such as garbage collection, janitorial services, and hotels and restaurants) would collapse without the foreign work force. The same holds true for most other European states.

States of the southern geographic fringe of Europe—Spain, Portugal, and Italy—that in the earlier stage of European postwar reconstructon were "sending" countries did not perceive an immigration problem for many years. But as their economies developed from small-scale farming to large-scale exporting of crops, intensive tourism, and modern industry, their need for labor grew. This need could not be met internally, despite migration from the countryside to the city. In Italy, for example, the gap was filled mainly by migrant workers from North

Africa, who largely do the picking of crops and processing of food for export. In the words of Italy's interior minister, "more and more Italians refuse humble and dirty work."

In a country where tomatoes are almost sacred, the Italian press reported that unauthorized African migrants in the Apulia and Puglia regions picked almost 50 percent of the country's tomato harvest. Tomato prices, it was reported, were kept low by employing illegal African laborers at low rates of pay. Nearly 50 percent of the Italian fishing company Mazara's boats employ cheap Tunisian or Moroccan crews. Italian nationals are disturbed by such statistics, which represent what they perceive to be a profound infiltration of their country by foreigners.

Immigrants are utilized not only because the EC countries initially had shortages of labor but also, as was alluded to above, because European nationals do not want to do "dirty" jobs. In addition, industries like immigrants because the latter accept much lower wages than nationals would demand. Germany, for example, seems to be evolving a three- or four-tier pay system, with West Germans receiving the highest pay, followed by East Germans, then other eastern Europeans, and finally non-European foreign immigrants receiving the lowest pay.

As the reader has seen, women are receiving new protection under EC laws, but foreign workers have little protection from mistreatment due to their often illegal status, as well as to racism. One may look at England as an example, despite its "strong" antidiscrimination laws. Blacks from the West Indies are perceived negatively by many British. The 495,000 people of West Indian origin living in England represent the majority of blacks in the country; however, they make up less than 1 percent of the country's population. In 1976 England passed the Race Relations Act and formed the Commission for Racial Equality to combat discrimination in employment, housing, education and other areas against minorities and immigrants. Unfortunately, the law has weak legal remedies; it has no provisions for class-action suits or provisions for affirmative action to hire minorities. The commission was intended to help individuals pursue discrimination complaints through an industrial tribunal, which can award compensation of up to approximately $17,000. The commission, however, has obviously been unable to effect a significant change in racist attitudes. One study found that one-third of all employers would hire whites over equally qualified blacks without even giving black applicants an interview. Another study found that black workers were more than twice as likely as whites with similar qualifications to end up in low-skill manual jobs.

Internal EC borders were supposed to be dismantled by January 1, 1993, but extreme nationalism and xenophobia have reared their ugly heads. Thus, with England in the lead, the decision was made to postpone this important part of the EC. Though citizens of EC member states will eventually be free to move and to work wherever they choose, the revised borders will raise the question of how the EC will deal with foreigners (400,000 legal immigrants are expected to enter the EC annually, and no country has a good count on illegal immigrants). The question remains as to whether each country's individual government or the European Community should define immigration policy. Britain and Germany represent polar opposites, with Britain looking to maintain control over those entering its territory and Germany desiring to shift responsibility to the EC; the remaining nations seem to lie somewhere between these two.[13] Most began to narrow legal immigration in the early 1970s, when the oil shock caused a recession. The "economic miracle" had ended, and the guest workers who had contributed substantially to European economic successes during earlier years were asked to leave. France reduced drastically its number of illegal immigrants; Spain imposed visa requirements for visitors from Algeria, Morocco and Tunisia; and West Germany experienced decreasing net immigration after it began to limit Turkish immigration and encourage East German immigration.

The effort to create a "Fortress Europe" has been growing: in October 1991, twenty-seven eastern and western European nations agreed to tighten border controls to deflect the tide of illegal immigrants, arguing that an influx of uncontrolled migration would destabilize their countries.[14] Today, many of the EC countries further intend to control the stream of foreigners. Some favor temporary immigration. All agree that an immigrant requesting political asylum can seek such status only in one EC country and may not reapply in another member country if rejected; this eliminates the so-called orbiting of asylum seekers from one country to another and lowers substantially their chances of entry. The EC also plans to draw up a list of countries whose nationals will require visas to enter the community. Countries are debating also whether non-EC nationals legally residing in one community country can travel or work in another one. All of this points in the direction of increased protectionism. In the future, foreigners will have a much harder time as the EC becomes increasingly interested in what it perceives as self-protection (that is, protection of nationals), rather than the protection of its immigrant population. Immigrants will no longer enjoy even the scant rights that are theirs presently, according to a member of the twenty-five-member Migrants Forum, the advisory council to the EC that is made up of immigrant groups from each of the member states. While borders are opening up internally, they are closing to the outside.

In order to understand Europe's current immigration policies, its fear of foreigners, and its increasingly xenophobic, racist reactions against foreign people of color, it is necessary to look at the policies from a historical perspective. It should become very clear that the EC has an extremely long way to go in order to utilize effectively the potential of its diverse immigrant population.

France

In the beginning of the twentieth century, large numbers of Polish workers, followed by Algerians and Italians, came to France to work in the agricultural, mining, and manufacturing industries. During World War I, France looked to its colonies, especially in North Africa and Indochina, for workers to help in its war efforts. At the end of the war, however, these same people were declared foreigners and were forced to carry identification cards indicating their status.

During the years immediately after World War I, people from various European countries (such as Portugal, Italy, and Spain, as well as Belgium, Poland, and Yugoslavia) came to France for permanent or seasonal work. More recent asylum seekers have come from as far away as Southeast Asia, South America, and the Middle East. The presence of large communities of Algerians, Moroccans, and Tunisians, as well as people from Guadalupe, Martinique, and French Guinea, is inextricably linked to France's colonial history.

A case in point are the Algerians. After decades of trying to make Algeria an extension of France, tremendous animosity toward Algerians arose after the French defeat in the Algerian war for independence in the 1960s. Violence against Algerians started in the port of Marseille and spread all over the country. France also increased pressure to limit integration of its immigrants into society and went to the extreme of preventing family reunification and forcing repatriation. From that time to the present, many of France's ills, such as crime and drugs, have been blamed on immigrants from the Third World, and particularly on Algerians. In 1980 the French government passed the "bonnet law." It went after those now-illegal immigrants that the French government had formerly invited to France, but now wanted to be rid of. Under this law, France forced many foreigners to return to their countries of origin. Included were many French-born children who were, therefore, officially French citizens.

During 1983–84 a French media campaign accused asylum seekers, primarily from North Africa, of being terrorists. Meanwhile, authorities demanded greater documentation of persecution in their homelands and refused entry to a higher percentage of asylum seekers. In 1986 right-wing Interior Minister Charles Pasqua introduced a law that denied the basic right of due process to immigrants facing deportation. Under the law, more than one hundred Malians, chained together in a specially chartered aircraft, were deported. Only one year later, a total of seventeen thousand immigrants were deported. Although shortly thereafter deportation almost stopped, it remains a viable option. In July 1991, Prime Minister Edith Cresson proposed that France's illegal aliens be deported en masse aboard special planes chartered by the government.[15]

Recent polls indicate that 16 percent of the French people favor mass deportation, while 68 percent want to stop new immigrants from entering France. Two-thirds agree that illegal immigrants should be sent back to their countries in chartered planes. Three out of four believe that there are too many Arabs in France, and one out of two feel there are too many blacks. Nine out of ten believe that racism is widespread in France. In 1992, Deputy Marie-France Stebois read aloud in the National Assembly the names of Arab immigrants who had committed crimes against French citizens.

To deflect the growing popularity of extremist groups, the well-established mainline party politicians are jumping on the anti-immigrant bandwagon. President Mitterrand has stated publicly that immigration has now gone beyond "the threshold of tolerance," and former Prime Minister Rocard has announced that France is no longer "a country of immigration." Presently France is considering a wide range of measures to control immigrants, such as the deportation of undocumented aliens, the restrictions on new family members, and the expulsion of legal immigrants who hire illegal immigrants. Furthermore, some foreigners can now only receive transit visas, as opposed to tourist visas. France is also computerizing its immigration files in an effort to control the "problem." Ironically, a 1991 report states that the number of foreigners in France actually declined in the 1980s, dropping to 3.6 million legal immigrants from 3.7 million in 1982; however, only 46 percent were non-EC immigrants in 1982, compared to 64 percent in 1991.[16] There has also been an increase in attacks against foreign immigrants from the Third World.

It should be noted that the French have no sense of unease with the large numbers of Portuguese immigrants living in France; the Portuguese are more similar to the French in language, religion, race, and ethnicity. In 1985, 67 percent of the French said there was a significant amount of racism in France—in 1990 the figure was 72 percent. In 1990 France recorded fifty-two violent attacks against foreigners (thirty-seven against North Africans), killing one person and injuring thirty-six, as well as more than two hundred threats and insulting actions (almost all against North Africans). There is considerable evidence that the numbers not reported are much higher. Following are some specific examples:

- Four French youths from Avion attacked a second-generation immigrant girl from North Africa in Lyons and cut off most of her hair.
- Three Muslim girls were expelled from school for wearing head scarves, but were reinstalled after a ruling that they had a legal right to do so as long as it did not constitute religious propaganda. While the incident was ultimately a victory for the girls, the issue unearthed a great deal of anti-immigrant feelings. Fifty-three percent of the French disapprove of the minister of national education's affirmation that Islamic girls can wear veils.
- Some young French citizens of North African origins have been dismissed from school because various local officials have imposed limitations on the numbers of North African students allowed in the schools.
- A barman refused to serve a young Moroccan and called him "a dirty Arab," prompting the customer to throw a glass at

him, hitting him in the head. The barman, a white Parisian, sued for assault.

- A Sri Lankan student who held a night job in a modestly priced hotel reported that nonwhite guests were systematically refused rooms.
- A young woman from Mali who entered a police station to present her papers was searched and handled so roughly that her wrapped dress fell off, leaving her nearly naked while several male policemen taunted her.
- When a fifteen-year-old African boy had his front tooth smashed by the police, the youth reported that one of the policemen had pushed him away when he bled, saying, "You probably have AIDS."
- Recently fifty-eight graves of French Muslim soldiers who died defending France during World War II were vandalized by thugs.

Germany

The constitution of Germany contains two separate articles addressing the parameters of citizenship. The atrocities of the Nazi era compelled the democratic founders of West Germany to adopt asylum provisions that are liberal by Western standards. Article 16 of the German constitution therefore warrants that "persons persecuted on political grounds shall enjoy the rights of asylum." This article, as well as Germany's extensive social services, have made Germany the prime destination for asylum seekers: about 70 percent of those seeking political asylum in EC member states choose Germany.[17] The second provision is article 116, dating from 1913. It entitles people of German origin who were expelled from or had to flee foreign countries after World War I to German citizenship. This includes the former German areas of eastern Europe: Albania, Bulgaria, Danzig, Estland, Yugoslavia, Lettland, Lithuania, Poland, Romania, the Soviet Union, Czechoslovakia, and Hungary.

A person can become a German citizen through birth or naturalization. Every child born to married parents is German if the *father* is a German citizen. The emphasis on biology and patriarchy as a determining factor is clear: a resettler from Hungary or Poland who never visited Germany and who does not speak a word of German is automatically German, while the child of a German mother and an Italian father who has lived and worked in Germany for many years is considered Italian. A recent survey found that 40 percent of the Germans want the German race to stay "pure."

Germany did not have even minimal immigration of Third World people before World War II. After World War II, its constitution guaranteed asylum to political refugees; however, only naturalization can secure a foreigner's status as a resident, although there is no right to German citizenship. People may apply for German citizenship if they have been living permanently in Germany for at least ten years, are at least eighteen years old, meet all sorts of conditions (knowledge of the German language, reasonable living accommodations, economic security, and so forth)—*and* have decided to orient themselves toward Germany and the German culture, have integrated themselves into German society, and have a way of life that demonstrates no transgression of German law. The purpose of the restrictions is to maintain the purity of the German race.

These conditions and the high cost of naturalization are some of the main reasons why only 2.9 percent of the Italian, 2.8 percent of the Spanish, and 0.75 percent of the Turkish immigrants in Germany are naturalized. The vast majority of foreigners now residing in Germany are open to expulsion; although this has not been widely practiced to date, it remains a constant threat. Currently, the German government is offering non-German (not including former East Germans) immigrants $6,300 to go back home.

In 1979 a commission set up under the leadership of a former minister-president from Nordrheinwestfalen produced the famous Kuhn memorandum. After thirty-four years, this document acknowledged officially for the first time that there had been immigration into West Germany. On this basis it called for more attempts to integrate migrants, especially children and young people; legislation giving immigrants some security over residence; and the right for them to participate in local elections after a longer period of residence. But the government (a coalition of the Social Democrats and the Liberal party) rejected the proposals of this commission, instead, reinforcing further the principles of its so-called foreigners' policy: (1) to prevent further migration, (2) to encourage voluntary repatriation, (3) to better the economic and social integration of those who had lived in West Germany for many years and (4) to make the right of residence more precise.

As a result of large numbers of people seeking asylum (193,063 in 1990; 256,112 in 1991; 500,000 in 1992), Germany has imposed its first visa restrictions to prevent further arrivals. Germany also cracked down on illegal immigrants in August 1991 by sending extra guards to the borders of Poland and Czechoslovakia.[18] In addition, Germany has begun to make life as difficult and unpleasant as possible for asylum seekers who have already entered the country. Many have had to wait years for a decision on their application and have been prohibited from working during the wait. The social security they receive is much less than what German citizens receive.

In Europe as a whole, the percentage of asylum seekers granted asylum has decreased from about 65 percent in 1980 to 10 percent in 1990. Germany now accepts only 3 percent of those who apply. On December 7, 1992, Germany rewrote its asylum law to have its border guards stop anyone coming from countries that border Germany; those turned away can appeal, but from another country. Asylum seekers from countries that do not practice political persecution will also be turned back.

All is not well in Germany even between those from the former East Germany and West Germans. In October 1989, according to opinion polls, 63 percent of West Germans agreed East Germans should be accepted, but by February 1990 this had dropped to 22 percent. Even among those who felt their own economic situation was very good or good, 70 percent claimed that *Ubersiedler,* or East German immigrants, received too much in the way of state handouts.

"Out with foreigners" and "Living space for Germans instead of pseudo asylum seekers" were slogans that recently brought the right-wing Republican party under ex-Nazi Franz Schonhuber 7.5 percent of the vote and a seat in the Berlin Parliament. The number of identifiable extreme right-wingers rose from 32,300 in 1990 to 39,800 in 1991 to over 40,000 in 1992. Many Germans have expressed feelings that they pay too much for the "pseudo" asylum seekers, who are highly vulnerable. These prejudices and feelings of hate provoke violent incidents like the following: in the east German town of Hoyerswerda in September 1991, a gang of skinheads and right-wing radicals broke into the dwelling of asylum seekers, terrorizing and injuring the inhabitants. German officials reacted by evacuating all asylum seekers "for their own protection," and now Hoyerswerda is free of for- eigners—just as the mob wanted. Three men who admitted to attack- ing foreigners in Hoyerswerda because "they were frustrated at being unemployed, . . . had been drinking heavily," and were angry after a failed attempt to rob a Vietnamese street vendor were released on probation by a judge in March 1992. Human rights activists feared that such leniency would encourage violent, racist behavior.[19] While neo-Nazi skinheads in Germany generally limit their attacks to Third World people, they have been spreading their violence to southern and eastern Europeans; two Italians were beaten at a Portuguese-owned bar in Hamburg in the fall of 1991.

The German police have effectively squashed "anarchist squatters" and environmentalists with impressive displays of force, but they have been strangely unable to stem this current tide of neo-Nazi hate crimes (over 2,000 in 1992, up from 270 in 1990 and 1,483 in 1991). This lack of control may be explained by opinion polls that show an increase in German hatred of foreigners and feelings that the number of asylum seekers is a problem. News reports confirmed how German police and firefighters withdrew and watched skinheads firebomb a shelter for 150 Vietnamese guest workers, men, women, and children. It was not until after weeks of numerous attacks on foreigners that Chancellor Helmut Kohl's government took a "strong" stand. German business leaders strongly urged Kohl to move because they feared the negative impact the violence would have on foreign investment, especially in east Germany. While denouncing the violence as a "disgrace," Kohl called for a tightening of asylum restrictions.[20]

The 1992 killings of an elderly Turkish woman (who had lived in Germany twenty-five years) and her two granddaughters finally brought out anger among many German citizens. Despite the outrage about the deaths, Germans tend to blame the violent racist attacks on such things as no recreation facilities for youths (so they firebomb houses holding refugees). Rather than vigorously going after these bomb violators, the government has promised to pursue immigrants who exploit Germans' constitutional guarantees by filing fraudulent claims.

The outdated, overly authoritarian measures of dealing with and the violence against an important segment of the German population will eventually hurt the country. There are 140,000 foreign employers in Germany, giving work to thousands of Germans; of these, 33,000 are Turkish. Many foreigners who started businesses years ago doubt that they could experience the same success if they were starting in the current hostile climate. Germany must also start looking at its immigrants as the asset that they are. The studies of Hans Dietrich von Loeffelhoz (of the prestigious think tank Rheinisch-Westfalisches Institut fur Wirtschaftsforschung) confirm that Germany's immigrants have added $120 billion to the national gross domestic product since 1965, and that every 100,000 immigrants contribute $600 million a year in taxes. All in all, immigrants produce a minimum net gain of $15 billion per year for the nation.[21] Germany must change its immigration laws and address its negative attitudes toward foreigners or its economy and its society will suffer severely. In fact, German business leaders and some concerned politicians have heard increasing concerns from foreign business leaders and politicans on possible lower investments, or even boycotts of German goods. One out of three German jobs are dependent on goods produced in Germany but sold out of the country.

Spain

Spain has always been a country of emigration; it has only recently emerged as a country of immigration. The influx of foreigners was caused by two factors. First, the closure of official immigration into France in 1974 made Spain the alternative European destination for people from French-speaking Africa. The second and more important factor is Spain's entrance into the EC and its resultant economic well-being.

Since Spain required North Africans in 1992 to have a visa to enter the country (before it was only a passport), hundreds of North Africans have risked their lives to cross the Strait of Gibraltar, about ten miles of choppy water, and enter illegally. Spain currently has about eight hundred thousand immigrants of either African or Latin American descent. The province of Catalonia and its capital, Barcelona, have become immigrant territory, the obvious destination for those from West and Central African countries just a few hundred kilometers across the Mediterranean. Most of them are from Morocco, followed by Senegal, Mali, and Gambia. There are also constant arrivals from

Portugal, the Philippines, and Latin America, all of whom dream of "making it" in Europe.

In the province of Catalonia, where almost all Japanese investment in Spain and 25 percent of all other foreign investment is centered, immigrants are relegated to low-paying activities like fruit picking and agriculture, where they earn half of the salary of their Spanish co-workers. It is almost impossible for immigrants to navigate successfully the highly complex and very rigid immigration system in which residence and work permits go together, and immigrants find themselves in a vicious cycle trying to get one or the other and failing in both. Marriage to Spanish nationals does not help because it does not automatically confer nationality or resident status on a foreigner, and a child born in Spain to parents where one or both are foreigners does not gain Spanish nationality either. These antiquated laws invite employers to take advantage of the immigrants' powerless situation. To counter these practices, the Center for Information for Foreign Workers (CITE), a Barcelona-based organization supported by the communist party trade union, was founded. According to CITE, many employers deny contracts to their illegal employees so that the latter remain clandestine. Once immigrants get their work permit, their employers default on their contribution to the employees' social security payments; this results in the permits not being renewed and the immigrant workers lapsing back into illegal status. One hundred and twenty thousand applications for renewal of permits are received every year, but since Spain's entrance into the EC, most have been denied.

This is especially hard on Algerian immigrants. The number of Algerians in Spain rocketed after the revolt in Algeria in October 1988. Before this upheaval, there were only four hundred official Algerian residents and a minority of illegal Algerian immigrants in Spain. But the revolt forced thousands to flee the country, and many of them chose Spain as their destination. Spain, however, had just entered the EC and was not interested in accommodating the incoming Algerians, despite the many economic connections between Spain and the Maghreb countries. The only concession granted the incoming Algerians was permission to remain in Spain for three months without a visa. Algerians looking to work could only find jobs picking fruit on a day-to-day salary at the lowest wages. Reportedly, many of the hundreds of young Algerian girls who fled to Spain now work as prostitutes in the bars of the coastal cities. All of them are considered illegal by Spanish authorities and risk prompt expulsion if caught. When apprehended by authorities, most illegal Algerians are sent home in a matter of hours with a stamp in their passport saying that they are not welcome for three years. Spanish customs has not invested in a central computer fling system, however, and new passports are easily available in Algeria. Would-be illegal immigrants are also held in prisons or in police cells along with other prisoners, most of them drug dealers.

Racism in Spain exhibits itself in job discrimination against immigrants, even in jobs that Spaniards refuse. One Guinean immigrant said he had often been refused jobs because of his skin color, saying, "I've tested it with my white friends. I'd go in first and be told the job had been taken. Then they'd go in and be told it was still available." When talking to a reporter, one immigrant from Senegal complained about how racist the government and the police were in Spain. Authorities have also tried to limit the rights of workers through rigid labeling and special identification; in a small town in Catalonia, one local mayor tried unsuccessfuly to enforce an identification card system for black workers in the town. Lately Spain is experiencing, like much of Europe, a surge in racially motivated violence. For example, in Tarragona an illegal Moroccan construction worker was beaten to death by two Spaniards in a drunken fight.

Police brutality seems to be accepted as the status quo when dealing with immigrant workers. Since foreigners are so closely associated with crime by the Spanish authorities, they are often subjected to harassment by police. In the early 1990s, a massive police raid on the towns of Vic and Osona resulted in the arrests of seventy Moroccan workers, fifty of whom were deported. Trade unions, church groups and human rights organizations decried the incident for the brutality of the arrests, as well as the injustice of deporting workers who had been living in Spain for years. During the same time period, Nigerians who had applied for political asylum were beaten by police officers who found them sleeping in a downtown plaza. Apparently, many Moroccans sleep in parks for fear of being discovered and deported during nighttime raids on their homes by police seeking illegal immigrants. In November 1992, three dozen Dominican Republic nationals living in ruins were violently awakened by four masked Germans who fired indiscriminately, killing one and seriously wounding another. This was the first recorded death of an immigrant due to racially motivated attacks.

This mistreatment persists despite the fact that the Spanish retain two colonies, Ceuta and Melilla, on the Moroccan coast (although an opposition Islamic party has recently formed in Melilla, perhaps signaling a rising independence movement). Spain also has growing commercial interests in North Africa. It has spent $1.5 billion in aid and investment as Morocco's second-largest trading partner after France. Spain receives 15 percent of its oil from North Africa, and the Spanish state oil company, Repsol, is presently exploring for gas in Algeria.

Italy

The beginning of the 1970s marked a fundamental reversal in the history of migration in Italy. For more than a century before that, the transalpine peninsula had been one of the greatest suppliers of labor power, first to North America and Latin America, then to other European countries (especially France) and also to Australia. An estimated 25 million Italians migrated to the United States and other destinations between 1870 and 1970. Italian emigration, however, has diminished as the economic growth began to take hold in the northern and central regions. Falling birthrates have also helped reverse the trend.[22] Now the only Italian emigrants are those who put their mental abilities at the service of world industry. Thus, whereas most European countries began to erect legal barriers at the beginning of the 1970s to prevent immigration, it has only recently become an important issue in the Italian media and politics. As a new phenomenon, it poses questions and difficulties for Italian society, since Italy is much more accustomed to exporting its poor than to receiving them from other countries. Another problem for Italy is the scorn it is receiving from increasingly protectionist EC partners who view it as the " 'soft underbelly' into the Community for covert immigration."[23]

As far as Italian society in general is concerned, a placid acceptance of immigration has indirectly delivered a strong boost to the image of *Italiani, brava gente* ("Italians, a kind people") that Italians have promoted to the world. After a long period of public and also political indifference, however, Italian society has started to show increasing signs of unease and intolerance toward immigrants. In the early 1990s masked Italians ran through the streets of Florence, beating and knifing Africans. Protests were organized in Milan in which Italians carried signs reading, "Milan Is Becoming the Bronx of Italy" and "Casbah? No Thank You."[24] When locals in a prosperous suburb of Milan grew resentful of the presence of six hundred homeless and mostly unemployed Moroccans, who had created a shanty town in the midst of their neighborhood, police dragged the peaceful Moroccans from their lean-to homes. The immigrants were gathering in the suburbs to escape the dangers of downtown Milan, where a young male Moroccan had been murdered as he tried to sell cigarettes. An immigrant hostel in Bolzano, near Bologna, was burned down by Italian youths, leaving 120 North African immigrants homeless. The victims charged that the crime had been tacitly encouraged by the town council's ban of further local black immigration. In orchards outside of Naples, African fruit pickers have been attacked; African prostitutes in the same environs have been attacked by native Italian pimps and prostitutes angered by the new, "exotic" competition. In Turin and Verona, immigrants have been banned by local politicians from washing windshields at traffic lights. This occupation has often been the only source of income for many immigrants.

This racially motivated violence has occasionally been sanctioned and/or carried out by the authorities. In one incident, police razed a makeshift mosque, barbershop, surgery, and restaurant on the grounds that it was unsanitary. The true motivation was political, as left-wing politicians attempted to undermine the growing popularity of the anti-immigrant, right-wing groups by destroying an immigrant community: right-wingers presumably could no longer attract voters by their antiforeigner rhetoric if the left-wing proved itself just as anti-African. The ultraconservative Lombard League of Umberto Bossi has won widespread approval and votes with its anti-immigrant rhetoric; in a November 1991 election the league replaced the Christian Democratic party as the number one party in the town of Brescia, with 24.4 percent of the vote. Many believe the Lombard League could gain 21 percent of the vote nationwide.[25] Attacks continue; twenty Italian youths fell upon several North Africans, stabbing and beating them severely. Julio Salieino, an Italian sociologist, noted the increase in violence and said it is based in part on increased nationalism and clashes in culture and religion between Islam and Christianity, which bring out Italian xenophobia.

Until recently Italians had no regulation of foreign workers because of the latter's necessity to the economy; however, since the late 1980s things have changed. Italy now has approximately 1 million immigrants, with thousands arriving weekly. In Milan, the number of foreign workers exploded from 5,000 in 1988 to 70,000 in 1990. Italy's police and bureaucratic systems were not prepared to handle the situation,[26] and in 1989 Italy granted amnesty for illegal workers. Approximately 140,000 workers, primarily employed in the industrial north, were given legal status simultaneous with the new laws that were passed in an attempt to regulate non-EC foreign workers better by tying their entrance much more closely to labor market requirements. Employers in the agricultural south who want a mobile, flexible, low-skilled, low-paid work force, however, have not cooperated sufficiently with the laws to eliminate illegal workers. Also, for those immigrants holding low-paid, cash-only jobs as bricklayers and drivers, legality makes them less attractive and more expensive to their employers. For them the amnesty was no blessing, since authorization left them unemployed and starving. Many jobs shunned by Italians but desirable to North Africans go unfilled, because legal North Africans are now too expensive and Italian employers would rather seek out Italian employees than pay decent salaries to North Africans. A Milanese restaurant employing two Egyptians in its kitchen had advertised for an Italian cook, waiter, and dishwasher and received only one response in two months. A Milanese bakers' association had such extreme difficulty in finding Italian-born help that it offered to train 5,000 immigrants for the unfilled jobs.[27]

The Martelli law of February 28, 1990, banned new Third World immigration by imposing visa requirements on people entering Italy from Morocco, Tunisia, Algeria, Turkey, Mauritania, and Senegal. In June 1990 a computer system for registration and regulation of immigrants was established. At that time, Italy began deporting all those who had not "regularized" themselves by getting a residence permit. The irony is that Italy's population will fall from its current fifty-six million to forty-five million in 2045, with only one in four Italians of working age. Italy, despite its Catholic orientation, has one of the lowest birthrates in Europe and is already paying nineteen million pensions. Therefore, restricting immigration has no basis in logic but rather stems from attitudes of superiority and racism against people who are different.

Anti-Semitism

Although hatred against Jews and crimes stemming from this antipathy have existed for thousands of years, anti-Semitism as a term was coined only in 1879 by Wilhelm Marr. Jews and Greeks coexisted peaceably for years in Asia Minor and Egypt until the Jewish population grew too large to exist isolated in its independent communities. Assimilation into Greek society caused problems. In 175 B.C. Atiochos IV started a civil war against the Jews because he was afraid that they might join forces with Egypt, a hostile nation. In ancient Rome, the Jews had a contract promising them autonomy. This contract was supposed to be renewed in 140 B.C., but new troubles started and the Jews were merely tolerated. Julius Caesar would not allow any Jewish men into the military, because they could not train on Sabbath.

By the fifth century A.D. no Jew was allowed to work in public service. Instead, many went into trade. Jews suffered terribly during medieval times: Christian crusaders murdered them, and mobs killed those Jews who refused to be baptized. Times became so hard that more and more Jews began to migrate to the East; in the West, they were forced to wear the Star of David and special clothes. When the plague was decimating medieval Europe, the panicked society adopted the Jews as one of their scapegoats. Jews were accused of slaughtering Christian babies, and Christians claimed that comparatively few Jews were dying of the plague and that this made Jews morally suspect. Spain's anti-Semitic views were reflected in the government's national policies, as Spain did not recognize Israel until 1986.

While Jews were subject to atrocities in the West, even more were perpetrated in the East. From 1648 to 1654, Ivan the Terrible of Russia caused at least one hundred thousand Jews to flee back to the West after having only just abandoned it because of mistreatment there. One hundred years later, the nine hundred thousand Jews remaining in Russia were subjected to double taxation. When enlightenment finally dawned in Europe, it did not include the Jews: Voltaire called them "the most horrible people in the world," writer/philosopher Emanuel Kant called them "a nation of cheats," and Fichte, a pupil of Kant, thought it better to cut off their heads than give them civil rights. All of this hatred culminated in Hitler's extermination of six million Jews in concentration camps in World War II.[28]

In 1985, 37 percent of the French polled believed there was a significant amount of anti-Semitism in France; in 1990 the figure was 45 percent. While only thirty-two thousand Jews live in Italy, 11 percent of the adult Italian population displayed extreme anti-Semitic feelings by saying Jews should leave Italy. In West Germany, 57 percent of those surveyed did not want to have any Arabs in their neighborhood, whereas 22 percent did not want to live close to Jews. Education, however, seemed to help to improve prejudicial attitudes: while 27 percent of those with only basic education did not want to mix with Jews, only 14 percent with higher education stated the same view. Only 13 percent of the population in Germany claimed to know a Jew personally. (There are only thirty-five thousand Jews who have registered their religion with the government, plus approximately fifteen thousand who have not registered.) In France the percentage increased to 35 percent, and in the United States two-thirds of those surveyed knew a Jewish person.

Anti-Semitism survives, and anti-Semitic acts have increased with other racial violence in the early 1990s. The widespread desecration of Jewish cemeteries (such as that in Carpentras, France) is an example of such rising hate crimes directed against Jews.[29] In the entire year of 1990 there were 392 incidents of anti-Semitic acts; however, 172 took place in May after the Carpentras cemetery was desecrated. In Germany, a Jewish cemetery in East Berlin was desecrated, and the graves of Bertolt Brecht and his wife, Helene Wiegel, were daubed with the words "Jewish pigs." When Heinz Gabinski, a leader of German Jews, died, neo-Nazis delivered two pigs' heads (wrapped in joyous letters about his death) to a synagogue; Jews consider pigs unclean animals. In 1992 a monument in Berlin dedicated to the tens of thousands of Jews sent to the death camps by trains was severely damaged by explosives. In addition, a German who was thought to be Jewish was beaten and burned to death. In England, Orthodox Jews were attacked, five synagogues were vandalized with graffiti, and cemeteries and a memorial to those killed in concentration camps were desecrated. As a result of the attacks, London police began keeping track of them: in a short time, it had forty-six reported cases of physical assault, nine acts of vandalism, four cases of anti-Semitic literature, and six cases of verbal abuse.

Conclusion

As one looks into the future of the EC and its competitiveness, it is clear that serious problems will arise because of religious, racial, ethnic, lingual, and cultural differences. Although apparent even at the present time, these conflicts will become more prominent when the European common market becomes a reality and the EC member nations do not experience immediate utopia but rather a difficult period of economic adjustment and sacrifice.

Although the EC nations have created the right language to support diversity, this chapter has demonstrated that they and their populations have yet to "walk their talk." If the EC does not learn to deal effectively with these issues, we believe it will suffer nearly the same fate as the former Soviet Union and Yugoslavia. Having been made up of fifteen republics of diverse ethnic, religious, racial, cultural, and linguistic groups, the USSR had to deal with both open incidents of violence and the subtler issues of maintaining cultural traditions among various ethnic groups; selecting the official languages of republics and which language(s) will be taught in schools; which ethnic groups have access to universities and jobs; which groups have access to the limited housing; and so on. The communist state controlled, but did not solve, these problems through terror; its collapse has seen a resurgence of ethnic, gender, cultural, and religious violence in all of the newly freed countries. While we do not predict for the EC open violence on the scale witnessed in Russia and Yugoslavia, we do predict increasing incidents of violence that in some areas could reach the intensity of conflicts in the former Soviet Union.[30]

Since Europeans have difficulty dealing equitably with Asians and nonwhite immigrants, as the EC competes in the global marketplace, these attitudes will negatively affect their ability to work and trade effectively with nations of Asian and nonwhite peoples. Furthermore, even though the United States is a western European nation in many respects, the EC faces another difficulty as its ethnocentrism interferes with effective interactions with Americans. The fact that 50 percent of American managers either resign or are fired within eighteen months of foreign takeovers suggests the degree of the problem. Remember that the British, by far, have purchased more U.S companies than any other national group, including the Japanese.

For the EC to survive and prosper there must be both an economic union *and* a political union to enforce the equitable and fair treatment of all EC citizens and immigrant residents. If this is not achieved, the noncitizens living and working in EC countries will always be victims of hatred and discrimination, and the EC's productivity and unity will suffer. A tremendous effort will be necessary to effect changes allowing the diverse peoples of the EC to appreciate and value their differences. The place to start is a political union with strong laws protecting the rights of all humans, such as we have in the United States. Therefore, both internally and externally, the EC must overcome its ethnocentrism, racism, and xenophobia to survive politically and economically; in short, it must change or perish. We would be remiss not to note that in France, Italy, and Germany, citizens have rallied against racism and anti-Semitism; however, the numbers must grow, and the rallies must be more frequent.

Women in the U.S. Workplace

Current Status of Women

In the previous sections of this book, we have painted a clear picture of why the Japanese and European Community economies will have difficulty in the increasingly competitive and diverse global marketplace. The next four chapters will focus on diversity issues of gender and race/ethnicity in the United States that, if not dealt with more effectively, will hinder it in regaining economic dominance. At most, these difficulties could ultimately lead to extreme conflicts among diverse groups, resulting in the United States sinking in status to a second-class economic power.

Despite the fact that a recent survey of one thousand two hundred executives indicated a positive attitude toward women and their advancement (68 percent were eager to promote women to top executive levels, and 85 percent were eager to promote them to middle management; only 29 percent said women were not likely to be promoted as quickly as men), the reality is that women continue to be inequitably hired, renumerated, promoted, and rewarded, a clear waste of more than half of the U.S. population. This chapter will clearly demonstrate that corporate America, while ahead of Europe and Japan in the fair treatment of women both by law (see Appendix B) and in attitudes and behavior, has far to go in making women full and equal members in all job areas and at all levels of their organization.[1] Despite numerous suits and data presented, there are many corporate executives and managers—almost exclusively men—who will argue that women have not made significant progress not because of discrimination but because they do not have the necessary educational background, skills, work experience, and continuous careers (because of family responsibilities) to reach the higher levels. We will demonstrate that the reason women are not likely to become CEOs sooner is not what 201 CEOs from the nation's largest corporations say (as demonstrated in Table 10–1)[1] but neosexism or outright gender discrimination.

Here are some basic facts to consider. Over the past four decades, women have come to constitute an increasingly larger percentage of entrants into the civilian work force: 33 percent in 1960, 43 percent in 1980, and 45 percent in 1990. In the past three decades women have accounted for 60 percent of the total increase in employment. In fact, an estimated two out of every three people who will fill the 15 million new jobs between 1993 and the twenty-first century will be women. By 2000, women will represent at least 47 percent of the work force. In 1960, 38 percent of women were in the work force, compared to 84 percent of men; these figures in 1990 were 59 percent and 77 percent respectively.

Since the 1970s, the number of dual-career families and single heads of households has grown enormously, changing the profile of the

TABLE 10–1

Why Is a Woman Not Likely to Be a CEO Sooner?

Women lack long enough experience	64%
Are too concentrated in areas of the company that don't lead to the CEO post, such as communications	50%
Lack broad enough experience	45%
Have not built up solid networks of connections and support	31%
Personal lives and obligation to families get in the way of their careers	29%
Not enough in male-dominated industries, i.e., engineering, manufacturing	17%
It's a matter of time	12%
Current CEO will be in position for a while	9%
Are not aggressive or determined enough to make it to the top	8%
It's more than a matter of numbers	6%

Source: Anne B. Fisher, "When Will Women Get to the Top?" *Fortune*, September 21, 1992, p. 52

American family. Two-income couples made up only 28 percent of all married couples in the United States in 1960, but they made up 49 percent in 1985 and 54 percent in 1990. This rapid growth in two-income couples is projected to rise to over 60 percent by the year 2000. The greatest changes in the female labor force in the past fifteen years have occurred among women of childbearing age, as having young children no longer means leaving the work force. In 1990, 75 percent of mothers with children six to seventeen years old were employed, compared with 55 percent in 1975. The most dramatic increase in the labor force in recent years has been the percentage of working mothers with children under two years of age, from 32 percent in 1975 to 52 percent in 1990. In the 1960s there was a significant decrease in women in the twenty-five to thirty-four-year-old group working, but this is no longer so in the 1990s. Women who marry and have children are likely to remain in the work force; therefore, there is no dip of participation in the child-rearing years.

Despite the gains in the employment of women, they remain unequally remunerated for their work both in professions that are traditionally male dominated and in lower-paying female-dominated occupations. In 1979 women earned sixty-two cents for every male dollar; women in 1990 earned seventy-four cents for every dollar earned by a man. (Because of the recession, in 1992 women earned 72 cents for every dollar men made.) The 1979 proportion for sixteen- to twenty-four-year-old women was 79 percent; in 1990 it was 90 percent. For the twenty-five to thirty-four-year-old groups, the figures were 67 percent for 1979 and 79 percent for 1990. Pay inequality gets worse for older women aged fifty-five to sixty-four: they earn fifty-four cents for every male dollar.[2]

The larger discrepancy between older men and women than between younger men and women has several sources. The primary source is the residual of outright gender discrimination; another explanation for some older women is that their careers were more likely to be interrupted by larger periods of time to raise a family than younger women. Other explanations are the greater education gap between older women and men and the concentration of older women in fields less related to business. Obviously, there has been improvement, but at the current pace (and with the impact of recessions) parity will not be reached until 2017 or beyond. In fact, the disparity between male and female salaries is so bad that women with college degrees are earning roughly the same average salary as men with only high school diplomas. At every level of education, women make less than men at the same level, and female-dominated fields do not pay as well as male-dominated ones. A year of experience adds only seven cents an hour to a woman's pay, while it adds twenty-four cents an hour to that of a man. Women now receive more undergraduate degrees than men; in 1989 they received 53 percent of all undergraduate degrees, compared with only 42 percent in 1970.

In medicine, the situation for women is particularly bad. No American medical school has a female dean, and 98 percent of department chairmen are men. The health care professions remain segregated, with 84 percent of physicians being men and 97 percent of nurses being women. Women doctors have actually lost ground in the pursuit of equal pay; whereas they earned 63.2 cents for every male dollar in 1982, they now earn only 62.8 cents. And the disparity is not connected with experience and tenure: women who have been practicing between ten and twenty years earn an average of $99,400, compared to $158,000 for men practicing the same amount of time.[3]

The problem exists as well in government. Women on U.S. Senate staffs make an average salary of $30,131 while men make $38,407, and 22.7 percent of women compared to 18.3 percent of men are making less than $20,000 per year. All this is despite the fact that women Senate staff members on average have one-third more job experience and have held their positions 50 percent longer than their male counterparts.[4] In 1990, women held 31.3 percent of high-level state and local government jobs, despite the fact that women in lower-level jobs accounted for 43.5 percent of the entire government work force.[5] The fact that women can receive less pay and advancement even when they are more educated and experienced than men exposes as a fallacy the rhetoric that women are not getting ahead because they have yet to accumulate the experience or education of men.

Not only are women not paid equally for doing the same work, but they are not promoted equally for the same experience and excellence in job performance. Granted, there has been much improvement in the numbers of women promoted: in 1990, women represented 40 percent of management jobs in the United States, more than double the level of 19 percent in 1972. From 1972 to 1990, women working as executives, administrators, or managers more than doubled as well, from 5 percent to 11 percent. The percentage in the professional specialty occupations did not go up as much (12 percent to 15 percent), but this is still a 25 percent increase. A much-anticipated Labor Department study of nine federally contracted companies concerning glass ceilings for women and minorities, however, revealed instances of glass ceilings in each company. Former labor secretary Lynn Martin nevertheless toed her administration's line, saying that the instances were subtle as opposed to illegal, and therefore no punitive action would be taken. This response angered many women and minorities.

The 1992 Labor Department glass ceiling report noted that in the preceding ten years there had been little progress made in middle-management and higher positions in the country's one thousand largest corporations; people of color and women held less than 5 percent of these positions in 1990, and less than 3 percent in 1979. At the very senior levels minority women represented only 3.3 percent of the female corporate officers, who in turn represented less than 2 percent of *all* corporate officers. Of 1,315 board members of the one hundred largest American corporations, only 7.5 percent were women, and only 11.5 percent of top union leaders were women. The Labor Department concluded that its original directive to concentrate its analysis at the executive suite and highest levels of management was irrelevant, because there were few if any women at these levels. In the report's words, "To put it plainly, the glass ceiling existed at a much lower level than first thought."

Another report found that less than 0.5 percent of the highest-paid officers and directors of the top one thousand U.S. companies are female.[6] Only 2.6 percent of executive positions (vice president and up) at Fortune 500 companies are held by women. Women have made virtually no gains in the upper echelons of management in the past twenty years: where men before held 99 percent of senior management jobs, they now still hold more than 97 percent of those positions. The sheer number of women who have entered the work force, however, makes their eventual advance into the middle and upper levels inevitable.

Women have broken into some previously male-dominated careers over the past decade; for example, a woman is now the supervisor of one in twelve stock mutual funds. Women's new presence in the industry is attested to by the fact that only one of the sixty-nine women in this position was there before 1983, and 80 percent of the women running funds had been in charge less than five years.[7]

Not only are there few women at high levels, but those few who have made it are not in line or sales jobs but in staff positions related to human resources, research, or administration. This job segregation was found throughout the organizations. Some occupations of women, however, showed dramatic increases between 1972 and 1990; lawyers, 4 percent to 21 percent; doctors, 8 percent to 19 percent; computer programmers, 20 percent to 38 percent; bartenders, 26 percent to 56 percent; and bus drivers, 34 percent to 52 percent. Clearly the male/female socialization into certain occupations remains, as women still represent more than 90 percent of nurses and 95 percent of secretaries. And in the traditionally male occupations of construction and mining, women only represent 11 percent and 14 percent, respectively.

Inequality for women is widespread throughout our society. It infiltrates our culture from the classroom to the media to medical research and athletic scholarships. In February 1992 an extremely extensive, comprehensive study was released showing that grade-school and high school girls were the victims of sexual discrimination from teachers, textbooks, tests, and male classmates. The report, based on all current major studies on girls and education and more than one thousand publications on the subject, showed that teachers paid less attention to girls, tests remained biased against girls, schoolbooks ignored and stereotyped women, and teachers allowed boys to call out answers in class while reprimanding girls for doing the same.[8]

Despite the fact that the U.S. numbers look better than those for the EC and especially those for Japan, the overwhelming data indicate that women still face considerable discrimination in employment in the United States. Recent lawsuits support this notion; for example, in November 1991 a female worker at Texaco was awarded more than $17.6 million for unfairly being passed over for promotion in favor of men (her job performance had always been rated excellent). This settlement is believed to be the largest yet for a single plaintiff in such a case.[9] A gender discrimination suit filed in 1979 by 814 women employees of State Farm Insurance Companies was settled in April 1992 with the largest damage total ever paid in a civil rights case— $157 million (an average of $193,000 per woman).[10] Proponents of these suits say that the large awards will make companies take gender discrimination much more seriously (State Farm has already increased its hiring nationwide to 50 percent women). Others say such settlements will encourage unfair quota systems. Even with positive discrimination lawsuit results, though, sometimes the litigation goes on for years: sixty-seven Navy women were awarded a meager collective sum of $670,402 in back pay in November 1991 after filing charges in 1973![11] Also, many expect that the Civil Rights Act of 1991 will spur many more sexual discrimination suits because it gives plaintiffs the right to cash damages and a jury trial, unlike the 1964 law.

Stereotypes About Women in Corporations

Much of the lack of progress for women in corporate America is the result of gender stereotypes. Numerous studies have shown that society's negative stereotypes about women are carried into the corporate structure, where they grossly affect women's careers. Alarmingly, there has been an increasing trend toward stereotyping women since the late 1970s. Between 1976 and 1978, 16 percent of men and 7 percent of women surveyed agreed that women were not serious about their professional careers; in 1988, 20 percent of the women and 25 percent of the men agreed. In more than five hundred diversity seminars we conducted with approximately ten thousand employees at all levels in 1991, 1992, and 1993, we continued to hear numerous sexist stereotypes about women. In 1988, more than thirty thousand employees (our largest data base) were asked to respond to a series of statements of stereotypical views of women. The employees' responses are found in Table 10–2. Profound differences exist between the female and male views; these same patterns continue to occur in our seminars.

Other analyses of the same data show that different groups held different views about women. Black men responded very much like women themselves, whereas white and American Indian men displayed the most stereotypical views of women. One can attribute the lesser stereotypes held by African-American men to the fact that African-American women have been in the workforce in much higher percentages than white women. Therefore, a higher percentage of black men have been brought up in households with working women. Another possible explanation is the fact that black men, being subjected to numerous negative stereotypes themselves, are less likely to hold stereotypes about women. Among women, white women held the most stereotypical views; the former explanation for men could also explain why women of color hold less stereotypes than white women.

Some sexist practices and attitudes were related by employees who

TABLE 10.2
Sexist Stereotypes and Attitudes

Specific Questions	Women	Men
(Number = percent who agree or strongly agree)		
• Many women obtained their current positions only because they are women.	32%	43%
• Pluralism will force us to lower our hiring and promotion standards.	25%	40%
• The increasing employment of women has led to the breakdown of the American family.	30%	41%
• Many women use their gender as an alibi for difficulties they have on the job.	22%	27%
• Many women are not really serious about professional careers.	20%	18%
• Many women are too emotional to be competent employees.	9%	8%

participated in our diversity seminars in 1991, 1992, and 1993. Participants were asked to respond to the following two questions:

- Some people believe that in our society, everyone is socialized into exhibiting one or more of the following: sexism, racism, ageism, ethnocentrism, intolerance of foreign accents, other religions, sexual orientation, and so on. What do you believe are the most important issues that you must deal with about your own reactions to people who are different than you? Put another way, what problems do you have in accepting and dealing with people who are different than you?
- What are the major diversity issues you believe you must deal with in the work environment because of your age, gender, race, religion, native language, sexual orientation, family characteristics (child/elder care responsibilities), and/or physical and mental limitations, and so on?

Some comments were as follows:

I have problems with discrimination based on emotional decisions made by female supervisors (white, occupational, man)

Women are forced to wear dresses before they are considered properly dressed. What's wrong with a jacket and slacks? Isn't that what men wear? (Native American, occupational, woman)

Some of the men I have worked around want us to be sweet and pretty to be looked at. (Asian, occupational, woman)

Women get power happy! (Hispanic, occupational, man)

Some people think that women are inferior in science and mathematics. (Asian, lower-level, woman)

Regarding sexism, I still at times allow myself to question the physical ability of women in certain jobs. (white, middle-level, man)

Try to avoid people I have a hard time understanding. Have a hard time dealing with very aggressive women (men, too). (white, lower-level man)

I have problems with child care and the erosion of the family unit. (white, occupational, man)

I tend to categorize people, especially women, into those that I am interested in romantically, those I respect as a mother figure, and those I have no interest in. (black, middle-level, man)

A lot of women are only in the work force because of the good pay and not because they like their jobs. They know that the EEOC will protect them from being relieved of the jobs. (Hispanic, occupational, man)

Frequent discussions on women's "time of the month," pregnancy, and issues that would never be considered with males. (white, occupational, woman)

When unqualified women are placed in jobs they cannot do well, their failure sets a stereotype for the rest of us. (Asian, occupational, woman)

I think women sometimes have a tougher time against each other than against men, due to women being more petty/back-stabbing and management "turns the other cheek" when it occurs instead of NOT TOLERATING that kind of behavior. (white, occupational, woman)

I believe men or women who are the head of households or main providers should be given promotions and jobs *over* men or women who are providing only a second income in the family and are being promoted in order to accomplish "pluralistic efforts." (white, occupational, woman)

I think that some women try too much to be like one of the fellas and bring some things on themselves. (black, lower-level, woman)

I think women with young children at home are discriminated against, especially when interviewing for a job. Most people feel that they are not willing to make the sacrifices necessary, i.e. put in the extra hours. (white, lower-level, woman)

My experience in the short five years I have been in business is that the majority of women I have worked with are too emotional and too hung up on petty bickering/gossip/fashion/catfights and not focused on their jobs or their careers. The remaining *small* minority are the finest professionals in the workplace. (white, lower-level, man)

Inherent bias to prefer someone who looks/acts like me without consciously realizing it. Latent anger/disgust feelings with women who have children and then return to work within six months when they do not need to financially. I think it is somewhat selfish on their part (of course this implies that the male also works; it would be OK if he stayed home with the children). I have no problem with this in single parent families—that's necessity. Tendency to "wait and see" on the abilities of a minority in a job situation. (white, middle-level, man)

In meetings, I might look upon a women who is outspoken to be pushy and forward. I tend to work better with people who have proven their ability already. (white, occupational, man)

Physical attractiveness of females can be a distraction. Awareness of race in interactions can interfere with communications, i.e. this statement might be a racial negative—better be careful of what I say. (white, lower-level, man)

A denial mechanism operates in people with respect to these sexist views. We found that people who express the most stereotypes are the most likely to say that women are no longer looked at in a stereotypical fashion. Only 23 percent of those who agreed that women are no longer looked at in a stereotypical fashion did not agree with any sexist stereotypes; 60 percent who expressed at least a moderate number of stereotypes believed that women were no longer looked at in a stereotypical fashion. The denial of sexist stereotypes and their negative impact on the careers of women is a key reason women have made only minimal progress since the 1960s.

Gender Discrimination Since 1970

All the data we have collected since 1970 indicate that sexist attitudes and stereotypes such as "Women are too emotional to be effective managers." "Women are not really interested in a professional career," and "Women working leads to the breakdown of the American family" are translated into discriminatory actions against women. The protestations of many corporate managers that they can hold these beliefs privately without acting them out in the work environment are pure fantasy.

Between 1964 and 1972 the percentage of employees who believed that being a woman would be harmful to advancement in their company decreased. For example, Bowman found that 77 percent of employees in 1964, compared to 58 percent of the white managers and 72 percent of the black managers in 1972, believed that being a woman was harmful in business.[12] Between our 1976–78 and 1988 and beyond surveys, however, we changed the question about the effect of gender on advancement to relate specifically to the respondent's own career. In 1976–78, 19 percent of the women and 47 percent of the white men believed their gender was harmful to their career advancement. In 1988, 45 percent of minority women, 28 percent of white women, and 29 percent of white men believed their gender was harmful. The responses of minority men were similar; 15 percent in 1976–78 and 13 percent in 1988 believed their gender were harmful to their careers. In 1991, we found that 51 percent of the women and only 9 percent of men (regardless of race) believed their gender would be harmful to their career advancement. Interestingly in 1993, the percentage of women who believe their gender is harmful decreased to 45 percent, and that of men increased to 21 percent. In focus groups, participants attributed this change to the new emphasis placed on utilizing a diverse work force: women are more optimistic, and men—especially white men—are more pessimistic.

Despite this positive sign, we should not forget that the Labor Department noted in its 1992 report that male and female managers were very similar in responses about job satisfaction, stress, and commitment to the organization, but women rated their own promotional opportunities as much lower than those of their male peers. In our 1988 study, 76 percent of the women and 25 percent of the men believed that women had to be better managers than men to get ahead in their company. In 1976–78 the figures were 72 percent and 27 percent; in 1991, 80 percent of the women and 27 percent of the men believed this. The figures remained about the same in 1993.

Over the years, we have found in our surveys that more than a majority of employees have witnessed the following examples of discrimination in their company (see Table 10-3): women have a harder time finding sponsors in the company (72 percent); women were excluded from informal networks (63 percent); women must be better

TABLE 10–3
Gender Discrimination

Specific Questions	Women	Men	Total
In general, women have a much harder time finding a sponsor, or mentor than men do	81%	55%	72%
Many women are often excluded from informal networks by men.	71%	43%	63%
In general, customers do not accept a woman's authority as much as they accept a man's in similar situations	45%	34%	58%
In general, women have to be better performers than men to get ahead	76%	25%	56%
Many women are faced with some type of sexual harassment on the job	62%	47%	48%
Many women have a difficult time initiating informal work-related activities such as lunch and socializing after work, because men misinterpret their behavior as a "come on."	58%	33%	42%
In general, women are placed in jobs with no future.	54%	17%	41%
In general, women are penalized more for mistakes than men	45%	9%	33%
(N = % who say at least frequently) How frequently do you hear language in your organization which you consider sexist?	34%	22%	29%

performers to get ahead (58 percent); and women are faced with sexual harassment on the job (56 percent). Almost six times as many women (35 percent compared with 6 percent of men) believed that there was a great deal of discrimination, but only 8 percent of the men and 19 percent of the women believed there was no gender discrimination.

Note that a 1990 analysis found that 79 percent of Fortune 500 CEOs conceded that women in their organizations faced barriers that men did not in getting to the top. The essential difference between women and men is not whether there is discrimination in the workplace, but the extent to which it exists. The following comments from our recent surveys and workshops graphically illustrate the reality of gender discrimination:

It seems like women discriminate against women quite often. (white, occupational, woman)

Gender discrimination in the company is demonstrated in the number of middle- and higher-level women management, compared with men. (Asian, lower-level, woman)

All people are more productive in a supportive environment. The subtle everyday messages women receive telling them they are not competent is not supportive and causes an enormous loss of production. (white, lower-level, woman)

Pregnant women seem to be more discriminated against. There is an inadequate attitude about mothers as employees. (white, middle-level, woman)

One of my peers is female, a little paranoid, and seldom listens to suggestions from anybody on the crew, no matter how helpful they try to be. As a result, we tend to let her stumble around and screw up. (American Indian, occupational, man)

The only problem white men face today is that they have been spoiled for too many years and are having a hard time adjusting to "sharing." They've been raised to think they get the whole pie. (white, occupational, woman)

The only way anyone gets moved in this office is if they know someone and that someone likes them. Then they get the opportunity. Otherwise, it doesn't matter how hard you try or what you do extra. If they don't like you, you won't go nowhere, except out when you've had enough and quit. (white, occupational, woman)

I personally do not feel I am taken as seriously about my work as I wish to be. (American Indian, occupational, woman)

Women, more and more, are joining the job market, which takes time away from home. Very few men are assuming home responsibilities to help. Often, the family has problems which are blamed on women. (African American, occupational, woman)

Tendency of business is to pigeonhole women in lesser jobs. For example, if someone is an outstanding secretary, she's not encouraged to seek other opportunities which would offer growth and advancement. (white, lower-level, woman)

In my company, although women hold jobs at all levels, most women are employed in areas which are traditionally considered "women's" jobs (customer service, admin. asst., etc.)—same with minorities and white men. These employees seem to make lateral career moves far more often than vertical ones, and more so than others in the company. (white, lower-level, woman)

My supervisors have indicated they are threatened by me, that I will replace them. So they look for ways to make my performance seem less by lack of direction, repeating the same function many times, miscommunicating, taking credit for my ideas. (white, lower-level, woman)

Personal discussions between men and women often center on the distrust of the sexes. Until this is relieved, both sexes will reflect discrimination within the company. (white, lower-level, man)

Because this company actively rejects sexist behavior I feel the men have reacted by patronizing women and blaming their failures on the advancement of women and also not crediting the advancement of women due to their abilities, but rather to their sex. (African American, middle-level, woman)

Sexual harrasment problems are ignored by middle levels and up. (white, middle-level, woman)

I believe many women feel more discriminated against than they actually are; they sometimes look at events and issues, trying (perhaps unconsciously), to find a prejudice that may not really exist. (white, officer, man)

What the data and comments clearly show is that the companies in our studies are not doing a very good job in respecting differences in the gender area.[13] They are not fully and effectively utilizing women, who make up between 30 percent to 70 percent of their work forces. This is suicidal in the new competitive global economy where companies must fully utilize their diversity and develop high-performance quality-oriented teams.

Women in International Settings

As the global marketplace emerges, those who move to the top will be required to have international assignments; however, only 5 percent of expatriate American managers are women. The main reasons companies give for not sending women for overseas assignments are (1) that they lack the technical qualifications and (2) local national prejudice. Moran, Stahl, and Bayer, a consulting firm, found that 80 percent of the companies in a survey said that there were disadvantages sending women overseas. Joyce Cross, human resources director for McDonnell Douglas, said that some contracts the company has with Japan and Saudi Arabia do not allow women on the job due to labor laws or social customs.

We believe a key problem in sending women overseas is not only the real sexist attitudes of foreign countries, but also that American corporations project their own sexist biases onto all countries and do not distinguish the various cultures and environments that exist not only among but within different countries and corporations. There are some areas where American women have been accepted better than their male counterparts, including parts of Latin America, Asia, and Europe. Women executives are perceived as being more understanding, more approachable, and not as aggressive. As noted in Chapter 7, the participation rate of women and their success rate vary greatly among EC countries.

In addition, it seems to us that in many cases being a foreigner is more of a disadvantage than being a woman. Recognizing that more women study foreign languages in our schools, corporate America is missing out on fully utilizing these women's talents. Moran, Stahl, and Bayer found that of those companies that have sent women overseas, the vast majority say women have performed in an effective to outstanding manner.

Sexual Harassment

A key factor negatively affecting women in the work force that has come to the surface in a blaze of light in the 1990s is sexual harassment. According to the U.S. Equal Employment Opportunities Commission (EEOC), sexual harassment is defined as "unwelcome sexual advances, requests for sexual favors, and other verbal or physical conduct of a sexual nature" when "submission to or rejection of this conduct explicitly or implicitly affects an individual's employment, unreasonably interferes with an individual's work performance or creates an intimidating, hostile or offensive work environment."

The legal history of sexual harassment is as follows. The Civil Rights Act of 1964 provided for sexual harassment protection but did not allow for cash settlements or punitive damages. The next time that sexual harassment was further defined in the law was in 1980, when the EEOC stated "that making sexual activity a condition of employment or promotion was a violation of the 1964 Civil Rights Act" and that creating "an intimidating, hostile or offensive working environment" was illegal. This ruling was not particularly effective, however, until 1986 with the landmark case of *Meritor Savings Bank v. Vinson,* when the U.S. Supreme Court sided with Michelle Vinson in her charges that her boss had publicly fondled her, exposed himself to her, and repeatedly raped her. This case was groundbreaking because it expanded the definition of harassment to include verbal or physical conduct that creates an intimidating, hostile, or offensive work environment or unreasonably interferes with an employee's job performance. The Civil Rights Act of 1991 provided that victims of sexual harassment—who previously could be awarded only missed wages—could collect a wide range of punitive damages and attorney fees from employers who mishandled a complaint. January 1992 saw two major precedent setting sexual harassment cases: in Florida, a female shipyard worker successfully sued on the basis that nude pinups in the workplace constituted illegal harassment, and in San Francisco, a controversial decision (discussed below) was made using a "reasonable woman" guideline.[14]

The Numbers on Sexual Harassment

Is all this attention to sexual harassment in the workplace warranted? You bet. In our 1976–78 survey, we did not ask any questions about sexual harassment, but we have since incorporated them. The 1986 survey found that 71 percent of women and 51 percent of men believed that women face some type of sexual harassment on the job. The figures in 1988 were 62 percent of the women and 47 percent of the men, and in 1992, 75 percent of the women and 52 percent of the men. From 1985 to 1990, an average of 5,000 cases were filed with the EEOC; however, the number jumped to more than 6,600 complaints in 1991 (an increase of 23 percent) and to 7,465 through September 1992.[15] Ninety percent of victims of sexual harassment, moreover, do not file formal complaints.

Nearly 90 percent of Fortune 500 companies have received complaints of sexual harassment, and more than one third have been sued at least once (almost a quarter have been sued more often). In 1991 $5.2 million in damages were awarded to women on sexual harassment charges; through September 1992 the figure was $7.6 million. Sexual harassment can be very costly to an employer in productivity as well as cost of litigation and settlements. A 1988 study of sexual harassment in one hundred sixty Fortune 500 service and manufacturing companies reported that sexual harassment cost these companies an average of approximately $6.7 million a year in lost productivity. According to the United States Merit Systems Protection Board, absenteeism, job turnover, and lost productivity caused by sexual harassment costs the U.S. government an estimated minimum of $189 million a year. We should add that an atmosphere where sexual harassment goes on is not conducive to forming high-performance teams.

Confusion and Outcries

As states are now each individually creating their own legislation on the matter, they are causing confusion among many and eliciting outcries from others. The most controversial ruling so far is the 1991 precedent-setting ruling by the Ninth Circuit Court of Appeals holding that the traditional "reasonable man" standard should be redefined in cases of sexual harassment as the "reasonable woman" standard. In other words, an act or comment is sexual harrassment if a reasonable *woman* would consider it to be so. Many claim that this ruling will cause problems and increase confusion over sexual harassment; as Philadelphia lawyer Jonathan Segal says, "something highly offensive to Minnie Pearl might be an inviting dare to Madonna."[16]

Title VII of the Civil Rights Act of 1991 allows the government to punish offenders who use offensive language to create "a hostile environment" for women at work. This clause has caused an outcry among many who say it is a violation of the First Amendment guarantee of free speech. This issue has divided the Florida branch of the American Civil Liberties Union, as two separate divisions of the group may file opposing briefs. The concept of language creating "a hostile environment" is expected to be challenged and to reach the Supreme Court to redefine sexual harassment.[17] The Civil Rights Act clause has been called "cultural fascism" by some, and others argue that lawsuits would be devastating to small businesses. Many have decried the sexual harassment laws as part of a new puritanism that will lead to mass consorship.[18]

Clearly, men and women hold very different views of what does or does not constitute sexual harassment or a "hostile" working environment. One survey reported that 67 percent of men would feel flattered if propositioned by a female colleague, while 63 percent of women would be offended if propositioned by a male colleague. A survey by *Redbook* magazine and the *Harvard Business Review* reported that 24 percent of women found a man giving a female worker the "once over" to be harassment; only 8 percent of men agreed.[19]

Men lately have complained that any remark they make can be interpreted as sexual harassment, and one article purported recently that sexual harassment laws were a ridiculous attempt to legislate good manners. Cynthia Fuchs Epstein, sociology professor at the City University Graduate Center, however, says that such attitudes are an overreaction. "Cases that need to be pursued are those that step over the bounds of 'bad taste' and into the realm of emotional discomfort. If the intent is mere casual joking, that's one thing. It may be obnoxious or unpleasant, but it's not harassment. But if there's an intent to make you uncomfortable, it's beyond the border." Epstein does add, however, that "men in many workplace settings . . . have that kind of ethos of bawdiness . . . [and] feel their comments were not harassing—that they're just doing what the good ole boys might do."[20]

Finally, employees and employers must become educated to the fact that men can be harassed by women and that same-sex harassment exists. In the case of homosexual or lesbian sexual harassment, "many people are afraid to come forward because their alternative lifestyle may cause other problems for them in the workplace," said one expert, "but [homosexual harassment] does happen." Also, although the vast majority of sexual harassment cases involve a man harassing a woman, 440 of the 5,690 complaints filed with the EEOC in 1990 were reported by men who were predominantly being harassed by women.

A danger in the corporate setting is that men will not interact productively with women because they are afraid of committing some form of behavior that will be defined as harassment. Women will lose out by being excluded from important projects and from the informal social networks necessary to succeed. Another negative is that employees are not as effective in their jobs when the atmosphere is hostile.

Work/Family Issues

Impact of Dual Roles on Women's Careers

As we noted earlier, one of the fastest-growing groups in the work force is that of women with young children. We also noted that many women are not leaving their jobs for any extended time (that is, are not interrupting their careers) because of family obligations. Finally, we noted that almost two out of three new jobs created in the 1990s will be filled by women and that 80 percent to 90 percent of these women will become mothers while employed. Thus, in order for the United States and its corporations to be successful, it must develop more family-friendly programs in order to utilize all women effectively regardless of family status.

In our book *Politics and Reality of Family Care in Corporate America,* we found that only 24 percent of women with children eighteen and under did not have problems balancing work and family conflicts, and only 22 percent of the women with elder care responsibilities said they had no problems. Having what effectively are two full-time jobs creates stress conflicts both at home and on the job. A certain level of on-the-job stress (caused by employment uncertainty, office politics, budget crunches, tight time frames, lack of corporate resources, and sometimes long hours) is inherent for most employees. For upwardly mobile employees, factors such as high expectations for performance are added to extraordinary work loads. For all employees, on-the-job stress along with family stress can create an overload of too much to do, with too little time in which to do it. Ultimately, owing to both physical and mental problems that are its by-products, overload lowers corporate productivity.

Sixty percent of the women, single or married, and 53 percent of the single men we surveyed experienced stress on the job related to the balancing of work and family conflicts. Similar numbers had stress at home for the same reasons. By contrast, only 38 percent of the married men with children under eighteen had such stress at work, and 42 percent at home. The figures dramatically demonstrate the unique, comfortable position in which many married men find themselves, but that comfort may be short-lived. As career opportunities for women increase and as the pressure of these careers intensifies, wives will become increasingly intolerant of the extreme imbalance in responsibilities at home, and more and more married men will begin to feel the stress and conflict of dual-career lives. As this happens, married men may find themselves no longer immune to dealing with family problems in the workplace. Data from a 1984 survey we conducted on child care compared to a 1989 survey showed a dramatic increase in the percentage of men who have stress at home and at work. For example, in 1984, 22 percent of the men had stress at home, compared to 39 percent in 1989.

Single-parent women, who are an ever-increasing demographic group in our country (one out of four children are born to single mothers), have unique challenges in balancing work and family life. In our seminars, work/family issues are among the key diversity issues that are creating problems in corporate America. The conflicts created lead to ineffective teamwork, lower morale, and lower productivity. That the United States as a nation and its corporations as economic entities have not effectively dealt with work/family issues is based in large part on the fact that our society has not yet decided what should women's roles really be. Ellen Galinsky, a leading child care expert, has frequently said if men had children, work/family issues would have been solved years ago.

Pregnancy

The United States Discrimination Act of 1978 and forty state, city, and county ordinances prohibit discrimination against pregnant women. The EEOC handles three thousand pregnancy discrimination charges a year; however, it believes this is only the tip of the iceberg. For example, the National Association of Working Women in Cleveland handles fifteen thousand calls a year from women claiming such discrimination.

The working mother is forced to cope with the problems at work and family long before her baby is born. From the moment the new mother is informed of her pregnancy, she must begin to consider the implications it will have on her career. When should she inform her boss, and how will the boss feel about the news? Will she be skipped over for promising long-term or demanding assignments? Will her job be there for her when she wants to return? Stereotyping of and discrimination against pregnant women may occur long before a woman has ever considered beginning a family. Felice Schwartz, in her book *Breaking with Tradition: Women and Work, the New Facts of Life,* points out that a woman will often be questioned during a job interview on her intentions to begin a family.

A recessionary economy, coupled with inflexible corporate personnel and health insurance policies, gives many women no choice but to be dishonest with employers. Though many employers may complain that they grant female employees a certain amount of time for maternity leave only to have them quit immediately prior to their anticipated return, they fail to realize that most corporate health insurance plans will allow women to retain their coverage only if they are on a leave of absence.[21]

A 1990 Bureau of Labor Statistics survey found that only 37 percent of women in firms of one hundred or more employees are covered by any type of maternity leave policy.[22] Those who are covered often find these policies to be inadequate. A survey by the Wellesley College Center for Research on Women and *Working Mother* magazine reported that almost 40 percent of respondents felt their company's maternity leave policy was miserly or nonexistent. Forty-five percent said their company's policy was adequate, while a scant 16 percent called it generous. Almost half of the women who felt that their company's maternity leave policy was generous reported being very satisfied with their jobs, while only 27 percent of those women offered miserly policies reported being very satisfied. The women who reported the most satisfaction were those who had taken six months of maternity leave, 72 percent of these women felt they were allowed enough time with the baby.[23]

The United States finally has caught up to the rest of the industrialized world in its implementation of family-friendly policies with the passage of a family leave policy in 1993. Industrialized European nations, however, far outdistance the United States in proffering child care alternatives.

In effect, many women face a four-tiered process of discrimination in regard to work and family issues. First, many women are methodically quizzed and even refused jobs as a function of their ability or actual plans to become pregnant. Second, when a woman does become pregnant, she is often treated as less than capable in her workplace. Says Joan Vertin, associate director of the American Civil Liberties Union's Women Rights Project, "When times are tough, pregnant women are seen as expendable." Third, as pointed out above until 1993, the majority of U.S. corporations did not offer maternity leave options, and many others offered plans considered less than satisfactory by female employees. Since the family leave law passed, many women still are not covered or will not be covered because they work for small corporations, less than 50 employees which are not covered by the law. Finally, the oft-documented hardships of taking care of a family while forging a career or just "working for a living"—especially without adequate family-friendly policies such as affordable and/or on-site day care, flextime, and work sharing—are inevitably crippling to both the corporation and the working mother (and, increasingly, the working father).

The economic necessity and/or need for fulfillment that drives women into the workplace often sets them up for discrimination vis-à-vis contemporary corporate American attitudes and policies. In fact, Patricia Ireland of the National Organization for Women notes that after sexual harassment, pregnancy discrimination is "the number one complaint we get about job discrimination." U.S. corporations are being forced to become more sensitive to contemporary work/family concerns as other industrialized nations offer dependent care options and as working mothers increasingly begin to win cases filed against discriminatory corporations. This issue will become even more pressing as the American birthrate begins its sharp climb in the coming decade. Should the United States wish to compete in a global marketplace in which work/family issues are being addressed, it is crucial that governmental and corporate entities develop fair and consistent family-friendly policies.

Recognizing that our population is getting older and that women are still the primary care givers for the elderly, the stress on some working women will increase as they take on this new role. One of the fastest-increasing family structures in the 1990s will be the "sandwich generation"—families who are responsible for caring for both children and parents. Many women try to make up for their lower productivity by taking work home and coming to work on the weekends, but this effort, while laudable, further increases stress and work/family conflicts by consuming limited time. Corning, one of the top scorers in a Families and Work Institute study, reports that turnover has plummeted 50 percent since the introduction of family-friendly policies, and Aetna reports that since the company has adopted an extended maternity leave policy, the number of mothers who do not return to work has fallen by 50 percent. Other companies find that more flexible policies have enabled them to retain key employees, saving money as a result.

Conclusion

Although American women have made significant strides toward equality—more so than in practically any other country in the world—there is still a great deal of work to do to achieve actual equality. For the same experience and skills, women are still inequitably paid, promoted, and hired; they are also widely victimized by sexual harassment. Men and women have become more educated about sexual harassment, but the immediate results are increased confusion and even animosity between the sexes. It is clear from the discussions in the chapters on Japan and Europe, however, that women who work in companies owned by these nations will face a great deal more social-interactive problems than those who work in American companies. This applies more to Japanese companies than European ones.

Women also face negative attitudes from society that they are less capable, that they can only perform certain "female" tasks, and that working women are responsible for the breakdown of our society.

Women also face increased stress as they are called on to be super-women, working full-time and carrying for children and dependent parents. They are breaking ground and winning concessions on work/family issues, but as in cases of sexual harassment and discrimination, there is much more room for improvement. Women must have equal and fair opportunities in all aspects of the U.S. society, if the United States wants to retain its lead as the major economic power in the 1990s and beyond.

U.S. Immigration Policies

How Much Better than the EC and Japan?

Fears of unmonitored immigration and attempts to draft an EC-wide immigration policy are hot topics in Europe. Japan, as noted here, has never allowed much immigration. With an all-time worldwide high in the United States of more than one million legal immigrants in 1990, however, immigration is currently a very contested issue here as well. Historically U.S. immigration law, although one of the most open policies in the world, has been marred by ethnocentrism, racism, and political maneuvering. Furthermore, various ethnic immigrant and native-born groups have clashed throughout U.S. history in degrees rivaling those of current European unrest. Recently U.S. immigration laws attempted to eradicate racial biases, but U.S. policy remains family-based (and, therefore, Eurocentric) despite the 1990 Immigration Act encouraging the admittance of more economically beneficial immigrants.

Anti-Asian Immigration Policy

The history of Asian immigration is perhaps the darkest chapter in U.S. legal immigration. Chinese laborers in the nineteenth century were often referred to as coolie labor because of their reputation for working under worse conditions for less money than any other immigrant group. Following the anti-Chinese riots in various cities in the 1870s and due to pressure from labor organizations, Chinese immigration was ended with the Chinese Exclusion Act of 1882, which was extended every ten years until its repeal in 1943.[1] This began an anti-Asian immigration policy that could be called anything but open.

Japanese laborers were used to replace the Chinese after the Japanese government allowed citizens to work abroad in 1884. Many Japanese emigrated to Hawaii and the West Coast, but ultimately they were manipulated as strikebreakers like the Chinese and were the object of the same anti-Eastern sentiments and violent incidents. They were excluded from further immigration in 1908 through the "gentlemen's agreement" in which the Japanese government agreed to stop issuing passports to those wishing to emigrate to this country. Filipinos, after the annexation of their country by the United States in 1898, filled the void left by Japanese until the need for their labor was lessened by increased competition from Mexican workers in the 1920s and the Great Depression of the 1930s, which increased the numbers of white Americans seeking employment. The Filipino Exclusion Act of 1934 effectively ended Filipino immigration with an annual quota of fifty visas a year. As part of a large restrictive immigration law in 1917 the "Asiatic Barred Zone" was created, banning most immigration from Asia.

Even today, Asian immigrants are apparently the victims of more discrimination and racially motivated violence than other immigrant groups. A Federal Civil Rights Commission report issued in February 1992 stated that Asian Americans "face widespread discrimination in the workplace and are often victims of racially motivated harassment and violence."[2] Japanese communities in Southern California have been the victims of increased verbal abuse, hate mail, graffiti, and vandalism.[3] One cannot help but conclude that Asian immigrants were and are subjected to harsher discrimination and exclusion than European immigrants because they are "more different."

The First and Second Waves

From 1607 to the early 1830s a total of only one million immigrants entered what would constitute the United States; they were almost exclusively British emigrants and African slaves. After that period, immigration to the United States can be divided into four waves. The first signified the beginning of mass immigration: from the early 1830s to the mid-1850s five million immigrants arrived, consisting mostly of English, Irish, German, and French-Canadian settlers. With this first mass influx, immigration already was becoming "the subject of extensive domestic controversy," as the immigrants' arrival was not viewed as "a benign development."[4] Preexisting arrivals were threatened by the numbers and comparative diversity of the new immigrants, as well as by their economic impact. This created a precedent for future negative reactions and the erroneous connection between immigrants' diversity and their sometimes negative effect on wages, working conditions, unemployment levels, and labor organization. The second wave between the early 1860s and the early 1880s, consisted of more than five million mostly German, British, Irish, and Canadian immigrants (much like the first wave), but with the addition of significant numbers of Scandinavians and Chinese. Because of severe labor shortages in the north during the Civil War, the first immigration statute in U.S. history was passed in 1864. The Act to Encourage Immigration was designed to attract urban workers to produce munitions and arms. It allowed employers to recruit foreign workers by paying for their transportation and living expenses; workers signed contracts pledging wages to repay these costs. Outraged domestic workers protested that the immigrants were being used as strikebreakers, and the act was repealed in 1868.

The Third Wave

With the third wave, beginning in the 1880s, immigration soared to new heights. More than 5 million entered the United States in the 1880s, 3.6 million in the 1890s; and 8.7 million in the first decade of the new century. Immigration continued to reach record levels until the outbreak of World War I. This third wave was ended by legislation in the 1920s that effectively limited immigration until 1965. The wave signaled a new immigrant population more representative of eastern and southern European nations. Whereas between 1820 and 1890, 85 percent of all immigrants came from northern and western European nations, by 1910, 70 percent were from southern and eastern Europe, compared to 20 percent for northern and western Europe.[5]

Once again, the preexisting population and the ruling powers were feeling threatened by the "adverse effects" of mass immigration. The United States adopted a literacy test in 1917 in the immigrants' native languages, set an annual immigration ceiling of 358,000 and created the aforementioned "Asiatic Barred Zone." The Immigration Act of 1924 (also known as the National Origins Act) continued the preference for northern Europeans by creating quotas stipulating that 82 percent of immigrants originate from northern and western Europe, 14 percent from eastern and southern Europe, and 4 percent from non-Asian Eastern Hemisphere nations. The seeds of this very anti-diversity law were planted with the Immigration Commission report of 1911. The commission, appointed by Theodore Roosevelt in 1907, linked the negative economic effects of immigration (low wages, poor working conditions, labor organization problems, and unemployment) with the difficulties of assimilating the racially, culturally, and ethnically diverse immigrants. The very "otherness" of these third-wave immigrants was deemed detrimental to the economic and social well-being of the United States.

1952: Anti-Communism and the Status Quo

The 1924 act proved to be inflexible, discriminatory, and out of step with immigration trends. Great Britain, for example, was allotted 42 percent of the visas but left many slots unfilled each year, while countries like Italy and Greece acquired application backlogs. President Harry Truman planned to replace this policy in 1952 with the support of many reformers in Congress and across the nation. Truman advocated a system based more on humanitarian principles, one that would assist those truly in need. But the Senate study conducted in response to Truman's request argued for maintaining the status quo "to best preserve the sociological and cultural balance of the United States."[6] The only open-minded provision of the subsequent Immigration and Nationality Act of 1952 (the McCarran-Walter Act, which was enacted by overriding Truman's veto) was that it abolished the exclusion of Asian immigrants. The conservatism of the new law was a reflection of the paranoia and anticommunism of the times; many in Congress were frightened that communist immigrants would infiltrate the country. The act was also the first law to institute a preference system within the quotas, specifying levels of training, abilities, and education. This law, like its predecessor, was proven to be obviously flawed: between 1952 and 1965, only 61 percent of the quota visas were used by the favored western European countries. Many refugees from other parts of Europe and China had to be permitted to immigrate under specially enacted temporary programs.

1965: Altruism Meets Politics

In 1965, President Lyndon Johnson also desired to pass an open-minded and fair immigration policy; however, both Congress and the administration were ultimately more interested in playing politics. Spurred by the civil rights movement, Americans were finally ready to award immigration privileges to those who truly needed it. Nevertheless, although the Kennedy administration and the subsequent Johnson administration sought to abolish national-origins priorities, the eventual Immigration Act of 1965 allotted 74 percent of visas to family reunification as a result of heavy lobbying by such groups as the American Legion (20 percent went for labor market needs, and 6 percent for refugees). This would ensure a heavy influx of northern and western Europeans, since they had been the dominant immigrating groups for so long. These groups and their congressional sympathizers wanted to "retain essentially the same racial and ethnic priorities that the national origins systems had fostered," even though the system was being abolished in name.[7] The seven-category preference system instituted with this act also shifted away from the skill categories of 1952 to a more family-based criteria.

The Fourth Wave

The 1965 Act resulted indirectly and unintentionally in a fourth wave of mass immigration because of its insufficient ability to handle the realities of modern immigration and the political maneuvering as well as the emergency humanitarian provisions enacted to make up for its weaknesses. On the same day that the 1965 act was signed, Lyndon Johnson announced that any Cuban desiring to emigrate to the United States was welcome to do so. Though humane, the gesture was largely viewed as a political move to embarrass communist leader Fidel Castro. From 1959 to 1973, 677,158 Cuban refugees entered the United States, mostly after 1965. These numbers were allowed above and beyond the 1965 immigration law quotas. The Cubans tended to settle in the Miami–Dade County area of Florida, where they invigorated the economy but where their presence resulted in four major race-related civil disorders in the 1980s. U.S. involvement in Indochina (Vietnam, Laos, and Kampuchea), ending in the 1970s, also brought in a stream of emergency refugees not provided for in the 1965 act—130,000 from April to December 1975 alone.

Two amendments in the late 1970s to the 1965 act helped to make U.S. immigration policy more egalitarian. The 1976 amendment imposed the seven preference categories under the new ceiling requirements of 20,000 per Western Hemisphere nation, and the 1978 amendment did away with hemispheric quotas and created a single worldwide ceiling of 290,000; this finally did away with national-origin preferences.[8]

Just as President Gerald Ford was about to crack down on the unlimited special-provision immigration of refugees from Southeast Asia and elsewhere, Jimmy Carter replaced him and expressed new interest in humanitarian refugee legislation. He used his presidential authority to temporarily grant admission to a total of 210,000 Indochinese refugees from July 1979 to September 1980. In 1980 the Refugee Act was enacted, effectively removing refugee admission from the legal immigration system by abolishing the seventh preference category for refugees. This act expanded the definition of refugee even beyond UN levels as "any person who is outside any country of such person's nationality . . . and who is unable or unwilling to avail himself of the protection of that country because of persecution or a well-founded fear of persecution due to race, religion, nationality, membership in a particular group, or political group, or political opinion."[9] It also included persons within their country of nationality when designated as such by the president. Furthermore, the act granted amnesty to those already in the States who were afraid to return to their country of origin. But while the Carter administration improved the humanitarian/refugee status of U.S. immigration law, it did not sufficiently address problems concerning illegal aliens and the need to recruit economically beneficial immigrants.

Western Hemisphere Immigration

Western Hemisphere immigration was not regulated or restricted until 1968; however, other policies did affect it. While the Immigration Act of 1924 reduced immigration from the traditional European sources, Canadian, Mexican, and Caribbean and Puerto Rican immigration dramatically increased in the 1920s.

The immigration of Mexicans is a major component of the fourth wave, but its origins and unique problems started much earlier. During the Mexican Civil War between 1910 and 1917, one million Mexicans (in a population of fifteen million) were killed. Many survivors fled to the four border states of California, Texas, New Mexico, and Arizona. They and their economic effect were largely ignored, as the region was in the infancy of its economic development—Arizona and New Mexico only had achieved statehood in 1912. Mexican labor was much needed for agriculture and irrigation projects, especially after the exclusion of Japanese in 1908, but this need decreased during the depression, when unemployed white Americans were preferred.

Illegal immigration existed from the times of the first immigration statutes of the 1870s; however, besides one major flareup after World War II (ended by the notorious border sweep known as "Operation Wetback" in 1954), illegal Mexican immigration did not explode until after the passage of the Immigration Act of 1965. The ending of the Mexican Labor Program at the end of 1964 caused many formerly legal Mexican workers to work illegally. Also, the caps on Western Hemisphere immigration caused Mexicans, who were immigrating annually at three times the legal rate of twenty thousand, to immigrate illegally as a massive backing of applicants quickly accumulated.

The fact that so many immigrants migrate to the United States illegally even when such factors as poverty, overpopulation, and political danger are absent can be blamed on the "Texas proviso." This concession to pressure by Texas agricultural employers was part of the Immigration and Nationality Act of 1952. It effectively kept U.S. employers from being penalized for employing illegal immigrants. Attempts to do away with this backward clause were not successful until the Immigration Reform and Control Act of 1986, which after much congressional stalemating and opposition from the Reagan administration did away with the proviso and allowed illegal workers under certain conditions to declare amnesty and seek alien status or eventual naturalization.

The Immigration Act of 1990

With the Immigration Act of 1990, the economic considerations of the United States were finally recognized in the admittance of immigrants (see Table 11–1). Family-based quotas were also increased, however, ensuring continued preference for northern and western Eu-

TABLE 11.1

The Preference System Created Under the Immigration Act of 1990 (In Effect As of October 1, 1991)

Category and Preference	Fiscal Years 1992–94	Fiscal Years 1995 and beyond
I. Family Immigration (total)	520,000	480,000
A) Immediate Relatives (projected)	239,000 (unlimited)	254,000 (unlimited)
B) Preference System	226,000*	226,000*
1) Unmarried adult children of U.S. citizens	23,400	23,400
2) Immediate family members of permanent residents	114,200*	114,200*
3) Married Adult children of U.S. citizens	23,400	23,400
4) Brothers and Sisters of U.S. citizens	65,000	65,000
C) Additional Family Legalizations (for relatives of IRCA amnesty recipients)	55,000	NONE
II. Independent Immigration (total)	180,000	195,000
A) Employment Based Immigration	140,000	140,000
1) Priority Workers (workers of extraordinary ability)	40,000	40,000
2) Professionals (with advanced degrees)	40,000	40,000
3) Skilled workers, professionals, and other workers (unskilled)	40,000 (10,000 limit on unskilled)	40,000 (10,000 limit on unskilled)
4) Special immigrants	10,000	10,000
5) Investor immigrants	10,000	10,000
B) Diversity Immigrants	40,000 (16,000 must be Irish)	55,000
Total Immigration	700,000	675,000

As the immediate family members are exempt from numerical limitation, the limitation on family immigration is determined by subtracting the immediate Relative total of the previous year from the Worldwide total of family-sponsored immigrants, but the family preference may not fall below 226,000. Hence, the indicated numbers are "pierceable" —they may be exceeded if the immediate family members are greater than is projected.

Source: Public Law 101.

ropeans. Essentially, the new law was very much the old one it replaced, except for allowing for much larger numbers of legal immigrants. Vernon Briggs, author of *Mass Immigration and the National Interest,* states that the law "perpetuates all the negative attributes of the Immigration Act of 1965" and that it is "highly mechanistic, legalistic, nepotistic, and inflexible." Many, however, truthfully state that the 1990 act goes further than any other in considering the economic benefits of contributions and skills of immigrants above race and national origin.[10] As we are viewing the immigration laws from an economic standpoint as well as one of diversity, we cannot help but agree with Briggs: the law does not go far enough in placing abilities and diversity above family reunification, and U.S. immigration laws are also growing more convoluted and unwieldy. Change is still needed to create greater fairness and more simplicity.

From 1992 to 1994, 465,000 of the 700,000 allotted immigrants will be admitted on the basis of family reunification; in 1995 the level goes up to 480,000 out of 675,000. The law, however, only increases employment-based visas from 54,000 to 140,000 per year, with five preference categories of workers.[11] Most amazing is the creation of a "diversity immigrant" category to deal with the concern that countries of former mass immigration (mostly northern and western European countries) were being closed out! Therefore, from 1992 to 1994, 40,000 visas will be issued to thirty-four specific countries (including Poland, Japan, Great Britain, Indonesia, Argentina, Germany, France, Italy, Norway, and Czechoslovakia), with 16,000 reserved for persons from Ireland.

What We've Done Right

Despite its history of policies favoring white Anglo-Saxon immigrants, the United States did make a major and lasting immigration policy decision early in its history. In 1818, the U.S. Congress did the right thing when it refused to respond to a request from the New York Irish Emigrant Society to grant a large segment of Illinois land for exclusive Irish settlement. The decision not to create homogeneous communities helped avoid the creation of separate ethnic states such as those in the former Soviet Union; the current ethnic turmoil there proves the untenability of such a policy.[12] We would further suggest that the mixture of cultures, particularly in urban settings, is responsible for the rich economy and culture of the United States.

The United States now must be careful not to adopt an attitude like that of German political leader Volker Ruhe, who in 1991 said, "We are not an immigrant nation and we will not become one."[13] Many other societies, such as Sweden, Japan, Scotland, Norway, and Korea, have unfortunate histories of discouraging immigration. As stated often throughout this book, the diversity of the U.S. population is the key to its current and future competitive edge. It is partially the openness of U.S. immigration, however faulty, that has led to this diversity advantage. (We must remember that the U.S. also owes much of its diversity advantage to the nonimmigrant Native American population and the forcibly enslaved African-American population.) Compared to other immigrant-accepting nations, the United States attracted far more immigrants between the mid-nineteenth century and the 1930s: United States, 30 million; Argentina, 6.4 million; Canada, 5.2 million; Brazil, 4.4 million; Australia, 2.9 million. The United States also has the most diverse immigrants of any immigrant nation (see Table 11–2).[14]

Immigrant Clashes and Strife

Dozens of articles since the 1980s have reported the increasing U.S. controversy over immigration. In Congress, both liberals and con-

TABLE 11–2
Diversity of Voluntary Immigrant Populations

U.S.	Australia	Canada	Argentina	Brazil
15% German	80% British	37% British	47% Italian	34% Italian
11% Italian		37% American	32% Spanish	29% Portuguese
10% Irish				14% Spanish
9% Austro-Hungarian				
8% Canadian				
7% British				

servatives are raising their voices in concern over continued and increasing mass immigration into the United States.[15] Former President Bush's refusal to allow the immigration of Haitian "boat people" is an example of negative attitudes toward immigrants (Bush argued for their return because they were fleeing economic hardship, not political persecution.)[16] President Clinton's administration has not kept its campaign promise to not deport Haitians without "due process." Sixty-eight percent of Americans in a *Business Weekly*/Harris poll answered that current immigration was bad for the country.

As a consequence, U.S. immigrants face harassment and discrimination that, though perhaps not as violent or widespread as that faced by asylum seekers in Germany, is profound and disturbing. This harassment, however, is not without extensive precedent. As noted earlier in this chapter, Chinese and Japanese immigrants were the objects of violent protests a century ago, and each group of arriving immigrants from the first wave of 1830 onward has been the victim of suspicions, prejudice, discrimination, and often violence. Among present-day immigrants, Asian Americans are once again a target of prejudice and increased harassment as the fastest-growing minority in the United States (their numbers have doubled to 7.3 million since the early 1980s); the next chapter will provide a number of examples of this.

Despite the long-held belief that immigrants lower wages, worsen working conditions, and cause unemployment for native-born workers, both elected representatives and the American populace should realize that today's immigrants offer practically only positive contributions to this society. Just as the past diversity of U.S. immigrants is very much responsible for our nation's present dominance, today's immigrants are the key to future U.S. economic global competitiveness. In the 1980s, a record 1.5 million college graduates immigrated to the United States; in fact, America is receiving better-educated immigrants than ever before. And in the future, America's high-tech industries, including semiconductors and biotechnology, will depend on immigrant engineers and scientists to remain competitive because the United States is not producing enough home-grown talent. Less-educated immigrants also contribute to the economy as workers, consumers, business owners, and taxpayers. The 11 million employed immigrants earn $240 billion and pay $90 billion in taxes, far outweighing the $5 billion in welfare that unemployed immigrants receive. Said sociologist

John D. Kasarda, "There is substantial evidence that immigrants are a powerful benefit to the economy and very little evidence that they are negative."[17]

Conclusion

With the Immigration Act of 1990 and the record number of immigrants accepted in both 1989 and 1990, the United States is clearly ahead of its European and Japanese counterparts in accepting diverse, well-trained and economically beneficial immigrants. Perfection, however, is a long way off. Our historical immigration policy, though certainly more open than all but that of modern-day Germany, has had its dark spots (as demonstrated, for example, by the government-sanctioned exclusion of and discriminatory populist behavior toward Asian and Haitian immigrants). The United States must make certain that it does not return to any such exclusionary or nonproductive policy. Rather, it must strive toward ever more inclusive immigration practices in order to ensure its global diversity advantage.

Racial Minorities
in the United States

While Japan and the European Community are basically homogeneous societies in terms of race, the United States is racially diverse and has been rapidly increasing its diversity since the 1970s. The white population has decreased from 83 percent of the total in 1970 to 73.1 percent in 1990. Between 1980 and 1990 time frame, the African-American population increased by 13 percent, the Asian-American population by 108 percent, the Native American population by 37 percent, the Hispanic/Latino population by 53 percent, and the white population by only 6 percent. Many of the changes in the racial makeup of the American population have come about due to several key changes in U.S. immigration policy; these changes began in the 1960s with the eradication of long-held quotas favoring northern and western Europeans and then southern Europeans. The ability of third World people to immigrate to the United States until the 1960s was minimal.

It is clear that economic issues are probably the chief factors in determining the level of racist attitudes within U.S. society. Although political and social competition are important, the competition for desirable land, money, education, and jobs in large part determines the intensity and depth of the threat felt by white society. Once a minority is perceived as obtaining something to which the dominant group feels entitled, it is subjected to harassment, exploitation, manipulation, and oppression from the dominant group.

The discrimination encountered by each minority group varies in type and degree. Although whites have developed negative stereotypes to justify the exploitation of and discrimination against all peoples of color, negative stereotypes are most common and resilient concerning blacks. Overwhelmingly positive concepts of blacks have not prevailed in any period of white American history. For example, in 1990, 57 percent of Americans believed blacks were currently in a worse situation than whites in terms of jobs, income, and housing because they lacked the motivation or willpower to pull themselves up out of poverty. Other people of color, however, have been viewed negatively and positively at different times. The actual size of the minority group and its skin color further determine the attitudes and behaviors directed toward its members. In return, the minority group's response to society is greatly influenced by the attitudes and behaviors directed toward them.

The greatest burden of racism appears to have fallen upon blacks. African Americans make up the largest minority group in the United States and also interact more extensively with the white population because of their residential locations throughout most of the country. African-American history illustrates the tremendous oppression African Americans have overcome in order to maintain their own cultures and establish their rights as American citizens.

Hispanics/Latinos are the second-largest minority group in the United States. More so than other minority group name, the term *Hispanic/Latino* encompasses a large, diverse group of people who come from distinctive ethnic and racial backgrounds and who have achieved various degrees of economic and educational levels. Mexicans, Puerto Ricans, and Cubans constitute the three largest American Hispanic/Latino subpopulations.

Asian Americans are more accepted by the white majority than blacks and Hispanics/Latinos in part because of their smaller numbers, business successes, and educational achievements. As a result of this greater acceptability, they have tried to assimilate into white society to a greater extent than the other minority groups—at least until the late 1980s, when the acceptability of Asians decreased among Americans. This negative change occurred because of their growing population and the fact that many Americans now perceive a threat from the economic successes of Asians abroad and in the United States. The three largest Asian subpopulations are Chinese, Filipinos, and Japanese, respectively.

Native Americans compose the smallest minority group in America, and research on this group remains sketchy at best. Nonetheless, the oppressive policies of the U.S. government toward the Native Americans who have survived have stripped the latter of most of their lands and many of their languages and cultures.

Only 19 percent of the overall U.S. population see blacks as hard-working, as compared to 64 percent for Jews, 53 percent for whites, 46 percent for Asians, and 24 percent for Hispanics. With regard to intelligence, 58 percent think Jews are very intelligent, with comparable figures being 55 percent for whites, 38 percent for Asians, 23 percent for blacks, and 22 percent for Hispanics. Note that 16 percent of white Americans would oppose a relative marrying a Jew, 57 percent a black, 37% an Asian, and 40% a Hispanic.

All people of color have faced severe discrimination and racial oppression. The long-hallowed myth of a melting-pot society has been debunked by a number of social scientists, including Melvin Steinfeld, who summed up the historical racial oppression that different people of color have suffered in this manner: "While Anglos and other immigrants from northern and western Europe were melting, Blacks were enslaved, sold, denied voting rights, and lynched; Indians were shoved off the paths of westward expansion and massacred; Chinese and Japanese were excluded or interred; [and] Mexicans were conquered and oppressed."[1] In brief, a common factor in the history of people of color is the power struggle with the dominant white population. Many whites view people of color as a threat to the status quo, which favors whites. They fear the loss of power, control, and economic and social position; thus, they overtly and covertly fight to maintain their privileged position in the United States.

In order to understand current diversity issues in the United States, it is crucial to understand the historical underpinnings of modern-day racism. Following is a brief history of each minority group: African Americans, Hispanics/Latinos (Mexicans, Puerto Ricans, and Cubans), Asians (Chinese, Japanese, and Filipinos), and Native Americans. This history will assist the reader in understanding the enormous problems the United States must overcome to realize the even larger potential of its diverse population.[2]

African Americans

Racism against African Americans as it is known today originated in the seventeenth century. In 1619, a Dutch sea captain sold the first group of blacks to Southern colonial plantation owners as indentured servants. The number of white indentured servants had rapidly declined, and they had gained considerable legal status; to fill the demand for labor, plantation owners began importing blacks. At first, plantation owners tried to keep the importation of blacks minimal, but the demand for labor steadily increased and so the importation of blacks kept pace. Southerners viewed blacks as an inferior race and feared African influence on their Anglo culture, or a possible rebellion; as a result, many whites felt the need to control the growing black population. Laws were continuously passed restricting blacks' rights, subsequently transforming the black indentured servant into the black slave. Over the decades, a crucial debate occurred among the states and between their citizens over slavery, culminating in the Civil War.

Southerners did not give up trying to control and disenfranchise blacks following the war. A series of codes were constructed during the initial reconstruction period (headed by President Andrew Johnson) that ended any debate over black equality and societal status. The codes effectively kept the freedmen in a state of subjugation and subservience, regulating marriage, employment, vagrancy, and civil and criminal rights. In effect, the codes restricted the new rights gained by the blacks under the Thirteenth Amendment and left them largely unprotected by American laws. White Southerners also employed violence and terror to maintain black subjugation.

Passing the Fifteenth Amendment of 1870 granted the freedmen suffrage, but the reallocation of Southern political power to include blacks was short-lived. By 1872 virtually all of the elite had resumed their place in the Southern political system and continued to control the South's land and industry. The Democratic party resumed control over Southern politics, and blacks experienced a substantial decrease in opportunities and status. The 1896 Supreme Court's ruling in the case of *Plessy v. Ferguson* provided the South with justification for establishing legal segregation policies. With this decision, the Supreme Court established the doctrine of "separate but equal" by ruling that separate accommodations for blacks and whites on railway cars were legal as long as the accommodations were equivalent. But although the South theoretically had to provide blacks and whites with equal facilities, it did not, allowing black public accommodations to decay. Black children attended substandard schools, and workers were excluded from well-paying jobs. By the beginning of the twentieth century, black Americans found themselves stripped of their civil rights and in a condition similar to slavery.

World War I changed the nation's focus from the struggle for internal freedom to worldwide salvation from oppression. Large numbers of blacks migrated to northern cities to fill manufacturing jobs created by the war; cities like Philadelphia, Chicago, and New York watched their black populations double and quadruple. With the conclusion of the war, whites returned home and began searching for work. Black Americans thus were in competition with whites for a limited number of jobs and resources. They penetrated white neighborhoods because traditionally black enclaves could not maintain their expanding numbers; as a result, race relations reached their breaking point in the summer following World War I. James Weldon Johnson, who headed the NAACP, referred to this period as "the red summer" because approximately two dozen outbreaks of violence occurred throughout American cities. The Ku Klux Klan increased its dwindling membership with new recruits, and lynchings, mob attacks, and race riots increased in number and degree throughout the United States. World War I had transformed race relations from a Southern problem to a national problem. Declining numbers of northern liberals campaigned for black equality. Many blacks could not understand the nation's new attitude: Americans had just finished fighting international oppression and tyranny, yet maintained similar conditions within their own borders.

Until the Great Depression, the standard of living for black Americans increased at a slow but steady rate. Black workers, along with other minorities, were the first to be fired in an attempt to preserve white jobs when hard times hit, and thus blacks' standard of living rapidly declined. Black action groups responded by mobilizing and protesting for black job opportunities. The NAACP began the "don't buy where you can't work" campaign,[3] one example of which occurred in Washington, D.C., in early 1933. A local grill located in a black neighborhood and supported by a black customer base fired all its black workers and replaced them with whites. Blacks picketed and refused to patronize the grill. Two weeks later, the black workers returned without an explanation.

Blacks' status in American society remained stagnant until World War II. They lived in segregated areas, attended segregated schools, and experienced lateral as opposed to upward employment opportunities. But World War II, like its predecessor, created a northern labor shortage. More blacks migrated to the north to fill these jobs, and the black standard of living rapidly improved.

More than forty thousand African Americans participated in World War II through military service. As was traditional, the African Americans who joined the military were placed in all-black combat units. Nonetheless, these regiments were commonly sent to the South for training, where they were expected to conform to the Jim Crow segregation system when they left the military facility. Many of these soldiers who were from the north were unaware of the unspoken, unwritten racial policies structuring Southern life and, therefore, deviated from the social norms; white Southerners responded with extreme violence, insults, and widespread discrimination.

After World War II's conclusion, African-American soldiers returned home expecting gratitude and a chance to participate in the freedom for which they had risked their lives, but they faced the same discrimination that they had left. Europeans were liberated from Nazism and fascism, but black Americans were not liberated from racism. No cries of appreciation were heard. Many African Americans who had worked in the private and public sectors lost their jobs to homecoming white soldiers. Significant numbers of African Americans became unemployed, and the opportunities and growth established during World War II quickly disappeared. In response, such organizations as CORE (Congress of Racial Equality) and the NAACP experienced increased membership in the fight to end discrimination and oppression.

In 1954, the Supreme Court decision of *Brown v. Board of Education* reversed the 1896 *Plessy* ruling of separate but equal. The Court now ruled that separate educational systems could never be truly equal and mandated the integration of all public schools. African-American activists celebrated this victory; *Brown* was the foundation for integrating every aspect of American society and achieving black equality.

Implementation of the Supreme Court's vague directive to end segregation in public schools with all due speed was left to individual states. Many states proceeded and integrated schools in good faith, but numerous Southern states avoided implementing the *Brown* decision until one tired black woman changed everything. On December 1, 1955, Mrs. Rosa Parks refused to give her bus seat to a white person and subsequently was arrested. At that time, Martin Luther King began capturing the hearts and minds of many Americans; his belief in non-violent protest forced white Americans to confront their treatment of African Americans. The media broadcast images of African Americans and their white supporters, peacefully asking for equality and a chance at the American dream, being met with police dogs, torrents of water, and bloody violence. By the mid-1960s, American disgust for violence and racial discord peaked, inspiring the passage of the 1964, 1965, and 1968 Civil Rights Acts. These acts prohibited job discrimination, set uniform voting requirements, prohibited the refusal of services on account of race, eliminated segregation at publicly owned or operated facilities, prohibited segregation in any federally funded program, and forbade housing discrimination. African Americans today enjoy a level of equality and opportunity only imagined by their ancestors. Nonetheless, African Americans still face discrimination and limited access to housing, education, health care, and employment.

Hispanic/Latino Americans

The definition of race can be based on a combination of national origin, tribal membership, religion, language, minority status, and physical characteristics; however, Americans usually treat race as a stable, enduring, hereditary characteristic largely determined by outward appearance. In the United States, people are largely unaware that other cultures define race using different criteria. In Brazil, an entirely different set of racial categories exist that is based not only on outward appearance but also on status. Thus, two full siblings whose appearances vary can be considered of different races. Also in Brazil, one's race can change as one achieves wealth and political power (and therefore status).

The American view that race is fixed can have important implications for minority groups, with one being the tendency to view minority populations as homogeneous groups with common values and expectations. No U.S. minority group has experienced this phenomenon more than the Hispanic/Latino population. Hispanics/Latinos come from a variety of highly distinctive racial and ethnic backgrounds; for example, a third-generation educated, white Cuban American has little in common with an uneducated Central American immigrant of mainly Native American ancestry fleeing civil upheaval

and political persecution. Yet they are both classified as His-
panic/Latino. Examining the histories of three main Hispanic/Latino
ethnic groups in America—Mexicans, Puerto Ricans, and Cubans—
explains the diverse history and backgrounds of the Hispanic/Latino
community.

Mexican Americans

Mexicans lived in and controlled large sections of the western part of
what is now the United States for hundreds of years prior to its conquest by white Americans. As Anglos moved westward in the early
nineteenth century and took over Mexican lands, they developed a set
of stereotypes to demean Mexicans and justify the land's conquest in
their minds. Mexicans' darker skin enabled whites to transfer many
of the existing black stereotypes to Mexicans (such as dirty, drunk,
ignorant, and cowardly). In addition, Mexicans were Catholic, and
thus Protestant whites classified Mexicans as nonbelievers and discriminated against them on religious grounds.

By the 1830s Anglos substantially outnumbered Mexicans in Texas,
and in 1836 Texas proclaimed independence. When Texas applied for
and received U.S. statehood in 1845, Mexico promised to invade. The
Mexican threat provided President James Polk the opportunity to send
U.S. troops into Western territory in the hope of obtaining substantial
Mexican lands. After Zachary Taylor's victories and the conquest of
the Mexican capital in 1848, Mexico signed the Treaty of Guadalupe
Hidalgo, ceding the territory now comprising California, Arizona,
New Mexico, Nevada, Utah and portions of several other states.

The United States curtailed its desire for additional Mexican land
because the remaining Mexican territory was inhabited by substantial
numbers of Mexicans. The U.S. government believed the incorporation
of too many Mexicans into American culture would be difficult and
dangerous; Mexicans' racial makeup was seen as inferior, and their
influence on American society could only harm it. It also was believed
that few Mexicans would stay in the newly conquered territories, and
thus the U.S. government said that Mexicans choosing to stay in this
new American territory for more than one year would become American citizens. Most of the Mexicans remained and became the first
Mexican Americans, much to the surprise of the government.

Prior to the U.S. conquest, many of the Mexican Americans owned land and participated in a sophisticated and ancient society. After the war, they became powerless, exploited laborers who were completely stripped of their land and dignity. Conflicts and violence soon developed between Mexican Americans and White Anglo settlers.

Since the United States wanted every possible square foot of territory meeting the low Mexican population criterion, it continued the acquisition of land from a weak, defeated Mexico in the Gadsden Purchase, which ceded the lower sections of Arizona and New Mexico to the United States. As a result, the border established between Mexico and the United States became quite arbitrary: it was merely a straight line drawn across desert, except in Texas where the Rio Grande served as a substantial territorial divide.

Over the decades, little changed for Mexican Americans. By 1930, many Mexican Americans' inability to speak English (primarily because of discrimination) excluded them from the economic mainstream. Mexican-American children during this time period were often segregated from white children under the pretense that both groups would receive a higher standard of education under these conditions. As with those for blacks, Mexican schools received less money, lower-quality teachers, and poorer supplies, resulting in many Mexican-American children remaining uneducated and lacking adequate job skills to improve their lives.

World War II offered Mexican Americans their first true opportunity for advancement in American society. The labor shortages caused by the war allowed Mexican Americans to enter jobs previously unavailable to them. These jobs paid better wages and gave Mexican Americans new job skills. The drastic shortage of workers also caused the U.S. government to approach the Mexican government for farm laborers to maintain Southwestern agricultural output; for the first time, Americans (albeit hesitantly) welcomed Mexicans into the United States. Nevertheless, discrimination had not vanished. Mexican Americans were still refused service at restaurants and hotels and still could not obtain jobs commensurate with their skills. Not until the Civil Rights Acts of 1964 and 1965 did Mexican Americans experience equal treatment in public accommodations.

Conditions have improved for Mexican Americans since 1965, but the level of improvement remains questionable. Mexican-Americans' average family income is the lowest of Hispanic groups in America. Mexican Americans' education level is lower than that of whites,

Asians, and African Americans. Fifteen and a half percent of all Mexican Americans have completed less than five years of school, and their dropout rate is much higher than that for blacks. The situation of Mexican Americans is not a positive factor in the U.S. effort to regain its competitive edge in the new global economy. (Remember that Hispanics/Latinos, 60 percent of whom are Mexican Americans, represent the fastest-growing minority group in the United States.

Puerto Ricans

Puerto Ricans have experienced a unique relationship to the United States since the Spanish-American War. On April 25, 1898, three months after the formal declaration of war against Spain, the United States landed military forces in Puerto Rico. To gain Puerto Rican support and successfully remove Spanish resistance from the island, Major General Miles promised the Puerto Ricans relief from oppression and the "blessing of the liberal institutions of our government."[4] The majority of Puerto Ricans allied themselves with U.S. troops, and on August 12, 1898, a peace accord was signed between Spain and the United States providing for the evacuation of all remaining Spanish military forces from Puerto Rico. On October 18, 1898, Spain completed the withdrawal of its troops, and on April 11, 1899, the signing of the Treaty of Paris officially transferred Puerto Rico to the United States and ended 390 years of Spanish rule.

Puerto Ricans optimistically awaited the opportunity to enjoy the rights of the U.S. constitution. The U.S. Congress, however, dampened these hopes by passing the Foraker Act of 1900, which turned Puerto Rico essentially into a colonial dependent. The act denied Puerto Rico territorial status and the promise of eventual statehood; instead, it imposed a set of tariffs aimed at generating revenue for Puerto Rico's internal improvements. Theoretically, Senator Foraker and his supporters opted for a tariff system over internal taxation because the latter would fall to finance Puerto Rico's social programs; however, a hidden agenda backed this legislation. Domestic interests wanted and needed to protect their own infant beet sugar and tobacco industries; a tariff system could accomplish this protectionism, while internal taxation could not.

As demonstrated by the Foraker Act, self-interest and fear of foreign competition entered early into the determination of Puerto Rican status in the United States. The Jones Act of March 2, 1917, offered Puerto Ricans a new source of hope for the establishment of their rights. It declared that all inhabitants of Puerto Rico were to become United States citizens and be able to travel freely and immigrate to the United States and its protected lands; however, this act did not guarantee the eventual incorporation of Puerto Rico into the United States.

The first wave of substantial Puerto Rican immigration to the United States occurred during and after World War II. Like other minority groups, Puerto Ricans filled the job vacuum for unskilled, semiskilled, and skilled workers that the war had produced. Puerto Ricans began to experience a new level of economic prosperity, and the number of Puerto Ricans moving to the mainland continued to rise.

As the economy slowed in the late 1940s, job opportunities for Puerto Ricans disappeared. Returning white U.S. soldiers reclaimed their previous jobs, and recently arrived Puerto Ricans found themselves facing declining employment opportunities. This downturn in the economy briefly curbed Puerto Rican immigration, but, by the early 1950s, the Korean War once again offered excellent job opportunities. Substantial numbers of Puerto Ricans immigrated to the United States to seize these new opportunities. In addition, the military enlisted forty thousand Puerto Rican volunteers to fight in the war, bringing many of them to the mainland for training; after the war, many of these Puerto Rican soldiers elected to remain in the United States.

By the mid-1950s well over one million Puerto Ricans had entered the United States, with 60 percent residing in New York City. New York's large Puerto Rican population caused many white New Yorkers to view this immigrant group with disdain, especially the darker Puerto Ricans. Of all large groups of Hispanics/Latinos in the United States, Puerto Ricans are the most likely to have African ancestry, and our studies show that the amount of discrimination experienced by darker Puerto Ricans is akin to that faced by African Americans.

New York's large Puerto Rican presence (and the presence of other Hispanics, such as Dominicans) has transformed the Big Apple into a bilingual city. Spanish can often be overheard, and in certain sections it is the dominant language. The presence of a large Spanish-speaking population has made bilingual education and the integration of bilingual workers into social and health services a necessity. These changes are viewed by many white New Yorkers as costly and unnecessary and, therefore, serve to increase the hostility directed at Puerto Ricans.

Many Puerto Ricans feel a split in loyalties between the mainland United States and the island of Puerto Rico. Maintaining residence on the island preserves one's culture and language while exposing the individual to less discrimination. Advancement and economic opportunities are quite limited on the island, however, and the standard of living remains substantially lower than that of U.S. residents. Migration to the United States offers Puerto Ricans the opportunity to enjoy the full rights of U.S. citizens, including voting in U.S. elections and access to U.S. social services. Both the benefits and detriments of immigration seem immense for Puerto Ricans, but as increasing job opportunities arise in the United States and the island's economy stagnates, it seems likely that the mainland will once again see a large influx of Puerto Ricans who will further influence American culture.

Cubans

Cubans represent the third-largest ethnic Hispanic/Latino subpopulation in the United States. Economic, political, and family considerations have contributed to Cuban immigrations. Despite the fact that 10 percent of the Cuban population lives in the United States, most Cuban Americans remain loyal to their homeland and culture.

The influx of Cuban immigration to the United States is generally broken into seven distinctive phases, with the first stage (which had several periods) ranging from the mid-1800s to the Castro-led revolution in January 1959. During this time period, Cuban politics created a substantial number of dissidents resulting from the failed 1850s overthrow of the Spanish government. These Cubans had two choices: remain in Cuba and face persecution, or emigrate to the United States. Needless to say, many of them chose emigration. Supplementing the Cuban-American political refugee population were Cuban laborers who migrated as Cuban cigar manufacturers moved their operations from Havana to the United States in the 1860s and 1870s; the expanding U.S. economy also attracted Cuban immigrants who were searching for economic prosperity. The depression and World War I slowed Cuban immigration, but as the U.S. economy recovered Cuban immigration was revived.

The second wave of Cuban emigration occurred after Castro's seizure of power. From 1959 to 1962, more than 215,000 Cubans fled to the United States. Supporters of the overthrown Batista regime emigrated to the United States to avoid persecution, while a large number of the economic elite and landholders left Cuba to flee Castro's socialist reforms. This group of immigrants settled in Florida and eastern New York, where the first wave of Cuban immigrants had settled: Miami's climate was similar to Cuba's, and New York and New Jersey's burgeoning economy offered immigrants a multitude of employment opportunities.

The high concentration of Cuban Americans greatly influenced future trends in Cuban-American demographics. The second group of Cuban Americans set up informal networks to aid future Cuban immigrants and to offer mutual support. In effect, these Cuban Americans replicated many facets of their native culture to attract future immigrants.

The Cuban missile crisis of October 1962 cut off U.S.-Cuban relations and all air traffic between the two countries. Until September of 1965, Cuban emigration to the United States was illegal; however, approximately 56,000 Cubans (the third group) escaped here, usually by way of Mexico or Spain. On October 10, 1965, the fourth stage of Cuban emigration began with the "freedom flights." Castro allowed Cuban citizens with family residing in the United States to apply for exit visas. Closeness of family relations was supposed to determine the priority an individual had in receiving passage, but Castro allowed a high proportion of the elderly to leave (to avoid paying them social benefits) and prevented the majority of seventeen- to twenty-six-year-old males from leaving (due to their military commitments). About 302,000 Cubans emigrated to the United States through the freedom flights. Once again, these immigrants had higher educational and economic levels than the average Cuban and chose to live in Miami or New Jersey in order to be close to family. On April 6, 1973, Castro suddenly ended the policy.

The fifth wave of Cuban immigration began on September 30, 1979. During this wave about 38,000 Cubans traveled to Mexico or Spain to apply for entry into the United States. The sixth stage consisted of an airlift of 14,000 persons at the end of 1980. This airlift was sudden and unexpected and the only one Castro allowed during this time; the immigrants reflected the mixture of Cuban society much more closely than previous populations. Upon their arrival in the United States, the 1980 immigrants often took skilled and semiskilled jobs at a lower level than they had held in Cuba.

The seventh stage of Cuban immigration to the United States was the April 1980 Mirai boat lift, during which 124,779 Cubans arrived in America. Castro did not expect such a large and embarrassing exodus; 1 percent of the Cuban population left during this period. Therefore, five months after the boat lift began, Castro once again stopped issuing exit visas, but in the last months he filled the boats with the mentally ill, the disabled, and criminals. He planned to rid Cuba of this "nuisance" population while tainting the image of Cuban Americans.

Castro's strategy was somewhat successful. The Cuban-American community had been unified and working for the betterment of all Cubans. The boat lift, however, with its large numbers of poor, mixed-blood heritage, and criminal Cubans, strained the Cuban-American population, and it caused a change in Anglo-American sentiment toward Cubans. Prior to the boat lift, Cubans were looked upon favorably. Cuban Americans earned the second-highest income of all U.S. immigrant groups and achieved the highest educational level of any Hispanic/Latino subpopulation. Just as importantly, most Americans considered them noble political refugees who had fled their homeland to avoid the perils of Castro and communism. The increase in violent crimes in the Miami and the New Jersey areas, however, along with the influence of the Colombian drug cartels on violence in Miami, changed many Americans' sentiments. In the 1980s, Cuban Americans became associated with criminals, despite the fact that few Cubans were involved in drugs and crime. Also, the recession of the 1980s and poor U.S. economic conditions, combined with the growing American sentiment to limit immigration, created hostility toward Cuban Americans, who were depicted as taking over Southern Florida. The Cuban-American community responded by no longer considering itself a unified group, instead differentiating between "new" and "old" immigrants, with the "old" Cuban Americans trying to disassociate themselves from the new (many of whom were of mixed racial ancestry).

Asian Americans

American attitudes toward different Asian immigrant groups have ebbed and flowed between positive and negative perceptions. American children, youths, and adults have been trained to subscribe to the European worldview, which has for centuries feared and misunderstood Asia's various cultures and ethnic groups. Asians have been perceived as a threat since the days of the Roman Empire. From this point up until the Middle Ages, "Europe lived in terror of Asiatic invaders." This fear increased when the first Europeans to gain entrance into Asian countries found many of the latter's practices to be far superior to European culture, science, and societies; the Chinese were the originators of paper, the printing press, and gunpowder. Kotkin and Kishimoto note that

> even after Europe's supremacy had been clearly established, Asia— its strange social and governmental systems, huge continental land mass, and enormous population—loomed as a vague, dark threat in the European imagination. As early as 1873, English politicians fretted over the eventual industrialization of China as a potential challenge to European industrial supremacy. Germany's Kaiser Wilhelm worried obsessively about "the yellow races."[16]

As noted in Chapter 11, Asians faced greater legal exclusion than any other immigrant group. They also are the most visible and targeted minority group today for racially motivated violence and discrimination.

Chinese, Filipinos, and Japanese are the three largest Asian groups in the United States. Filipinos are perceived by many Americans as Hispanic/Latino rather than Asian: many are Catholic, have Hispanic/Latino surnames, and are much darker than most Chinese and Japanese. Thus, just as Puerto Ricans face greater discrimination than other Hispanic/Latino Americans, Filipinos face more discrimination than Japanese or Chinese. We will briefly review the up-and-down history of these groups in America.

Chinese Americans

Between the years 1849 and 1854, the California gold rush brought the first large influx of Chinese immigrants to the region. Similar to other minorities, the Chinese came to the United States to find better economic conditions than those in their depressed homeland. Initially, these Chinese immigrants were welcomed because the majority worked in gold mines already abandoned by white miners or on the transcontinental railroad, where they filled the labor shortage in the newly expanding California. But as the Chinese population increased from one thousand in 1850 to one hundred thousand in 1880, economic conditions in California worsened.[7] The growing Chinese population expanded into more occupations, which made them more visible competitors to the white working class. As early as 1852, the governor of California recommended that action be taken to restrain the tide of "the yellow peril." As a result, the Chinese became targets of racism. These people, who had been regarded as a godsend and as desirable workers because they were a cheap and efficient labor force, were subjected to cruel and outrageous expressions of bigotry.[8]

Much of this racism manifested itself in the form of political platforms and discriminatory legislation. Because of the competition for mining employment, a "foreign miners' tax" aimed at reducing Chinese miners was passed in 1852. In 1854, the Chinese were included in a legislative ban preventing blacks and Native Americans from bearing witness against whites in court. This ban denied the Chinese basic political and legal rights, especially in mining claims and labor disputes. In the presidential elections from 1876 to 1890, both the Democrats and Republicans adopted anti-Chinese platforms hoping to change existing treaties with China to limit the number of Chinese subjects entering the United States. Political clubs such as the Workingman's Party, formed in 1877, were organized to force cheap Chinese labor out of the country.

Other discriminatory laws were passed including statutes banning interracial marriages between whites and African Americans, Chinese, and other Asians. These laws were not overturned by the U.S. Supreme Court until 1967. In 1882, the U.S. Congress passed the Exclusion Act, a ten-year suspension that restricted Chinese laborers from immigrating to the United States. It was both the first anti-immigration law and the first time such a law was passed on the basis of national origin. This act began a series of anti-immigration laws that limited non–northern Europeans from the United States for the next eight decades (see Chapter 11). Although the Chinese laborers already living in the United States could leave and return to the country, they could not become naturalized citizens. This discriminatory act was continually renewed until 1943, when China was a U.S. World War II ally. It was repealed and replaced by a new act allowing only 105 Chinese to enter the United States each year.

After the war, while mainland China developed into a communist state and battled against the United States during the Korean War, Nationalist China (Taiwan) remained a respected ally and a valuable U.S. trading partner. These now-separate Chinese nations greatly influenced American attitudes toward the Chinese, both negatively and positively. More recently, the normalization of relations between the United States and mainland China has eliminated most negative attitudes Americans had toward the Chinese mainland; in fact, as our trade increases with China, the need for Chinese employees is crucial.

Presently the Chinese in the United States are seen by many Americans as a "model minority," an excellent example of an American success story despite their early hardships. In reality, however, many Chinese still suffer from racial discrimination, poverty, and the resultant problems. The social problems of poverty, illiteracy, disease, broken families, and racial victimization have not entirely disappeared from Chinese-American life, as anyone who has visited Chinatown in San Francisco can attest.

Japanese Americans

Most Japanese laborers came to America after 1884, when the Japanese government lifted restrictions that prohibited its citizens from emigrating. In the late 1880s, as the demand for menial labor increased and the abundant supply of Chinese labor was prevented from immigrating to the United States, American employers encouraged Japanese people to immigrate to fill this need. While these new Asians were not warmly welcomed (because of the racism that had developed toward the Chinese), the substantial need for labor, as well as specific characteristics of Japanese society and culture, made the Japanese acceptable to Americans and allowed them to survive.

In 1890 only several thousand Japanese resided in the United States, but by 1900 the number had swelled to around one hundred thousand. This sharp increase in the number of Japanese and the resulting competition with the white population quickly kindled pervasive racist attitudes and behaviors. As early as 1890, white male union members were participating in physically violent forms of racist behavior. With the antagonism toward them increasing in the cities, Japanese immigrants increasingly turned to farming for their livelihood. Their successes in this endeavor, however, also posed a perceived economic threat to whites. The California legislature responded by passing severely restrictive legislation regarding alien landholding.

The wave of racism against the Japanese culminated in the "gentlemen's agreement" of 1908, in which the United States pressured Japan to restrict U.S. emigration, and the Johnson Immigration Act of 1924, which banned the immigration of persons "ineligible for citizenship." The latter act was directly aimed at the Japanese and was not repealed until 1952. Throughout this period, Japanese Americans discovered that college degrees, a good work ethic, and middle-class values did not guarantee them first-class American citizenship.[9]

The next significant event in the history of Japanese Americans occurred at the beginning of World War II. Anti-Japanese attitudes and feelings broke loose after Japan attacked Pearl Harbor. The hatred culminated in 1942 with the decision to place the Japanese-American "menace" in so-called detainment centers, which in reality were concentration camps. This violated the constitutional rights of 110,000 people, 70,000 of whom were American citizens. Since Germans and Italians—many of whom were new immigrants—were not placed in such camps, one must conclude that the U.S. government and many citizens did not perceive white-skinned German Americans and Italian Americans as a threat, while regarding "yellow"-skinned Japanese with suspicion because of racism. Lt. General John L. De Witt, commander of the Western Defense Command, in justifying these policies, stated:

> In the war in which we are now engaged, racial affinities are not severed by migration. The Japanese race is an enemy race and while many second and third generation Japanese born on United States soil, possessed of United States citizenship have become "Americanized," the racial strains are undiluted. . . . It therefore allows that along the vital Pacific Coast over 112,000 potential enemies, of Japanese extraction, are at large today. There are disturbing indications that they are organized and ready for concerted action at a favorable opportunity. The very fact that no sabotage has taken place to date is a disturbing and confirming indication that such action will be taken.[10]

Japanese were shipped to the Midwest and to the East Coast in order to comply with these discriminatory statutes. Others joined the U.S. military to fight for "their" country in Europe. In the exploitative tradition of racism, the same individuals who were locked up and denied constitutional rights were also subject to the military draft as citizens. The drafted Japanese were placed in a segregated unit in Europe, where they distinguished themselves as one of the most decorated units in any branch of service. Others worked as teachers at U.S. Army language schools or worked for U.S. intelligence.[11]

Despite this shameful treatment, attempts to hamper their progress resulted only in enhancing Japanese Americans' determination to succeed. This determination generated one of the most remarkable processes of upward mobility in American history. The economic, educational, and professional achievements of Japanese Americans rank as high as those of any other ethnic group in this country. In recent years, however, Japanese Americans and other Asian Americans (most Americans cannot or do not care to distinguish among different Asian groups) have been subjected to increased hostility and violent incidents, which will be discussed later in this chapter.

Filipino Americans

As a result of the Spanish-American War, the United States gained control of the Philippine islands and set out to Americanize them. English became the second language of the country; Filipinos were educated in American universities so they could return to the islands and assist the Americanization process. Most returned and took Philippine government positions. By 1938, about fourteen thousand Filipinos had come to the United States to study under the Pensionado pension plan.

When Japanese immigration was stopped by the gentlemen's agreement in the early 1900s, the U.S. demand for cheap farm labor, especially in California, resulted in the greatly increased immigration of Filipinos. These early immigrants were uneducated and had poor language skills in both Spanish and English. After working in the United States for a period of time, more than half of the Filipinos returned to the Philippines. This was due largely to the fact that early immigrants were young, unmarried men.

Although most anti-Asian laws were directed against Chinese and Japanese, they also applied to Filipinos. In 1902, the Cooper Act said that "as an American protectorate, Filipinos owed their allegiance to the United States, and were free to exercise all the privileges of any American citizen, except the right to vote, become naturalized citizens, join the U.S. Armed Forces, establish a commercial business, own real estate, . . . " Thus, their only privilege was the right to carry American passports that permitted them to enter and leave the United States freely.[12] In 1918, however, the United States offered any Filipino who served in the U.S. Navy or Marines (they could only be stewards) for three years the right to petition for American citizenship. Other discriminatory laws prevented Filipinos from marrying whites until 1933, when California courts ruled that Filipinos did not fall under the antimiscegenation law because they were considered Malayan, not Asian. The state legislature, however, passed a new law prohibiting Malayans from marrying whites. This law was overturned fifteen years later.

Anti-Filipino feelings surfaced in the 1920s and 1930s as whites saw Filipinos as competition for scarce jobs. On many occasions white farm workers attacked farms where Filipinos worked, burned their homes, and beat and even killed them. Violence against Filipinos also increased as many Filipino males began to associate openly with white women, something few Chinese and Japanese did. In 1934 the Tydings-McDuffie Act established a quota of only fifty Filipino immigrants per year and established 1944 as the date for Philippine independence. (Independence was not granted until 1946 because of the war.)[13] During World War II, except for their positions as stewards in the navy, Filipinos were excluded from the military until 1942, when an all-Filipino battalion—led by white officers—was formed. In part because of their role in World War II, Filipinos living in the United States became eligible for citizenship.

Since World War II, Filipinos have been attacked and discriminated against to a greater extent than Chinese and Japanese because of their darker skin and the continuing negative stereotypes. They, in contrast to Chinese and Japanese, have not been viewed as model minorities. Like the Chinese and Japanese, Filipinos have had relationships with the majority white population that have been characterized by acceptance when the United States needed them to perform certain duties (particularly those that white Americans did not want to do) and by rejection and discrimination when they were perceived as no longer necessary for the needs of the majority population.

Current-Day Problems

In the modern-day history of Asian Americans, another factor is contributing to anti-Asian attitudes—the economic successes of Japan and other Asian countries. A tide of anti-Asian sentiment is currently rising, especially along the West Coast, in large cities on the East Coast, and in the Texas area. Asians are faced with increasing discrimination as their numbers in the United States grow (from 3.8 million in 1980 to an estimated 7.3 million in 1991[14]), and as they begin to compete more vigorously with native-born, non-Asian Americans for education and jobs. Another factor contributing to the increase in anti-Asian sentiment is the success of the Japanese, and to a lesser extent of the South Koreans and Nationalist Chinese, in producing quality products more cheaply than the American labor force. Loss of jobs to Asian countries and U.S. importation of large amounts of Asian goods have fueled negative reactions to all Asian Americans because many Americans do not distinguish between Chinese, Japanese, Vietnamese, or any other Asian group.

A growing number of Americans view Japan's power in particular with increasing uneasiness. In a nationwide survey in the fall of 1990, 60 percent considered Japan's economic strength as a "critical threat" to U.S. interests.[15] Americans also seem to be most threatened by Japanese foreign investment: although British companies own far more American property and businesses than their Japanese counterparts, this fact causes nowhere near the amount of alarm in the American psyche as the Japanese presence. European companies even use many of the same practices as the Japanese (protectionism, government support) in their multinational companies with little or no negative American reaction.[16]

The presence of Europeans does not provoke the fear and nasty comments elicited, for example, by Mitsubishi's purchase of Rockefeller Center. One writer projected having to visit the Christmas tree and skating rink down at "Hirohito Center" in the future. When Mitsubishi's purchase of the center was announced in the fall of 1989, the Fox television affiliate in New York ran a film clip of the bombing of Pearl Harbor with the news story. Frank Wu, in a *Washington Post* editorial on another aspect of anti-Japanese sentiment, wrote that he (as a Japanese American) was asked to be understanding of residual American anger over World War II and Vietnam, as well as current Japanese foreign policy, but that Lee Iacocca (an Italian American) was never asked to be accountable for Italy's role as an Axis power or for its current political policies. Wu noted further that "60 Minutes" commentator Andy Rooney typified the loss of objectivity of some press members, as well as the feelings of many Americans, when he recently stated, "I'm vaguely anti-Japanese. Don't ask me why. Just prejudice, I guess. I'm very comfortable with some of my prejudices and have no thought of changing them now."[17]

Apparently non-Asian Americans cannot distinguish between the various Asian groups and vent their hostilities on any and all Asians. Therefore, we have the killing of a Chinese American, Vincent Chin (apparently mistaken for a Japanese national), who was beaten to death outside a Detroit bar by angry autoworkers in 1982. Other racially prompted killings include the death of Jim Loo in Raleigh, North Carolina, in 1989 and the massacre of five Indochinese students and wounding of 30 others in Stockton, California, that same year.[18]

After a two-year investigation, the U.S. Civil Rights Commission issued a report in March 1992 entitled "Civil Rights issues Facing Asian Americans in the 1990s." This report stated that "politicians who denounce Japan are fueling bigotry against Asian Americans, who already face widespread discrimination and even violence." Besides mentioning the everyday racial prejudice to which Asian Americans are subject, the 233-page report detailed racially motivated violent acts against Asians.[19]

Leaders of Asian-American organizations report that anti-Asian sentiments are being manifested in such forms as vandalism, graffiti, hate mail, and rock throwing. In February 1992, stones were thrown through the windows of a Japanese home in a suburb of Los Angeles. And Dennis Hayashi, national director of the Japanese-American Citizens League, says that he now receives daily complaints from Japanese and other Asian Americans receiving verbal harassment and hate mail. Ron Wakabayashi, executive director of the Los Angeles City Human Relations Commission, reports that anti-Asian incidents seem to be more and more premeditated in nature. Southern California in late 1991 and early 1992 was also the scene of anti-Asian acts such as smashing the windows of Japanese automobiles, burning a cross in front of an Asian restaurant, and making threats to the Japanese American Citizens League.[20] Signs have been posted in predominantly Asian-American neighborhoods asking that the last American to leave turn out the lights.[21]

Prior to 1965, more than 75 percent of Asian immigrants to the United States were laborers. Since then, however, approximately 50 percent of the Asian immigrants arriving in the United States have been highly skilled. This is due primarily to the change in the immigration laws to give preference to skilled immigrants and their family members. Today, the majority of Asian Americans have not been born in the United States; this holds true for all Asian groups except Japanese.

In 1990, Asian Americans' median household income was $36,102, compared to $30,406 for non-Hispanic/Latino whites, $21,921 for Hispanics/Latinos, and $18,083 for blacks.[22] One of the reasons, aside from education, for the average higher family income for Asians is that they generally have a larger number of family members working who contribute to the family income. Furthermore, they are concentrated in states with high income levels.

Upon interviewing our seminars' participants about their views concerning Asians, we found that of the four major racial minority groups discussed in this book, stereotypes about Asians are the most positive. Participants in our seminars characterize Asians as hardworking, well organized, intelligent, motivated, diligent, analytical, well educated, respectful, and family oriented. Very seldom are these adjectives used to describe Native Americans, blacks, or Hispanics/Latinos. Even many of the stereotypes that can be considered negative are not as negative in meaning and degree as are those applied to other racial minorities. Stereotypical negative views of Asians include characteristics such as being passive, shy, short, humble, cliquish, soft-spoken, submissive, and sneaky. We should also note that Asians used many of these same positive and negative adjectives to describe themselves.

Native Americans

A large, diverse group of people already inhabited North America when the Europeans first arrived. This group of people, later to be known as Native Americans, discovered the North American continent in approximately 25,000 B.C. Ten thousand years later, they had spread out across the continent and entered the borders of South America. At least two hundred tribes dotted the North American continent's landscape, possessing distinctive cultures, languages, agricultural and hunting methods, political organizations, and population sizes. For these reasons, communication between tribes and their unification against the Europeans was almost impossible, although efforts to form pan-Indian alliances were made by the Ottawa chief Pontiac in 1763 and by Tecumseh many decades later.

During the seventeenth century, the French established trade with the Huron tribes from the Great Lakes, while the English traded with the Iroquois near the Hudson river valley. In exchange for animal furs and skins, the Europeans provided the tribes with guns, gunpowder, alcohol, clothing, and other European goods. Conflict ensued when the rival trading tribes, representing England and France, began invading each other's land in search of pelts. The French and English also competed for hunting land, which resulted in the French and Indian War (1754–1761); with the aid of the Iroquois, the English won.[23]

Pontiac's 1763 call for intertribal military unity and a return to traditional values failed to remove the English from the continent but demonstrated that the unification of Native American tribes could still be a threat. In response, the English issued the Proclamation of 1763 in an attempt to regulate trade between the colonists and the tribes. Land west of the Appalachians was declared "Indian country," and all future land acquisitions had to be done legally and publicly. The U.S. Congress also observed these arrangements after the Revolutionary War, but the expanding population of frontiersmen ignored the proclamation.[24] Often Native Americans only partially understood the treaties that they signed, or were simply forced or deceived into signing them. In addition, the whites often disregarded treaties and simply seized whatever land or supplies they needed or wanted.

After hundreds of treaties were broken, the majority of tribal lands seized, the food supplies decimated, and the Native American culture under increasing attack, Native Americans began to fight openly for their lands in the legal system and on the battlefield. The result was an exorbitant loss of Native American lives. Under President Jackson's Indian Removal Act, eastern tribes were forcibly evacuated from their lands and moved west of the Mississippi river on the "Trail of Tears."

From 1607 to the Wounded Knee massacre in 1890, approximately one-fourth of all tribes permanently disappeared, and the Native American population decreased from an estimated 2 to 5 million to 200,000, an attrition rate unmatched by the Black Plague, the Thirty Years' War, or any modern war.

The General Allotment Act of 1887 (also known as the Dawes Act) returned the American attitude toward Native Americans to the Jeffersonian vision of civilizing them by turning them into small, private farmers. The act granted each Native American family its own plot of land and nulified the tribal land title, undermining the Native American traditions of communal living and survival. In effect, the act told Native Americans that their culture and life-style would no longer be accepted or tolerated in America. In addition, Native American tribal lands were allowed to be sold to non–Native Americans. Theoretically, money derived from this land was to be set aside for special Native-American programs; however, in the forty-six years that the General Allotment Act was in effect, ninety million acres of Native-American land was sold and few special programs developed.[25]

Education also played a key role in "Americanizing" Native Americans. Many Native American children were forced to attend boarding schools that were often far away from their family and tribe. In these schools, Native Americans learned white history and received a traditional European-based education. Native-American history and culture was completely excluded from the curriculum.

> Tens of thousands of Native American children were "legally" kidnapped and forced to attend schools hundreds of miles from home. Often their parents could not pay for their transportation home during vacations, so the youngsters had to remain at school all year. The school curriculum made no concessions to the cultural history or needs of Native American children. Rather, it was designed and applied with the idea of eradicating all signs of Native American culture.[26]

In the 1920s and 1930s, the U.S. Congress changed its policy toward Native Americans. No longer did it want to integrate Native Americans totally into American society. Instead, it recognized the tribe as a fundamental unit to Native American life and culture, reestablished the tribal land title, and began buying territory especially for the purpose of increasing tribal lands. In 1924, Congress granted all Native

Americans U.S. citizenship and began to establish tribal-based schools and social welfare programs.

World War II changed America's focus from internal to foreign affairs. As a result, no fundamental change was made in Native American policy until after the war's conclusion, when Americans began questioning the federal government's paternal role toward Native Americans. The growing American sentiment was that the federal government should terminate its guardianship role and grant Native Americans the autonomy necessary to control their own economics and social programs. As a result, the first termination bill passed Congress in 1954, and five more were passed the following year. But although the termination policy was supposed to help Native Americans improve their standard of living, it had the reverse effect.

> In the ten years, following the passage of the termination act, none of the major goals of the termination policy were realized. A major goal was to give the Indians full control over their property, both personal and collective. By the time of termination, virtually no trace of this intention to grant economic freedom remained. The Menominees were·given more than ample responsibility but they gained no significant new freedoms. The high burden of taxes thrust upon the Indians, the high cost of government services, the low profits of the tribal saw mill, combined to place the Menominees into a worse position than they occupied before termination.[27]

By the end of the 1960s, America's termination policy had failed, and its implementation had halted. President Nixon in 1970 outlined a new Native American policy. It mixed the prior radical termination and paternalistic policies so that the government could stop arguing over *whether* it had a commitment to Native Americans and focus on *how* government could best fulfill its responsibility. By 1972 Nixon's innovative policy was being undermined by special interest groups; however, Native American youths refused to silently allow a group of whites to hamper their opportunities further. In 1972, for example, the Native American Movement protested in Washington, D.C., against the long and continuing history of Native American oppression.[28] Native Americans' protests against white oppression continued throughout the 1970s, but by the early 1980s the protest had moved into the courts. Native Americans began suing the United States government in order to force them to uphold previously signed treaties.

Through the courts, Native Americans have recently upheld the right to protect sacred ancestral lands, control water vital to the Native American population and economy, and raise children on the reservations. Nonetheless, Native Americans continue to face a multitude of challenges, many of which derive from more than two hundred years of oppression.

Today the traditional Native-American family unit, economy, and culture struggle to survive. Only fragments of Native American traditions and customs remain intact; a legacy of despair and poverty fills the void. Native Americans are the poorest of all Americans, with 23 percent living below the poverty level. The median income of Native Americans is merely $13,678, the lowest among all racial minorities, and their unemployment rate is ten times the national average. Adding to Native American hardships is the fact only 55.8 percent of Native Americans twenty-five or older have completed high school, and only 7.7 percent have completed a minimum of four years in college.

Although the physical living conditions on Native-American reservations are poor, the land itself is rich. Much of the 2 percent of U.S. land that the Native American population of 2.52 million controls contains important mineral deposits: Native Americans control one-third of the country's easily accessible low-sulfur coal, one-half of its uranium, and substantial oil and natural gas deposits. As the demand for energy increases, these mineral reserves are becoming increasingly valuable as the white population, once again, desires Native American lands. Native Americans are effectively combating white Americans in the legal system, however, and beginning to reverse the effects of two hundred years of oppression.

Intergroup Conflicts

The rate of ethnic, racial, and religious clashes between minority groups is rising; it can partially be explained through intergroup competition. The recent rise in both the Hispanic/Latino-American and Asian-American populations has decreased African Americans' influence on minority issues and concerns, and it has increased competition for jobs. These minority groups also compete for funding of programs, access to public social and health services, and residence in low-income housing. Instead of blaming the discriminatory American infrastructure for their limited opportunities and their low standard of living, minority groups blame each other.

Often it seems that when one minority group gains power, either economically or politically, instead of aiding other minority groups, the "in-power" minority further oppresses them. For example, African Americans control a great deal of the Washington, D.C., political system and Hispanic/Latino Americans feel that African Americans exploit them. One incident illustrating Hispanic/Latino-American concerns occurred after African-American police officers arrested a Salvadoran immigrant for public drinking. Police report that the immigrant lunged with a knife at an African-American rookie officer, who subsequently shot him. However, the Hispanic/Latino-American community viewed the police version as a cover up and when a rumor spread that the Salvadoran was shot in the back while handcuffed, Hispanic/Latino Americans filled the streets. Two days of rioting ensued, resulting in 12 injured police officers, two hundred twenty five arrests and two million dollars in property damage.[29]

In South-Central Los Angeles in October 1991, tension and hostility between Koreans and African Americans mounted when a Korean store owner shot a fifteen-year-old African-American female as she left the store after struggling over a $1.79 bottle of orange juice that the owner accused her of shoplifting. "This incident embodies all of the problem areas," said a member of the Los Angeles County Human Relations Commission. "It has come to symbolize what is wrong in the situation."[30] The situation referred to was South-Central Los Angeles's depressed economy. Numerous storefronts remain empty; however, scattered throughout this poverty are prosperous small Korean groceries, service stations, and liquor stores that remind African Americans that they are at the bottom rung of the American economic ladder. This "situation" after the Rodney King verdict exploded into the riots (or uprising, as many referred to it) of April 1992, resulting in dozens of deaths, hundreds of injuries, and the loss of millions of dollars of property. The second verdict in 1993 which led to the conviction of two of the four police officers did not lead to violence for several reasons: the efforts of the various racial communities leadership, the massive police presences, and the verdict.

The above examples of racial violence point to a growing crisis in America. Whites and minority groups are accepting each other less and using each other as targets to vent their frustrations. The rise of racial and ethnic unrest threatens to eliminate the competitive advantage that the United States presently has over the European Community and Japan with regard to utilizing diverse workers. The twentieth-century marketplace will require that people from different races, cultures, backgrounds, and religions harmoniously work together to give the United States the competitive edge.

Conclusion

As seen above, each U.S. minority group shares a common history while maintaining a certain uniqueness. African Americans, Hispanics/Latinos, Asian Americans, and Native Americans all have faced discrimination and negative stereotypes that have hindered their opportunities. They have all heard promises of equality and the fulfillment of the American dream while whites ignored or postponed the implementation of Civil Rights legislation and progressive Supreme Court rulings. Nonetheless, opportunities for these groups have slowly improved, especially since the passage of the 1964, 1965, and 1968 Civil Rights Acts. In the 1990s, members of these minorities possess rights and opportunities that their ancestors, no matter how bright or capable, would have been denied solely on the basis of their race.

Even though the process is far from complete, the United States has made important strides in achieving equality for all its residents. The Civil Rights Act of 1991 exemplifies the nation's continued commitment to racial and other forms of equality. Its long history of accepting and integrating immigrants and minorities into American society better equips the United States to deal with its diverse work force and the increased reliance on foreign and immigrant labor that the twenty-first century will require to be competitive. Japan today remains a highly homogeneous population, and the EC, although attempting to integrate itself, continues to foster ethnocentric and xenophobic tendencies. Neither the EC nor Japan have laws to protect the rights of minorities (though the EC is thinking about requiring members to do so). As a result, we believe Japan and the EC will experience great difficulty in utilizing diverse workers as their native labor supply decreases and fails to meet the demands of an expanding economy. The United States has both the experience and legal framework to utilize immigrant workers, but the growing racial tensions that exist between whites and minority groups and among various minority groups threaten to diminish the U.S. diversity advantage. In addition, as we shall see in the next chapter, corporate America has a long way to go to provide equal job opportunities to minorities and to utilize fully the talents and skills of members of these groups.

13

Race Discrimination in Corporate America

The previous chapter clearly demonstrated that over the years all U.S. racial minorities have faced discrimination in all aspects of their lives. In this chapter we will focus on discrimination in corporate America. The discrimination encountered by each minority group is in some areas unique, both in kind and in degree. Each group has its particular legacy of both positive and negative stereotypes; these stereotypes come not only from the white majority but also from the minority groups themselves.

Over the years, blacks in our surveys and seminars have always been by far the most critical group of employees about discrimination against minorities in corporate America. In 1976–78 we found that Hispanics/Latinos were significantly more critical than Asians and American Indians, but in 1988 the responses of Hispanics/Latinos, Asian Americans, and Native Americans to questions about discrimination against minorities were no longer significantly different. In data collected from numerous seminars and surveys in a variety of corporations in 1991, 1992, and 1993, we found considerably more agreement about discrimination in corporate America among these various minority groups. There are a number of possible explanations for this convergence, including that as the number of Hispanics/Latinos becomes increasingly larger, they are more frequently becoming targets of corporate discrimination and are recognizing it. Within the umbrella term *Hispanic/Latino* are five distinct groups: Mexicans, Cubans, Puerto Ricans, Latinos from Central and South America, and other Hispanics/Latinos (primarily from Spain). When responses were analyzed in various surveys and seminars, we consistently found that

Puerto Ricans, many of whom have black origins, respond more similarly to blacks than other Hispanic/Latino groups. People who classify themselves as having "other Spanish" origins (that is, from Spain or its colonies) are usually white in color and respond similarly to whites. This strongly implies that the skin color of the Hispanic/Latino group members influences their responses.

It seems that as the numbers of Asian Americans increase in corporate America and anti-Asian attitudes increase because of Asian countries' economic successes, the amount of discrimination faced by these Americans has increased. In addition, Native American perceptions of increased discrimination could be due to the increasing resentment among whites as Native Americans become more aggressive in fighting for their legal rights. Thus, for these various reasons, in the late 1980s and the early 1990s we no longer have large significant differences among Hispanic/Latino, Asian American, and Native American perceptions of discrimination in the corporate world. We still do have significant differences, however, between the perceptions of these three groups and those of blacks. The latter's opinions about discrimination in corporate America have remained quite constant into early 1993 except for a slight dip in the early and middle 1970s.

Where Are Minorities in Corporate America?

When one looks at the hierarchy of corporate America, considerable progress has been made in providing job opportunities for people of color at nonmangement and lower management levels; however, there has been only minimal progress at middle-management levels and only token progress at upper levels of management. For example, the EEOC indicated that black women constitute 1.8 percent, black men 2.7 percent, and white women 21.1 percent of officials and managers of major corporations, even though they represent 6.2 percent, 5.9 percent, and 34.4 percent, respectively, of total employment in corporate America. The U.S. Labor Department glass-ceiling report noted that in ten years (1981 to 1991) the number of minority officials and managers employed by ninety thousand federal contractors reporting increased from 246,503 to 264,449, an increase of 7.3 percent. The report also found that minorities had better opportunities in smaller federal contractors (500 to 1,000 employees) than in Fortune 100 companies. For example, minorities made up 10 percent of the officials and managers in the smaller establishments, compared to 7 percent in Fortune 100 companies. Yet the minority officials and managers increased 49 percent in the latter companies, and only 18 percent in the former.

In confidential data from ten major corporations we obtained, 1 percent of the top managers were people of color, as were 5 percent of the middle managers. This is despite the fact that people of color made up approximately 13 percent of managers at the lower levels, and a significant number had been with their firms a long period of time. In addition, those who made it to middle and upper management were, in general, better educated than their white counterparts.

In addition to not advancing as quickly or in significant numbers, people of color seem to be directed into certain job categories. For example, especially above the lower levels of management, Hispanics/Latinos and blacks seem to be placed in areas such as human resources, public relations, and marketing/sales jobs related to their particular communities. Also, there is an increasing number of these two groups in the legal and information services areas. Even though Asians overwhelmingly start off in technical jobs, they seldom become managers of those areas. They are often only valued for their technical skills. Native Americans, though few in number, seem to be dispersed throughout job categories, especially if they do not "look" like Native Americans.

Data on Race Discrimination in Corporate America, 1964 to 1993

In 1964 Garda W. Bowman, in her study of two thousand corporate employees (who were almost exclusively white) found that 77 percent believed that being black was harmful for advancement in business; 71 percent believed this was true for being Chicano (Mexican), and 68 percent that it was true for being Asian. In 1972, we found those numbers substantially lower: for example, 68 percent of blacks, and only 58 percent of whites, believed that being black was harmful to advancement in business.

In 1978, black males and females (46 percent) and white males (45 percent) were most likely to believe that their race would be harmful; 6 percent to 16 percent of other race/gender groups felt this way. In

1988, the percentage of white men who believed their race was harmful decreased to 39 percent and that of African-American employees increased to 50 percent. In a 1992 survey, the numbers became even more different: 20 percent of the white males, compared to 60 percent of the black employees, believed their race was harmful to their career advancement.

In comparing data on a number of identical questions asked in 1972, 1976–78, 1988, and 1992 (for example: Do minorities have a more difficult time finding a mentor? Are minorities excluded from informal work groups? Must minorities be better performers than whites?), it becomes clear that most employees, regardless of race, believe that racial discrimination decreased between 1972 and 1976–78, increased between 1976–78 and 1988, and remained about the same between 1988 and 1993. For example, on the question of whether minorities had to be better performers than whites, 88 percent of the black employees and 33 percent of the white employees believed in 1972 that the statement was true. These figures dropped in 1976–78 to 82 percent of the blacks and 17 percent of the whites; by 1988, however, the figures swung higher, with 87 percent of the blacks and 35 percent of the whites believing that minorities had to be better performers than whites to advance. Between 1988 and 1993 the figures stayed about the same (88 percent blacks versus 37 percent whites).

What these data suggest is that when there is a national commitment to correct racism, discrimination is reduced. In the 1980s and the 1990s, the Reagan and Bush administrations did not have such a commitment; thus, discrimination against minorities in corporate America remained the same or increased slightly. When Reagan was first elected, many white males openly expressed to one of the authors that they could now promote the most qualified person, and they were not talking about minorities. A survey cited by *Time* magazine in 1992 found 31 percent of whites and 54 percent of blacks believed that discrimination against blacks was more prevalent in recent years than in past years.

Table 13–1 shows our 1988 data, which have been confirmed by numerous seminars conducted during the past four years and smaller surveys conducted in 1991–1993. We use the 1988 data because they include large numbers of people of color and the results are quite similar; however, the smaller surveys contained smaller numbers of Asians, Hispanics/Latinos, and Native Americans. When we form the

TABLE 13–1
Race Discrimination

Specific Questions	American Indian	Asian	Black	Hispanic	White
To what extent do you agree or disagree with each of the following statements about People of Color employed in your company? (N = % who agree or strongly agree)					
• In general, People of Color have a harder time finding a sponsor, or mentor, than Whites.	44%	57%	87%	54%	35%
• In general, People of Color are often excluded from informal work networks by Whites.	44%	42%	87%	42%	36%
• In general, People of Color have to be better performers than Whites to get ahead.	67%	58%	87%	53%	32%
• In general, customers do not accept the authority of a Person of Color as they accept that of a White in a similar position.	33%	33%	56%	38%	32%
• In general, People of Color are penalized more for mistakes than White employees.	44%	23%	80%	30%	14%
• How frequently do you hear language in your organization which you consider racist? (N = % who say frequently or very frequently)	38%	12%	46%	29%	16%

questions into an index to see the percentage of employees who perceive racism on all, some, or none of the areas, we gain some interesting insights. For every group except white males, at least twice as many employees perceived racism in three to six areas compared to those who perceived no racism. The same percentage of white women believed there was no discrimination problems as believed there were three to six problems.

Most minorities and women at middle levels and above remained consistently critical of the treatment accorded minorities and women. Contrary to white men's responses, minorities and women did not develop a more optimistic evaluation of their careers and work situations as they moved up the corporate ladder. One explanation is that managers from the dominant group feel more a part of the group that helped them get there. For women and minorities, group identity diminishes as they progress up the management ladder, because fewer same-sex or same-race superiors, peers, and subordinates are found at the higher levels. As their status becomes more obviously "token," they feel more isolated and thus become more alienated. Finally, as minorities and women move up the pyramid they are usually placed in nonoperational, less-powerful departments. Naturally they develop an increasing sense of powerlessness, in contrast to their white male peers, whose situations hint at a string of further advancement possibilities.

We have consistently found over the years that, on the whole, frequency of contact with minorities on the job does not significantly alter responses of employees about race discrimination in a company. For white women, but not white men, the more frequently they have social contact with minorities outside of work, the more likely they are to believe that a great deal of racism exists in the company.

What this pattern indicates is that perceptions of racial discrimination on the job in many cases have nothing to do with the actual experience of working with minorities, but with personal feelings. The fact that social contact outside the work place modifies white women's perceptions of race discrimination and not white men's suggests the tenacity with which white males cling to their subjective perceptions, in large part because they sense that their privileged position is under attack. It is easier to reconcile the obvious inequalities by believing that minorities face many problems as the result of minorities' own deficiencies. Yet we must keep in mind that 60 percent of white males see discrimination in their company, and 31 percent see a great deal of discrimination.

In order to put some life into these statistics, we present below some seminar participants' comments about discrimination they face in corporate America. In reading the comments, notice how blacks talk about discrimination based on race; Asians talk about discrimination based much more on style, culture, and language; and Hispanics discuss a combination of race and culture. The participants were asked to respond to the following two questions:

- Some people believe that in our society, everyone is socialized into exhibiting one or more of the following: sexism, racism, ageism, ethnocentrism, intolerance of foreign accents, other religions, sexual orientation, and so on. What do you believe are the most important issues that you must deal with about your own reactions to people who are different than you? Put another way, what problems do you have in accepting and dealing with people who are different than you?
- What are the major diversity issues you believe you must deal with in the work environment because of your age, gender, race, religion, native language, sexual orientation, family characteristics (child/elder care responsibilities), and/or physical and mental limitations, and so on?

Some comments of black employees were as follows:

Major diversity issues that I must deal with is that I am a black female who has a position that has been held by a white male and the people that I deal with are accustomed to dealing with a white male or female. Those people tend to think I don't know my job. (black, upper-level female)

Limitation on career advancement due to race. Stereotyped image with being a black male. Difficulty in commanding respect and cooperation of superiors and subordinates due to race. (black, middle-level, male)

I have not yet reached the age of difficulty. However, throughout my entire life and career, I have had to deal with comments, innuendos and prejudices as a woman first and also as a black. As a woman the questions have been: Does she have the strength of will and character to do the job? Will she get pregnant at a time when we need her most? Will she be emotional in a bad situation? Is she going to be a liability to the organization? Then there is the thought that "we don't need to pay her as much as we would pay a man." As a black the questions have been: Is she dependable? Is she intelligent enough to really do the job? You know how loud angry blacks can be, will she be able to carry herself in such a manner that makes the organization look good? Is she able to speak well, without a lot of slang? (black, upper-level female)

Lots of people (especially whites) are very offended by blacks (especially women) who are successful, assertive and intelligent because they fear blacks will take over their jobs (corporate setting), so therefore they feel we should stay at the bottom and only accomplish enough to stay happy but not to supersede them. (black, lower-level, female)

There just aren't enough blacks in upper management. Young blacks have nothing to shoot for. We don't see any blacks as executives of our company. We do have one token in—that's not enough. (black, occupational, male)

Employees of color seem to be disciplined more severely than whites for the same infractions; at least this is the perception. (black, lower-level manager, male)

Interactions with white males are sometimes strained due to my aggressiveness. It is very hard to do more than sympathize with discrimination for those who are not of color. The white female is a catalyst for black/white disharmony. (black, lower-level, male)

Trusting that the other races will be fair. Learning not to generalize my negative feelings toward whites. (black, lower-level, male)

The following Asian comments are representative:

Some Americans tend to spend more effort to understand European's English but not Asians. Some people think that Asians cannot speak good English. (Asian, lower-level, male)

Asians are usually quiet in the meeting. This happened to me that I did not speak or talk enough in the meeting and other people think I am stupid and cannot participate. (Asian, lower-level, male)

Being an Asian/Pacific Islander male we seem to be "taking over." Not conforming to A/PI stereotypes (politeness, etc). Not being plugged into the "patron/old boy network." (Asian, lower-level, female)

Being reminded "continually" of my race/gender. (Asian, lower-level, female)

Different cultural values. Different work ethics. Differences due to diversity. We are more close knit, we work harder and value things differently. (Asian/Hindu, lower-level, male)

Assumption that Asians cannot be managers. Not accommodating to cultural diversity in making stereotyped assumption. (Asian, occupational, male)

Lack of interpersonal skills: Do not know how to play politics with peers or supervisor. Do not know how to sell myself. Put the credit into other people's account. Sometimes, you solve a problem on your own. The other person sells the ideas gets the credits. Been stereotyped by your supervisor, then you won't get any visible assignment. (Asian, occupational, female)

Let's now turn to comments of Hispanics/Latinos and Native Americans:

I have been criticized because I try to live by my cultural heritage. I take the earth seriously and I am an introvert. (Native American, lower-level, male)

My accent has caused my career to slow down considerably since I made it to middle management. (Hispanic/Latino, middle-level, female)

My white female boss has a real problem with me because of her perceptions of Latino males. (Hispanic/Latino, lower-level, male)

When a person of color makes an error, an entire group of people is judged, not just the individual. This is unfair to American Indians and other people of color. (Native American, lower-level, female)

As a Native American woman I am constantly stereotyped as being passive or exotic. My abilities are ignored. (Native American, lower-level, female)

My supervisor has no interest in minorities for advancement. (Hispanic/Latino, occupational, male)

I believe the company should help excellent employees advance. Most of the time supervisors show favoritism toward whites. (Hispanic/ Latino, middle-level, male)

I should not believe that if another is not nice to me, he/she is prejudiced. He/she is not treating me nicely just because I am a minority woman. But I cannot ignore this fact because it is happening to me in my day-to-day life. (Hispanic/Latino, occupational, female)

I come across as being "stuck-up" when actually I am a quiet person who mostly listens in a group I don't know. (Hispanic/Latino, occupational, female)

The animosity I feel from them [white males] came about when I began facilitating pluralism workshops. None have gone, or want to go, and this animosity is intensified every time they see or hear the word pluralism. (Hispanic/Latino, lower-level, female)

The previous data and comments clearly suggest that U.S. corporations have significant improvements to make in order to utilize fully a diverse work force. Our data suggest that neoracism and institutional racism still play crucial roles in limiting the full utilization of many qualified people of color who have not only the education but also the service time to make greater contributions.

Problems of White Males

When discussing managing differences, we often focus on the problems created by discrimination for people of color and women. In this section, we will explore the problems that white men perceive, because a diverse high-performance team requires that all employees— including white males—feel understood, valued, and fairly rewarded by their companies. Many white males believe that what they now face in the U.S. workplace is reverse discrimination, that qualified white men are losing out on jobs and promotions to unqualified women and minorities. In our 1993 surveys we found that 87 percent of the white males and only 40 percent of the white females and 20 percent of the people of color believe white males face reverse discrimination.

I personally have been turned down for jobs and promotions because I was not female or nonwhite. The explanation was "off the record" of course! (white, lower-level, male)

I am a white male. I am discriminated against because I'm not gay, I'm not a minority, I'm not a woman, I'm not handicapped and I'm white; therefore I get no favoritism, only the opposite. Our company is so busy trying to be fair to those who say, "You are neglecting me because I have this particular (whatever)" that they hold off the average white male, which is discrimination in reverse. (white, occupational, male)

While we make up for the lack of women in middle and upper management, many qualified white males will go unrewarded. Many females promoted are deserving. Others were obviously not nearly qualified. (white, middle-level, male)

We are all individuals regardless of our color or sex and we should all be treated the same, as far as promotions, raises and opportunities. If a white female and a black or other minority were both qualified for a position, the minority would receive the position. Whatever happened to seniority? (white, occupational, male)

In another survey, we found that 44 percent of all employees (including white males) believed white males got their positions only because they were white males. Only 27 percent of the white males, compared to 83 percent of the black women, concurred. Following are some typical comments expressed by women and members of other races about their perceptions of white males' opportunities.

No problem being white and male, they have it made. (Native American, occupational, female)

White men have it made. They make, enforce and carry out company policy. (Hispanic/Latino, lower-level, male)

Some white men complain about "limited" opportunity, but they do not create opportunities by attaining additional education, certificates, etc. (Asian, lower-level, female)

The only problem white men face today is that they have been spoiled for too many years and are having a hard time adjusting to sharing. They've been raised to think they get the whole pie. (white, occupational, female)

I get angry at white males. Not only do they think that they're better than colored men and women, they think that they're the next best things to perfect. They can do no wrong. (black, occupational, female)

White males are still in control or in power positions. There appears to be a reluctance to share this control and become pluralistic. This creates anger and hostility against them. (black, middle-level, male)

Whenever we give a speech on mobility in corporations, we like to start out by asking, "Would you prefer to compete for a promotion with thirty-three people or one hundred people?" Most respondents say they would prefer to compete with thirty-three people, because they would have a much better chance for promotion. To understand this is to understand the problem white men face in their desire to move up the corporate ladder, and the psychological move toward great commitment to equal opportunity employment.

Until the Civil Rights Act of 1964, white men in corporations had to compete against only 33 percent of the adult population, for that is the percentage who are white men. After 1964, however, white men, at least by law, had to compete on a more equitable basis with the other 67 percent (that is, women and people of color). Essentially this meant that white men who were average or below average in abilities began to have a more difficult time in advancing, because they were now competing with women and minorities who had credentials and abilities superior to theirs. Despite this, white men who are above average—especially those who fit the image of the promotable manager—have little trouble advancing in work. The numerous and powerful decision makers were and are white men. Even average and below average white men still, in many cases, have an advantage over above average women and minorities.

Greatly increased competition with large numbers of people who white men believe, at some level, to be inferior or deficient in some way naturally leads to psychological dislocation and to cries of unfair treatment and reverse discrimination. Corporations should recognize that this is a normal reaction of people who are at risk of being displaced from a privileged position. It is especially painful because white men, always a minority of the population, have perceived themselves to be a majority. As a white lower-level manager said to us, "The company in effect has produced a new minority—the white male."

White men's sense of reverse discrimination is based in large part on the nontruths they hear from their own corporations, from the media, and from educational institutions. Since 1970, we have observed many white men who believe that they are victims of reverse discrimination because their companies and managers implicitly or explicitly do not tell them the truth. Some are directly told that their careers are going nowhere, or that they did not get a promotion or job because of women and minority quotas. In fact, none of the companies in my studies ever had quotas; they had goals and timetables for management positions up through middle management. The goals and the timetables were minimal, and there was no penalty for failing to meet them. Most managers or occupational workers who believe they were discriminated against actually were not promoted because of lack of skills, ability, or potential, or because of some subjective evaluation on the part of the company. Also, companies promise many more opportunities than they are able to deliver and have not developed ways of satisfying the high expectations of many workers. Since most white men believe they are being discriminated against, it is much easier to blame their lack of advancement on women and minorities than to tell them about their own limitations. White men, who feel much more in-group loyalty to the company than other groups, are less likely to take formal action against perceived discrimination than women and minorities.

Corporations have done a disservice to white men by not explaining the true facts about their opportunities, and society, which is controlled by white men, has done the same. News media, books, and articles have basically presented an image that all it takes to succeed is to be a woman or a minority person. The statistics from such sources as the Labor Department glass-ceiling report, however, show the opposite. Probably the one factor that has caused more psychological trauma in white men than any other is the Reagan/Bush administrations' constant attack on equal employment opportunities and affirmative action. How can white men believe that they are going to get a fair shake when the two most popular presidents tell them that they are discriminated against? During the Reagan administration there was a clear erosion of the federal commitment to make racial equality a reality in America. This has led to a significant backlash among whites, especially white males. It has also led to an increase in incidents of social hostilities.

It is crucial for corporate America to be sensitive to the concerns of white males and to assist them in understanding the value of diverse work forces and in understanding that a true diversity strategy is inclusive, not exclusive. White males must be an integral part of diverse high-performance teams.

Conclusion

Despite the tremendous progress made by minorities in the past decades in corporate America, very few minorities or whites find their companies free of racism. Minorities, like women, are faced with a whole host of problems that white males do not have to face. These range from such general factors as combating stereotypes about their abilities to the daily necessity of being better performers than whites in order to get ahead. They must perform with the additional handicaps of not having the same power and authority to get their jobs done, being excluded from informal work groups, and having more difficulty finding mentors.

We would ask those who want to dismiss the claims of discrimination by minority groups to consider a 1991 Urban Institute study that substantiated African Americans' perceptions. The researchers paired equally qualified African American and white males and tailored their dress, manner, and biographies to be closely matched. These pairs then applied for 476 entry-level positions. In one out of five situations the African-American applicant did not receive an application, interview, or job when his white counterpart did. The Urban Institute explained that the twenty percent differential between the African-American and the white applicants' treatment was caused by negative attitudes and stereotypes about African Americans. Another similar situation occurred in 1989 when four Manhattan employment agencies were charged with violating civil rights laws by routinely asking companies if they had a preference in the racial makeup of job candidates and then systematically meeting the companies' requests.

If the United States wants to regain its competitive position, it must become more proactive in providing people of color real and equal opportunities throughout society. As the U.S. population becomes more diverse and less white, the nation will become more dependent on its minority population for its successes. But in the process of dealing with the discrimination issues faced by people of color, corporations must be careful not to exclude or discriminate against white males. Ignoring diversity problems or not proactively solving them, regardless of their origins, could lead to increased conflicts among racial groups and loss of competitiveness.

Some Important Realities

Diversity Issues in the Three Economic Entities

The preceding chapters present a picture of three economic powers at the crossroads of either moving forward to be economic powers in the twenty-first century or being incapable of molding diverse populations into competitive work forces. If the latter occurs, they will be relegated to second-class economic status. In this chapter we will review the current situation for each of the powers and discuss two realities, beyond diversity, that each must understand and effectively deal with to be competitive in the twenty-first century.

Japan

Japan is further back than the EC in having a philosophical, legal, and proactive personal commitment to a diverse nation and work force. Its cultural mind-set also creates great problems for Japanese in valuing differences in their endeavors outside of Japan. All our data suggest that philosophically many Japanese are racist and extremely ethnocentric. Many have a sense of superiority comparable to that of far right-wing political parties of Europe and extreme racists in the United States. In the last two cases, these parties and groups are not large; in Japan, it would seem a large percentage of Japanese are of this mind-set. Despite the small numbers of immigrants living and working in Japan, and despite the fact that Japan in most years in the past did not (and as we look into the future, will not) have sufficient workers, it has recently passed added restrictions to its already strict immigration laws.

To overcome its problems with diversity, Japan would have to come to accept it as superior to the homogeneity long valued in its national culture. Japan has proven itself an adaptable nation in the past, and perhaps it can make this change; its ability to adopt Western manufacturing and quality systems have, in part, made it the economic power it is today. Japan also has been known, however, to stick ill-advisedly and stubbornly to a failing program, as it did during its ignominious defeat in World War II.

Despite the temporary recession in Japan, which has almost eliminated its critical labor shortage, we believe Japan must learn to use its female, elderly, and immigrant labor forces to compensate for the inevitable labor shortages that will be caused by changing demographics. In the late 1980s more than 20 percent of companies' capital expenditures went toward dealing with labor shortages. Although the government is trying to extend the working age past fifty-five and sixty, corporations continue to give incentives and create pressure for employees to retire younger, because their system of pay increases based on seniority has made these employees too expensive. As Japan's demographics change, however, corporations should be retraining these employees to fill the positions previously filled by new college graduates. Women should be provided with better higher education opportunities and should be taken seriously by employers when they say they want a career. Presently many corporations refuse to see women as anything other than temporary employees and/or candidates for jobs at low levels. Although many Japanese women are happy to stay in the home—they do not envy the long hours and slavish devotion of their salaried men, husbands, brothers, and fathers—Japan is losing out on half of its creativity and brainpower and must learn to court this untapped labor source.

Regarding foreign labor, the Japanese must realize that the methods that work so well in Japan are successful there partially because they are deeply rooted in Japanese culture. In a society that deeply respects and values group effort, in which individual distinction is frowned upon—the nail that sticks up must be hammered down—consensus decision making and team circles are second nature. The Japanese must learn to modify and adapt their methods to diverse cultures, however, when they export their manufacturing and business operations. They must also learn to promote and hire local workers into all work areas at all levels. As we shall see in the next chapter, far from compromising the quality of their operations, these changes would increase productivity and enhance quality.

All these factors suggest to us that Japan will not maintain its dominant economic position in the 1990s. If it does not change it philosophy and general values about women and non-Japanese workers, it could face a drastic economic decline as the United States, Europe, and other Asian nations become more astute competitors. It is evident that the Japanese are nowhere near taking the personal, proactive diversity steps that will be increasingly crucial to economic success in the 1990s and beyond.

The European Community

The European Community is also suffering from a birth dearth and a rapidly aging population. In the coming years, the EC will have to find new sources of workers and people to keep its economic machine running. While only about 3 percent of the EC's population is made up of foreign immigrants, primarily from Africa and Asian countries, the EC countries act as if they were being overrun by millions of nonwhite immigrants. Thus, rather than opening their doors to foreign immigrants, they are closing them, and some want to send nonnationals (especially nonwhites) back to their lands of origin.

This extreme ethnocentrism and racism is going to be very detrimental to the EC's ability to have a viable marketplace and economy. Without immigration, the EC countries' populations will decrease in the twenty-first century; the ability to finance their social programs will become limited, and social disintegration could occur. As the nonwhite world becomes more stable and economically powerful, the EC countries will be certain to face pressures to open their borders to and improve the treatment of Third World immigrants.

Also detrimental to the EC are the ethnocentric attitudes based on hundreds of years of hostilities among member nations that, among other things, have forced the postponement of the legal right of the EC population to freely move from country to country to live and work. These attitudes will create great conflicts and hinder the ability of the EC to utilize its diverse population effectively and to form necessary corporate mergers and acquisitions to make European companies more competitive. If managed improperly, these conflicts could lead to ethnic and racial fighting similar to that of Russia and Yugoslavia's former republics.

The EC Commission is more progressive philosophically than individual EC countries with regard to women. Although the commission has forced member nations to pass laws to provide women equal employment opportunities, some laws still have traces of sexism, and most do not have any legal sanctions against those who would discriminate against women. Thus, while there are laws to protect women, they are ignored to some extent in most countries. With the increasing shortage of qualified workers, though, EC countries must turn to women to fill the gaps.

If the European Community really is interested in becoming a world economic power, it would treasure immigrants and women rather than ostracize the former and overlook the latter; it would rush toward unification instead of constantly bickering over directives, monetary unity, and border control; and the current rash of nationalism would be replaced by a mood of solidarity. Europe as a divided continent will not be a world economic power. Its primarily small and medium-sized businesses will not be competitive in a global marketplace. Europe must realize that by embracing its diversity—by respecting and utilizing all its various cultures—a more unified continent could exist that acknowledges its differences and celebrates its commonalities. Instead, many European leaders, particulary leaders of the right wing, believe that diversity must be denied to maintain national identity. Instead of embracing diversity, Europe is denying diversity resulting in increased violent acts against immigrants and increased ethnic nationalistic movements.

United States

As the 1992 Los Angeles riots revealed, the United States has many problems to face regarding people of color and the urban poor. More money and effort has to be poured into education and programs for hiring and utilizing these labor bases. U.S. corporations must realize that African Americans, Hispanics/Latinos, and Asians make up a substantial and growing portion of their customer base. Many dollars are to be gained by courting consumers of color, and there is no better way to do this than by hiring the people who know what those markets want, what they respond to, and what they need.

Despite enjoying more progressive attitudes and laws than their counterparts in Japan and the EC and despite having made more strides in employment and other areas, women in the United States are a very underutilized segment of our society. As women receive more degrees relative to men and receive them in relevant business areas, as they become a larger part of our work force, and as their consumer and political power grows, the male-dominated United States cannot afford to discriminate against this valuable resource.

There are, however, several positive and progressive elements that are being practiced and implemented in the United States. It is the most diversely populated nation of the three economic powers; we have the capability of utilizing Americans in business, social, and political activities who are natives of practically every country in the world. Also, by having more liberal immigration policies, we are able to modify partially such negative demographic trends as the "baby bust" and an aging population. Thus, we will have a sufficient number of people to keep our economic machine running. The United States will not have businesses closing, as in Japan, because of insufficient numbers of skilled people to fill the jobs.

The United States has a proud history of different racial and ethnic groups coming to the country, facing discrimination, and finally achieving some degree of acceptance and generally peaceful coexistence. We have not resolved all of the gender, racial, ethnic, and religious problems; we have made mistakes, and we are still making some of them. We have the experience, however, to accommodate, if not accept, differences. Because of our experience with immigrants, racial minorities, and women, we are better positioned to accept the aged, the disabled, and those with different sexual orientations.

Philosophically, the vast majority of Americans have accepted the concept of valuing diversity. We have the best laws in the world to protect the rights of all people living in the United States, regardless of race, ethnicity, gender, religion, age, and disability (see Appendix B). No other country formally and legally supports equal opportunity, the right to privacy, and the undisturbed pursuit of happiness as uncompromisingly as the United States does. In addition, we are trying to make our immigration policy more equitable, in direct contrast to what the Japanese and Europeans are doing. In short, our philosophy is right, and our laws are right.

But the competitive advantage the United States has in its people is not a given. We are at a crucial stage in becoming the first nation in the world to have economic, legal, and social systems that truly accept and appreciate diversity and to recognize people as its most valuable resource and its competitive edge.

The crucial step we must take is to move from the philosophical and legal to the proactive and personal. The United States and all its citizens and non-citizens living and working here must begin to walk (that is, act) like they talk. We must recognize that we are as much a part of the problem as we are a part of the solution. This will be the most difficult step because it requires all of us to become personally involved in making the American dream, and thus the competitive advantage we have in our people, a reality for all.

In summary, we believe that any country or group of countries that wishes to be a competitive economic power as we approach the twenty-first century must mobilize its work force and fully utilize all of its people regardless of their diversity. The conflicts discussed in the previous chapters clearly suggest that unless the United States and the European Community do a better job than Japan in getting their diverse people to understand and value one another, Japan will continue to be the leading economic power. Japan's society does not have anything akin to the diversity of the United States and Europe's populations; Japan's low birthrate and aging population dictate that it allows more immigrants into the country. Its culture of xenophobia, racism, and sexism, however, will continue to prevent it from utilizing these people not only in Japan but also in countries whose markets it is trying to retain or penetrate, all to the detriment of Japanese competitiveness. The EC has a long way to go also in dealing with cultural conflicts within and among its member nations. The EC must also move effectively eliminate racism, sexism, ethnocentrism, and xenophobia in order to compete in a global market base. The United States, in contrast, has a history of more than three hundred fifty years of dealing with diverse people from numerous countries, and it has moved faster in providing women equal opportunities. There is much work to be done, however, if the United States is to utilize its diverse population effectively for its competitive advantage.

The Corporate Environment

In order to utilize diverse work forces effectively, to develop appropriate solutions to human resource problems, and to be competitive in the 1990s and beyond, corporations must understand some realities regarding the current mood of employees, the true nature of corporations, and human nature.

Employee Perceptions

Let's first review the attitudes of U.S. employees toward their companies. Information about employees in the EC and Japan is not as extensive; however, we shall cite some comparative statistics that clearly suggest they are having problems in similar areas and that their employees' dissatisfaction is greater than ours.

There are some fundamental problems that must be overcome to produce effective, efficient diverse teams and quality products and services. Many employees perceive their companies as unimaginative and authoritarian, as well as having untrustworthy leadership, a debilitating environment not conducive to risk taking, a plethora of politicking, insufficient opportunities, a lack of proper recognitions and rewards, and discrimination based on race, gender, age, language, and other characteristics. The following data from major studies that we conducted in 1988, 1990, 1991, and 1993 support this statement:

- Only 36 percent of whites, 16 percent to 18 percent of American Indians, Asians, and Hispanic/Latinos and 2 percent of the African Americans do *not* believe there is any discrimination against people of color in their firms.
- Only 1 percent of the women and 8 percent of the men believe there is *no* gender discrimination in their companies.
- Only 33 percent are *not* bothered when they hear employees speak in a language they do not understand.
- Only 35 percent of the white men, compared to 34 percent to 47 percent of the race/gender groups (except black women, 59 percent) believe white men's backgrounds are *not* conducive to being successful in a diverse work environment.
- Only 24 percent of the women and 45 percent of the men do *not* have any problem dealing with work and family conflicts.

- Only 43 percent of occupational (compared to 72 percent to 87 percent of management) employees believe their companies value them.
- 35 percent of the employees are seriously considering leaving their company.
- 64 percent of the employees believe their contributions exceed or greatly exceed their formal rewards.
- Only 56 percent of the employees believe that their top managers are open and honest.
- 46 percent of employees believe their supervisors do *not* encourage risk taking.
- 83 percent believe that there are many internal turf issues in their company.
- 44 percent say they are *not* satisfied with their involvement in decisions that affect their work.
- 50 percent believe their top managers are *not* creative.
- 51 percent believe top managers are *not* long-term focused.
- 56 percent believe top managers are *not* approachable.
- 58 percent believe top managers are *not* risk takers.
- 61 percent believe top managers are *not* flexible.
- 62 percent believe top managers do *not* have a participatory management style.
- 72 percent say top managers are *not* proactive but reactive.

In 1992, Louis Harris conducted a global survey (the first ever) of 3,707 middle managers in fifteen countries.[1] The surprising findings (see Table 14–1) were that in five out of ten areas more than a majority of American managers responded favorably; in only two areas did 50 percent or more of the EC country managers respond favorably, and 50 percent or more of Japanese managers responded favorably to only one area (feeling protected from layoffs)—and this has probably changed in 1993, since job security is becoming somewhat of a thing of the past. In only one category (believing that doing a good job greatly helps them achieve their life goals) did fewer Americans respond favorably than Japanese and EC managers. Also notice that the Japanese responded more favorably then EC managers in only one area (management is sensitive to family needs). Thus, overall, American workers are significantly more satisfied than their EC and Japanese counterparts; nevertheless, although a much higher percentage of

TABLE 14–1
Office Workers Rate Their Jobs

	U.S.	EC	Japan
Are proud of their company's products and services	65%	37%	35%
Are very satisfied with their work	43%	28%	17%
Say the pay is good	44%	26%	15%
Believe management is honest and ethical	40%	33%	16%
Feel they can contribute significantly to the company	60%	35%	27%
Believe doing a good job greatly helps them achieve their life goals	53%	65%	31%
Think management is sensitive to family needs	35%	19%	21%
Try to do it right the first time	67%	40%	33%
Work too many hours	21%	31%	33%
Feel safe from layoffs	56%	56%	50%

Americans responded favorably in areas such as satisfaction with their work, less than a majority of Americans are satisfied. These negative attitudes by many managers will negatively influence corporate efficiency and the bottom line.

Leading-edge or world-class companies understand that their competitors have access to the same training, equipment, technology, and financing, and to a lesser extent (depending on their reputation) the same people. What distinguishes companies and gives them a competitive edge is the extent to which they truly recognize that their people are their most valuable asset and the extent to which they invest in their employees' training and development in order to eliminate as much as possible the problems we have just cited. The goal is to create skilled workers not only in the technical, professional, and administrative aspects of the job, but also in the interpersonal skills required to do it well. Emphasis should be placed on teaching employees how to understand their strengths and weaknesses and to respect and appreciate each other regardless of differences. In order to achieve high-performance, competitive work forces, two further realities must be recognized by leaders of corporations: the true nature of corporations and of human beings.

The True Nature of Corporations

Many corporate executives, professors, and consultants maintain that the corporate world is basically an objective, rational, efficient, and fair meritocracy. Others, however (including the authors), do not agree with this notion. It is obvious from the information in previous chapters that corporations are not operating in an efficient, harmonious, and fair manner. The glaring flaw of the former group in understanding the true nature of corporations is the omission of the human element. If corporations are made up of individuals, can they function separately from the human mind, human nature, and human neurosis?

Corporations do not operate smoothly or according to logical rules. Corporations are arenas in which individuals compete and struggle for limited commodities such as authority, power, status, money, promotion, and recognition. A fundamental characteristic of corporate thought is that it treats problems as administrative rather than as political. Behind all the rational laws and rules of corporations, though, are the socially fashioned interests of specific groups. Order, therefore, is based not on reason but on socially conflicting, irrational forces that become reconciled in the "rational" order—in short, a very political process.[2]

K. E. Ferguson, a noted sociologist, supports these views of the political nature of corporations. "A corporation," she writes, "is not just a structure but also a process that orders human interactions. Because it is both structure and process, a corporation can be understood only in its social context . . . a context in which social relations between classes, races, and sexes are fundamentally unequal."[3] Corporations use their image as rational, efficient, and fair organizations as a filter for control. If one agrees with the observations that corporations are political processes and controlling institutions, the implications for forming effective teams and for improvement of employee involvement (two cornerstones of the quality process) are serious, as the reader shall see.

Another serious problem with corporations is that many rules and regulations that are necessary to ensure their predictable, rational, and efficient functioning are frequently transformed into absolutes and become ends in themselves.[4] When this occurs, corporations have great difficulty in adapting to special conditions and new situations not envisioned by the rule makers. Moreover, it is difficult for many of the initial rule makers to divorce themselves from the symbolic meanings that the rules have for them. One need only to think about the numerous businesses that have disappeared because they were not quick enough to see the change in the marketplace that dictated similar change in their process to produce quality desired products and services. One can readily see how such rigidity will sound the death knell to any continuous improvement process, which necessitates continuous change to satisfy customer needs. IBM and GM are prime examples of corporations that are in trouble because of their inability to change outdated practices.

Additional problems are created in corporations by their hierarchical nature, which dictates that few people reach the top even while most believe that they should and must do so—in part because this goal is promoted by corporations as the most valued reward employees can achieve. This phenomenon, together with the fact that the higher one rises in the corporation the more likely he or she is to be "elected" rather than selected, creates a stressful, uncooperative environment.

Opportunities in all three economic powers presently are severely limited and will shrink further as corporations downsize, rightsize, merge, and simply eliminate managerial levels. The factors that determine success are far more complex and subjective than sheer determination and hard work. In addition, another problem with corporations is that despite their claim of recognizing and rewarding employees who are deserving, corporations have too few advancement opportunities, resources that are too limited, and reward systems that are too out-of-date and inflexible to reward diverse work forces equitably.

Machiavelli's analysis of human nature reveals that human beings consistently expect more rewards than they are capable or deserving of attaining, much like the stereotypical obsessive gambler spurred on by the million-dollar jackpot. We ignore the odds, pin our hopes on winning, and walk away in anger and resentment when we lose. We find scapegoats—usually the people who are most different from ourselves—to justify our lack of successes.

The hierarchical structure inherent in corporations also emphasizes differences, such as privileges for higher-level managers. Such differences and privileges do not encourage cooperation, teamwork, and open communications; they foster divisiveness, selfishness, and poor communications, which lead to poor quality and loss of competitive position.

The division of labor, designed to enhance efficiency, unfortunately leads to further inefficiencies. The hierarchical nature of corporations, coupled with individual competitiveness, creates divisiveness and in some cases alienation among people in various functions and departments as they compete for scarce resources and opportunities. As we develop more complex goods and services and as our customers become more sophisticated and demanding, the need for cooperation in organizations to endow them with the competitive edge is absolutely crucial.

All of these factors (strict rules, regulations, and procedures; limited resources to reward and value employees; and the hierarchical nature of corporations) create anger, frustration, and alienation, leading to physical and emotional problems and ultimately resulting in conflicts among diverse groups, lack of effective teams, lower productivity, and poor-quality products and services. As a result, the economic health of the corporation suffers.

Some Basic Concepts About Human Nature

"Always assume that people are vitally interested in the quality improvement process. They will act to fulfill your conviction. No one knows for sure what is going on in other people's heads. Assume the best and that is usually what happens."[5] This philosophical position, as espoused by leading quality consultant Philip B. Crosby, is admirable but does not apply to reality unless companies do much more to change their cultures, implement programs and policies to bring out the best in people, and ensure that employees adopt positive, people-oriented corporate values.

Conflict between an organization's goals, regardless of structural definition, and the employees' aspirations, needs, and wants is inevitable. P. Selznick, a leading management consultant, accurately notes that although bureaucracies attempt to mobilize human and technical resources as a means of producing goods and/or services,

the individuals within the system tend to resist being treated as means. They interact as wholes, bring to bear their own special problems and purposes; moreover, the organization is imbedded in an institutional matrix and is, therefore, subject to pressures upon it from its environment, to which some general adjustment must be made. As a result, the organization may be significantly viewed as an adaptive social structure, facing problems that arise simply because it exists.[6]

Most corporations' intellectuals appreciate that there are extreme cultural differences both within and among countries. These cultural differences are based on the norms, values, and beliefs that significantly affect the behavior of individuals. The complexity of each individual is due, in part, to her or his membership in a multiplicity of cultures. One of the authors of this book is, for example, an American, a Cape Verdean, and an African American. As a youth, his cultural origins were based in a small country town in Massachusetts. He was Catholic and also Harvard and Berkeley educated. Furthermore, he is the single parent of three daughters. He is not a member of any one specific culture, nor does he represent a particular culture; rather, all of the above factors and many more have influenced his own unique culture, as well as his mental health. Although culture has become a popular notion in the corporate world, mental health has not; analysis of this much-neglected aspect of human nature is crucial in examining and understanding the corporate world's difficulty in forming diverse, high-peformance, quality-oriented teams in the 1990s and beyond.

The concepts of individual subjectivity and neuroses may be unpopular; however, corporate survival will depend on the organization recognizing these elements of human nature and developing strategies and systems to minimize them. (Corporations can only minimize, not eliminate, these conflicts, regardless of what they do.) This will give these companies a competitive edge over its rivals because by understanding these realities of human nature, it will be able to develop the correct strategies and programs to build high-performance teams.

G. Prezzolini, a philosopher, makes some astute observations regarding Western human nature that apply to all three economic superpowers.

People seldom believe what seems reasonable, nor do they always willingly accept what is expressed clearly, because logic and clarity have a weaker hold than imagination and mystery. Propositions that run counter to common morality do not create a desire for discussion or even contradiction but rather an urge to sidestep, ignore, or misinterpret. Life, which is full of such blindness to the most clearly expressed ideas, is ruled not by intellect but by desire and pride. Men (and women) want to live, not to understand, and they want to live in their own way. If an idea seems to contradict what they want to believe, they refuse to accept it. If they really understand it, they either suppress it or avert their gaze in order not to see it.[7]

R. W. White, a noted social scientist, supports Prezzolini in describing the value of psychoanalytic theory. White notes that "the constant play of impulse beneath and through the rational, conscious, goal-directed activities of everyday life" discussed by Freud shows that "beneath the surface of awareness lies a zone of teeming emotion, urge, fantasy, from which spring the effective driving forces, as well as various disrupting agents in our behaviors." White maintains that studies of culture and psychoanalysis have a great deal in common; namely, the belief that personality is more than the sum total of conscious, rational self-direction, also including irrational urges, anxieties, and overworked protective devices. Similarly, our customs, beliefs, and cultures exercise a tyranny over our unconsciousness through socialization.[8]

Initial psychological problems are compounded by socialization because the socialization processes do not always send either clear or objectively healthy signals about our worth, who we are, and what we are. Many of us have not taken the time to understand ourselves and, therefore, have no real understanding of our own neuroses. Rather, we employ a repertoire of defense mechanisms that allow us to survive (rather than flourish) in a neurotic world, characterized by an environment of conflicting signals and cross-purposes. The coping strategies of sublimation, repression, rationalization, projection, displacement, substitution, and denial are frequently employed by most human beings. Levinson delineates four basic ways that people cope: (1) channeling their energies into problem-solving or environment-mastering activity; (2) displacing energies onto substitute targets; (3) containing or holding on to energies by repression; and (4) turning energies against themselves, which leads to self-defeating behavior and accidents. All people use all of these models to varying degrees much of the time.[9]

The question is not whether we are mentally healthy but rather the extent to which we are unhealthy. Levinson would agree, but his definition further refines mental illness by allowing for the volatility of human nature. Most of us, for example, experience alternating periods of stability and instability. Given the inherent inequities, stresses, conflicts, and contradictions of bureaucracies, it is clear that some corporate American employees are in a constant state of stress and, as a result, are impaired in their abilities to value culturally diverse people; to form effective diverse teams; and to generate excitement about their company, their work, their products and services, and their customers.

T. Pettigrew, a leading social scientist, offers a definition for "positive mental health" that could exclude most of the human race:

> Six categories of human functioning have been suggested to define the concept of positive mental health: (1) the mentally healthy individual is self-aware, self-accepting, and enjoys a stable identity; (2) an individual's degree of development and actualization of his or her potential is also indicative of positive mental health; (3) so, too, is an individual's integration of the many psychic functions; (4) an individual's autonomy, relative independence from social pressures, and ability to act independently under internal controls are also important indicators; (5) the adequacy of an individual's perception of reality has also been advanced as a criterion by a number of writers; and finally, (6) positive mental health requires the ability to master one's environment at a reasonable level of competency.[10]

The issues and concerns expressed by employees earlier in this chapter will grow as the work forces and societies become more diverse and global, and as corporations restructure their organizations. Unless corporations recognize that they must develop strategies and solutions to assist their employees in developing better mental health, many of their efforts to develop effective and diverse high-performance teams will fall far short of their objectives.

Conclusion

The United States, compared to Japan and the European Community, has a diverse population and is on the leading edge of world philosophy and law to provide employees and all its citizens with fairness and equality. Each and every U.S. citizen, however, becomes positively proactive in their approach to deal fairly and equitably with people who are different than they are.

In addition to sexist, racist, ethnocentric, and xenophobic attitudes, popular misconceptions of the true natures of both corporations and human beings also create the constant conflicts alluded to by corporate employees. The continued denial of these problems by many companies has led to the ineffective utilization and underdevelopment of large numbers of corporate employees. Consequently, these corporations have been functioning inefficiently, and their team-building and quality efforts, as well as the corporate bottom line, have been and will continue to be negatively affected. We will now turn to how companies can develop diverse, high-performance, quality-dedicated teams.

What Companies Must Do to Be Competitive

It is clear that the U.S. population will continue to become more diverse. In addition, U.S. companies will continue to expand through acquisitions, mergers, and the transfer of facilities overseas. In the European Community, it is clear that while its policies will limit immigration from the Third World, the number of Third World people will continue to increase illegally. The movement of non-EC Europeans into EC countries will also continue to increase, especially as historical ethnic strife increases in the recently freed communist countries. Finally, in order for many European firms to survive in the global marketplace, they will have to merge, be acquired, and/or expand into other EC countries. Japan's demographics clearly suggest that it will eventually be forced to better utilize Japanese women and to open up its country to more foreign immigrants in order to run its economic machine. Japan's expansion abroad will continue not only in terms of starting Japanese-owned businesses in foreign countries, but also in terms of acquisitions and joint ventures.

All of these factors suggest that these economic powers will be faced with increasing diversity in their work forces. In our work with major clients, we are seeing increasing evidence that strongly supports the contention that work-team heterogeneity promotes more critical strategic analysis, creativity, innovation, and high-quality decisions and solutions.[1] Our findings have been supported by other social scientists, consultants, and managers.

Hoffman and Maier found that 65 percent of the heterogeneous groups observed in their study produced "high quality decisions" (solutions that provided new, modified, or integrated approaches), compared to only 21 percent of those of homogeneous groups.[2] Later studies also confirmed the positive effects of heterogeneity on group decision quality. Other studies show that given a creative task, heterogeneous groups adopted multiple strategies and identified more solutions than did homogeneous groups.[3]

Despite the great potential of diverse work groups, this potential does not manifest itself unless the diverse workers learn to understand, value, and trust one another. Without these efforts, homogenous teams are more effective than heterogenous teams in most cases, because more common norms, values, and behaviors produce better communication, fewer conflicts, and thus quicker (but not necessarily better) decisions.

The key strategy to deal with the complex issue of forming high-performance, decisive, quality-oriented teams is for corporations to understand the crucial link among diversity, team building, and total quality management. Unless people understand and value one another, organizations cannot develop trust, which is the key to effective teams. And without effective teams, corporations will not become world-class, competitive organizations that produce quality products and services. More succinctly, well-managed diversity leads to effective teams, which in turn lead to development of quality products and services; diversity equals teams equals quality. One cannot progress to any of these goals without successfully achieving the goal preceding it.

As world competition increases (especially because of the rise of the Asian economies), as the life cycle of products becomes shorter, and as customers become more demanding, we are increasingly hearing that employees are an organization's most important resource, and that employees at all levels make or break the company. Yet few companies even today proactively recognize that people are more important than the products or services the company offers. To varying degrees in these economic powers, many corporate executives/managers talk about the organization as if it were a complex machine whose people make up its millions of parts. They do not recognize that people decide the strategies to use to influence customers or potential customers, external influencers, and stakeholders who can influence the business, the resources needed, products and services to be offered, research to be done, technology to be used, tools to be utilized, employees to be hired and promoted, personnel policies and practices to be implemented, markets to be entered, and strategies to market products.[4] An organization is not a "thing" that functions; it is a living organism made up of people. The extent to which the organization functions effectively is dependent primarily on effective interactions between people (in other words, effective teamwork). The following are the key prerequisites of diverse, quality teams for globally competitive companies:

1. *Trust.* There is a high degree of trust and confidence among all team members.
2. *Respect.* As a result of trust and confidence, team members have a great deal of respect for one another.
3. *Clear Positive Values, Norms and Behaviors.* The team has developed clear positive values, norms and behaviors which have been accepted by all members and which foster better communication between members.
4. *Employee Value.* Members recognize that everyone has their strengths and weaknesses; however, everyone is valued despite limitations as long as he/she is doing her/his job well and giving 100% to the team effort.
5. *Acceptance of Different People.* Team members are understood, valued, respected and appreciated regardless of race, gender, age, religion, sexual orientation, language, family structure, disability, etc.
6. *Rewards.* While the individual is still rewarded and recognized, the team receives the greatest recognition and rewards. In short, rewards and recognitions should reinforce the idea of team effort.
7. *Quality.* Team members are committed to the quality processes and understand the linkage among diversity, team building and quality.
8. *Quality.* Team members are committed to improving processes to eliminate waste and defects.
9. *Quality.* Team members are committed to pleasing clients/customers.
10. *Clear Purpose.* The vision, mission, goal, or task of the team has been defined and is accepted by everyone.
11. *Intergroup/Intragroup Cooperation.* Team members recognize and clearly understand the necessity not to be turf-oriented.

12. *Specific Responsibilities and Expectations.* There are clear fairly distributed responsibilities and expectations for each team member. Team members accept and carry out their responsibilities with enthusiasm.
13. *Action Plans.* Action plans are developed with specific responsibilities, action steps and time frames.
14. *Climate.* The climate supports risk taking. Failures are looked upon as opportunities to learn, not to criticize or punish.
15. *Participation.* There is a lot of discussion, and everyone is encouraged to participate.
16. *Listening.* The members use effective listening techniques such as questioning, paraphrasing, and summarizing to get out ideas.
17. *Productive Conflict.* There are conflicts and disagreements, but the team is comfortable with these. It recognizes the importance of not avoiding, smoothing over or suppressing conflicts or disagreements. There are few hidden agendas.
18. *Consensus Decisions.* For important decisions, the goal is substantial—not necessarily unanimous—agreement through open discussion of everyone's ideas.
19. *Cooperation.* Team members cooperate in generating excitement, achieving goals and protecting team members in the process.
20. *Compromises.* Compromises are important as long as they do not adversely affect the quality of the products or services provided.
21. *Open Proactive Communication.* Team members feel free to express their feelings on the task, as well as on the group's operation. They recognize and accept the concept of proactive communication, i.e., if you need the information and are not getting it, go after the information—don't just complain about it.
22. *Shared Leadership.* While the team has a formal leader, leadership functions shift from time to time depending upon the circumstances, the needs of the group, and the skills of the members. The formal leader models the appropriate behavior and helps establish positive norms.
23. *External Relations.* The team spends time developing key

outside relationships, mobilizing resources, and building credibility with important players in other parts of the organization.

24. *Style Diversity.* The team has a broad spectrum of team-player types including members who emphasize attention to tasks, goal setting, a focus on process, promoters, analyzers, and those who question how the team is functioning.

25. *Personal Self-Assessment.* Each team member periodically does a self-assessment to make certain she/he understands her/his strengths and weaknesses.

26. *Team Self-Assessment.* Periodically, the team stops to examine how well it is functioning and what may be interfering with its effectiveness.

Teamwork not only allows companies to produce better and more cost-effective products and services, but it also has very important and beneficial human impacts. Productive, effective teams give employees a sense of empowerment, a sense of belonging, a sense of self-worth, and an improved sense of job satisfaction. Teamwork also helps in bringing down bureaucratic barriers.

Developing effective teams to create quality products and services presents crucial problems for corporations and is becoming increasingly difficult in the 1990s as a result of the following:

- Products and services are becoming more complex; thus, business is becoming more complex.
- Teams are becoming more complex. In order to solve complex problems or create complex services and products, teams are increasingly multifunctional, multidisciplinary, intercompany, and intercountry.
- Customers are becoming more diverse; their tastes and needs are becoming more sophisticated and demanding. These require more diverse teams that can better understand the new customers.
- Employees are becoming more diverse not only in terms of race, gender, and age but also culture, language, religion, sexual orientation, and ability.

- Change is the norm. It is rapidly occurring in many aspects of societies: in their economies, governments, societal norms, demographics, technologies, and relationships.
- People are becoming more aware of the need to subordinate some of their individuality to become members of the team. They must put aside their egos and work for the common good; however, this conflicts with their desire to compete as individuals. (Note this statement is true for the United States and the European Community. Japanese, as noted early in this book, are moving more toward the Western individualized mentality than the group mentality.)
- Constant mergers, acquisitions, downsizing, rightsizing, reductions in forces, and layoffs have created a great deal of distrust and lack of loyalty.

All of the above factors can be overcome if corporations spend the time and resources to train and develop their people and to reward those who epitomize the companies' values, norms, and principles. Failing to train employees properly in appreciating diversity, or in understanding team work, quality, and the other tools "for innovation, prevention, detection, and eliminating waste" will result in a waste of human resources and, ultimately, company assets.

Over the past several decades, starting in Japan then moving to the EC countries and the United States, total quality management (TQM) has become a leading corporate initiative. We define TQM as a process of constant evaluation, measurement, and adjustment of systems and processes to develop and train high-performance teams in order to provide the customer with the highest-quality products and services at the lowest cost. The only one who really determines quality is the customer, and the only way to retain customers is to have them completely satisfied about the products and services. TQM necessitates a flexibility and creativity in working style and thinking; one cannot possibly make readjustments if management rigidly defends the status quo. This requires trust and strong employee involvement. Quality is more than the well-known concepts of quality products and services. Quality consultants list a number of benefits that businesses reap from being quality leaders: "stronger customer loyalty; more repeat purchases; less vulnerability to price wars; ability to command higher relative price without affecting share; lower marketing costs; and share improvements."[6]

A number of quality consultants have noted the potentially devastating negative impact on a corporation when consumers receive a nonsatisfactory product or service. A recent study illustrated that while a satisfied customer will tell only a few people about his or her experience, a dissatisfied customer will tell an average of nineteen others. It has often been said that the best investment a person can make is in himself or herself. "Thus, the best investment employers can make is in their people."[7]

Being on the leading edge of innovative quality products and services requires an environment that fosters trust, respect, cooperation, risk taking, and flexibility. It requires employee involvement. More specifically, in any serious world-class quality effort, a key requirement is that all employees (regardless of race, gender, religion, culture, language, sexual orientation, age, and so on) at all levels are involved to their fullest abilities. Employee involvement is based on the principle that, in most cases, the person who does the job knows best how to solve the problems associated with that job. To have successful employee involvement, companies must create an atmosphere where people feel free to speak openly and candidly about any matter; value employees for their insights; and create an open atmosphere about all business issues. In addition, they must empower their employees to take appropriate steps to combat problems to ensure quality outputs; truly believe in employee development; and assist employees in understanding how their contribution impacts the organization's effectiveness. Finally, employees must have some sense of being treated fairly and some sense of job security in order to develop corporate loyalty. Edward Deming says that without job security (and, we would add, unfulfilled expectations generated by the corporation), employees will always fear change and will not perform at their best.[8]

A key to creating a creative, competitive diverse company with effective employee involvement is to rid employees of fear. Fear is the primary block to creativity: fear of making a mistake, of looking like a fool, of being criticized, of disturbing traditions, of losing the love and support of a group. The impact of fear is padded figures, diminished creativity, an emphasis on superiority over equality, superstition, unwillingness to ask questions, diminished productivity, and poor working relations. One could add constant conflict, displaced anger, and unfair treatment to this list.[9]

As quality and team building are continuous processes, so is people development. Employees (with the assistance of the company) should analyze themselves periodically and find internal and external ways to improve their effectiveness. This leads us to the concept of managing diversity.

Managing Diversity

It is very clear that teamwork and quality are linked. Few people, however, clearly understand that before companies can really have sustained teamwork and quality products and services that will provide a long-term competitive edge, they must deal with diversity issues. They must get their employees to value and respect people who are different from themselves in terms of such factors as race, ethnicity, language, culture, religion, age, ability, status, sexual orientation, and family structure.

Although many people believe managing a diverse work force is a new corporate initiative, in reality corporate America has always been faced with the problems and challenges of managing a diverse work force, and Japan and the European Community countries (for the reasons discussed in earlier chapters) are increasingly being faced with similar diversity issues. What makes it a new concept is that companies are recognizing that not only is their work force becoming more diverse more rapidly but also that their customer base is changing and so are key influencers and stakeholders. They are recognizing that they need to utilize all members of their work force better in order to have the edge in an increasingly competitive marketplace.

Managing diversity is a corporate strategy directly tied into the business strategy for managing organizational change and improving productivity in the 1990s and beyond. Managing diversity is a crucial strategy that has direct linkage with team-building and quality efforts. More specifically, quality efforts will not be totally successful and cost-effective if corporations do not have effective teams. Since the key ingredients to forming effective teams are trust and respect, effective teams cannot be formed without dealing with problems and conflicts associated with the diverse work force.

As today's work forces and customer bases in Japan, the United

States, and the EC countries continue to evolve and become more diverse in terms of race, gender, age, sexual orientation, culture, language, religion, disabilities, and other characteristics, it is necessary for corporations to shift their emphasis from homogeneity to diversity in their approach to managing people and courting different customer markets. As global competition intensifies, corporations must understand other cultures and have effective relationship management in the international political arena and marketplace, which are based on a pluralistic management philosophy. At the core of this philosophy is the belief that valuing diversity among employees will lead to greater creativity, more flexibility in responding to change, stronger commitment and better cooperation within heterogeneous work teams, and better-quality products and services to an increasingly diverse customer base. It will also lead to employees developing abilities to sway external influencers and stakeholders who can impact the business more effectively. Conversely, denying the existence of differences can often lead to lower commitment, greater conflict within the work group, poorer-quality products and services, and more difficulty in getting key stakeholders and influencers to support the company's business needs and direction.

Today it is an established fact that employees in the countries we are considering expect more from their employers and want more personal satisfaction from their work than at any time in history. As such, employees resist homogeneity in the organizational environment and, instead, seek situations in which their individual skills, styles, and views will be accepted, supported, and fully utilized as members of high-performing teams. As the marketplace, stakeholders, and influencers become more diverse, and as technology reshapes the way we operate and communicate, the diverse skills, values, experiences, and perspectives of all employees are becoming an increasingly critical resource within organizations that want to compete effectively and succeed in the future. As opposed to denying this diversity, today's successful corporation is acknowledging the need to understand, appreciate, and utilize the diverse skills of all employees in order to build effective teams, produce quality products and services, improve productivity, and improve their effectiveness in receiving external support from key influencers and stakeholders.

In order to understand diversity and its importance to the competitive process of companies, it is important for everyone to understand the difference between "managing diversity" and affirmative action/ equal employment opportunity (AA/EEO) initiatives. In Europe the issue of AA/EEO relates to women, and in Japan laws and society have not made AA/EEO an issue; however, recognizing the significant and increasing presence of Japanese and EC companies in the United States, understanding the differences is important for their successes in the United States. In addition, it will clearly point out that managing diversity is more than just awareness training—it is a corporate business strategy. The differences are clearly outlined in Table 15–1.

The United States, Japan, and the European Community must recognize that to survive in this new global economy, they must make all employees—regardless of race, ethnicity, gender, religion, age, sexual orientation, or disabled status—full participating members of their corporations. They must recognize and truly believe that a heterogeneous group will produce better ideas and strategies than a homogeneous group. A leading management consultant, K. Sale, makes this point beautifully, pointing out that "diversity is the rule of human life." He maintains that the human organism has evolved so far because of its ability "to diversify, not specialize: to climb and swim, hunt and nurture, work alone and in packs." Similarly, organizations thrive as healthy organisms when they are widely differentiated and capable of a full repertoire of responses. On the other hand, "they become brittle and unadaptable and prey to any changing conditions when they are uniform and specialized." In short, individuals and groups achieve full richness of potential when "able to take on many jobs, learn many skills, [and] live many roles."[10]

Is Diversity the Real Issue?

When approaching the subject of best practices to make companies competitive in the 1990s with its increasingly diverse work force and global marketplaces, it is important to understand certain concepts. We believe diversity issues are part and parcel of three other issues. One is the problems associated with any corporate structure and its associated policies and practices. Another is the issue of human beings, who are basically neurotic to some extent. The final issue is the problem of changing values about work and nonwork life. What makes managing the diverse work force so difficult is that in many cases we cannot tell which is the real problem, or what is the real issue.

TABLE 15-1

The Differences Between Managing Diversity and AA/EEO

Managing Diversity	AA/EEO
Reason: Proactive and based on business reality and needs	*Reason:* Reactive and based on government law and moral imperatives
1. Top management plays crucial leading roles	1. Top management delegates the leading roles to AA/EEO administrators
2. EEO/AA is a crucial part of the diversity strategy	2. EEO/AA is a separate strategy
3. Strategic part of the business plan	3. Nonstrategic, not tied into the business plan (except in progressive companies)
4. A strong linkage to managerial performance evaluations and rewards	4. No real linkage to managerial performance evaluations and rewards
5. A crucial strategy linked to team-building and quality efforts	5. A corporate strategy not linked to team-building and quality efforts
6. A wide variety of programs that affect the organization's cultural values and norms	6. Targeted special programs with little strategic focus that have no significant impact on the organization's cultural values
7. Long-term linked commitments that use ongoing acquired knowledge as building blocks for future strategies, plans, and goals	7. Short-term, unlinked commitments with very little building on acquired knowledge for the next steps
8. Emphasizes strategies to more effectively manage a diverse customer base, a more diverse employee body, a more diverse stakeholder base and a more diverse influencer base	8. Emphasize strategies to deal primarily with employees, not customers, influencers, and stakeholders
9. Inclusive (Focuses on all employees regardless of race, ethnicity, gender, age, religion, language, personality, sexual orientation, physical/mental limitations and so on)	9. Exclusive (primarily focuses on women and people of color)

TABLE 15–1 (continued)
The Differences Between Managing Diversity and AA/EEO

Managing Diversity	AA/EEO
10. Respects, values, understands, appreciates differences	10. Attempts to make individuals conform to organizational norms
11. Produces significant change in reward, recognition, and benefit programs	11. Reward, recognition, and benefit programs not changed
12. Both an internal and external strategy, i.e., a crucial aspect is to be actively involved in community and societal issues around diversity	12. Primarily an internal strategy, i.e., only a limited involvement in community and societal issues to meet governmental requirements

This is because all these problems and issues are intertwined. For example, an African-American, male middle-level manager who has excellent educational credentials and a good track record is becoming frustrated with his lack of upward mobility and his perception that he is not rewarded fairly. What is the reality? Is it because the bureaucracy is so structured that it does not have sufficient resources to reward all top people? Is it because the old bureaucratic way is to move people slowly? Is it because the man does not have an accurate self-perception, that he believes he deserves more than he should realistically receive? Is it because his "new breed" values are clashing with his company's old values on how to treat employees? Or is it that, as an African-American man, he is being discriminated against on the basis of race?

Another example: an Asian, female lower-level manager was not selected to head an interdepartmental team. She has a family and works little overtime but always gets her work done well and on time. She believes she was passed over because of her gender, race, and the fact that she speaks English as a second language. She is upset and is considering leaving her company. Her boss tells her that the reason she was not selected was because traditionally such teams are headed by someone from another department. What is the truth? Why did she not get the leadership role? Is it because of some bureaucratic procedure that says people from her department do not lead such teams? Is it because she does not place work above family (that is, she has "new breed" values)? Is it because she really is not capable of leading the team, but she thinks she is (her own neurosis)? Or is it because she is a foreign-born Asian female who speaks English as a second language?

Consider the case of a middle-aged white male who is in middle management and has become extremely frustrated with his career. He does not have a desire to become president, but he feels his loyal service and good job performance should merit a promotion to the next level of management. Throughout his career, he believes, various superiors have directly or indirectly promised him that he definitely will get to the next management level. His performance evaluations have always been positive, and he has been rated as a more than satisfactory (but not outstanding) performer. He joined the company right out of college and has remained for twenty years. He has not had any formal career planning and counseling during those years. Currently he feels that his career is at its end, and he is somewhat bitter. He feels that older white males are being discriminated against because of not only race and gender, but also age. Are his perceptions correct? Is it because most managers have never been trained to provide honest, candid feedback to employees? Is it because the company does not have a good career planning and counseling system? Is it because there are not sufficient promotional opportunities to provide all deserving employees with promotions? Is it because he, as the middle-level manager, does not have accurate perceptions of his strengths and weaknesses and believes he deserves more than he realistically deserves? Is it because his traditional value system is clashing with newer values? Or is he being discriminated against because of some combination of race, gender and age?

While corporations cannot eliminate such problems, there are many strategies they can use to minimize these conflicts and utilize their people more effectively to their competitive advantage. These strategies must recognize that inherent problems in the typical corporate structure, the employees' own neuroses, the workplace's changing value systems, and poor and/or improperly implemented human resource systems, *as well as* diversity issues, are potential problems to the full utilization of employees' potential.

The following pages are divided into three sections: (1) general strategies and recommendations; (2) strategies that specifically focus on diversity issues, and (3) general strategies that deal with all employees but have more impact on people of color and women because poor practices and policies have a more negative impact on their careers.

General Strategies and Recommendations

If corporations have diverse workers who do not understand, appreciate, respect, and value their differences; if they do not implement more consistent and fair performance evaluation programs; if they do not develop new creative ways to recognize and reward their diverse work forces, both as individuals and as teams; if they do not develop radical flexible-benefit systems that recognize the diverse work force; and if they do not have more systematic career counseling and planning to assist employees in understanding themselves and their strengths and weaknesses; they will never be able to have an employee body that is totally excited and committed to their company, their products or services, their customers, or their stakeholders and key influencers. Without effective, efficient teams, corporations cannot efficiently and effectively influence external stakeholders and influencers or develop timely, cost-competitive, quality goods and services. Their competitiveness will decrease, and their business ventures will ultimately end in failure.

To develop diverse, effective teams that are quality producers of goods and services will be much more difficult in the future not only because of the increasing diversity of the work force and customer base but also because of the continuing trend towards downsizing, buyouts, rightsizing, takeovers, acquisitions, diversification, restructuring, mergers, and the like. The opportunities of employees to develop and achieve their career goals are tentative, and job security is becoming something of the past even in such countries as Japan and Germany. Many employees are afraid, and their loyalty to their respective companies has decreased tremendously as their companies' loyalties to them have decreased. Also, as companies become "leaner and meaner," employees are beginning to feel tremendous imbalances between work and family. Employees are expected to sacrifice a certain portion of their personal lives for the good of the company. Finally, most employees perceive that their companies are demanding more but giving less in terms of rewards and benefits. All of these factors lead to considerable conflict that in turn negatively affects people interactions, teams, and quality.

Companies must remember that to have a world-class employee involvement process and quality effort requires that employers invest constantly in employees in terms of training and improving competencies. Employees must learn not only the new processes and tools but about themselves, their strengths and weaknesses, and how they are part and parcel of their company's problems and solutions. This latter point is extremely crucial for companies to be able to develop high-performance, quality-oriented teams effectively.

Companies must remember that their employees can learn to use the processes and tools necessary to produce quality goods and services; however, quality only results when this training is combined with employee training to improve awareness of their strengths and weaknesses, people skills, self-enhancement techniques, and problem solving. With these having been done, then the employees will be able to define their problems, develop solutions to the problems, implement the solutions, analyze the results, and start the process all over again. In other words, employees must truly be empowered to solve the problems they identify. If they are not, the solutions of others will not be readily accepted and implemented.

In addition to extensive training, companies must develop new structures and employment policies and practices that consistently reinforce the behaviors, attitudes, values, and norms conducive to organizations that espouse diversity, teamwork, and quality. To create an environment where diverse quality teams produce quality goods and services, companies must systematically develop human resource policies and practices that recognize the new diverse work force, the need for effective employee teams, and the need to have constant quality improvements.

In order to eliminate fear, produce a climate of fairness and decency, and develop trust, stability, and commitment among employees, companies must develop more systematic career planning and counseling. One of the biggest failures of corporate employment practices and one of the areas of greatest dissatisfaction among employees (because of tremendously false expectations) is the career planning and counseling area. Companies must assist their employees in understanding their strengths and weaknesses in order to deal with false expectations.

Performance evaluation procedures must include input from customers (clients), direct reports, and peers, in that order—not just from supervisors. Currently most corporations place emphasis on supervisors as the key evaluators and influencers of performance evaluations, with peers having some say and direct reports and customers little, if any, input on performance evaluations. In addition to having effective diverse teams, companies must place much more emphasis on team awards than individual awards. Because there are limited promotion opportunities, companies must be aware of the possible harm to those who are not recognized. In our view, one of the most destructive reward systems is the so-called merit award that is given each year to a select percentage of people for outstanding performance. Corporations that use this system create, from at least two months before the end of the performance period until the awards are announced, a great deal of tension and politicking as employees vie with each other and try to position themselves to be among the chosen few to receive the awards. The announcement of the awards has a very negative impact on the 90 percent of the employees who are not rated outstanding, especially because people in reality are rewarded on the basis of subjective as well as objective criteria. Team awards based on the results of the company as a whole or of individual units or departments generate much more harmony and cooperation.

To have a loyal and satisfied work force, companies must exhibit their team, quality, and diversity values by changing their system of promotions to reflect these values. With rightsizing, downsizing, and leveling, the former opportunities for promotions are not there; thus, companies must develop new ways to reward and recognize their work force in both formal and informal manners. Making on-the-spot awards for specific projects, activities, or accomplishments is also a way to help motivate people, because the reward is immediate and directly related to specific accomplishments.

In addition to team awards, we strongly urge companies to develop various pay incentive schemes and career tracks for those employees who are top talent but who are working in companies with few promotion opportunities; are seen as skilled in their areas but not management material; are satisfied with their job and have no desire to be promoted, but do have a desire to feel rewarded and valued; or are forced, for corporate reasons, to stay in jobs for long periods of time because of their expertise, thus being taken out of the mainstream of promotable candidates. For those employees, rewards can include flexible reward and recognition plans that take into consideration the increasing diversity of the work force.

Corporations also must develop a variety of informal, nonmonetary rewards. The ultimate goal of these new rewards is to bring corporate promises more into line with realities. In addition, radical flexible-benefit programs can be used as part of a compensation package. These plans should allow employees a wide variety of options to select from beyond the typical ones now offered. For example, they should include child care and elder care, vacations, sabbaticals, pay, and other options. We will now turn to what we consider to be the best practices in the areas we have just discussed. While no company is doing all of the best practices just yet, to become more competitive and remain so we believe it is essential for all companies to begin to implement all of them.

Specific Diversity: Best Practices

NORTHERN STATES POWER. Has developed a strategic multifaceted plan with the following components:

- Create employment policies and practices that support the company's commitment to diversity (including performance, potential, career planning and counseling systems, training and development strategies, diverse career tracks with appropriate resources, and leading-edge flexible-benefit packages).
- Integrate work-force diversity goals with all organizational design activities.
- Create an organizational structure to support the company's commitment to diversity.
- Establish link between diversity goals and performance review and reward systems.
- Establish shared values throughout the organization to support the company's vision of diversity.
- Develop a diverse mix of qualified candidates to ensure that the work force of NSP mirrors the communities in which it serves.
- Provide employees with the skills needed to perform in a culturally diverse environment.
- Create an atmosphere/culture in which all employees take own-

ership of the diversity problems and recognize they are part of the problem as well as the solution.

- Create an organizational culture where racist, ethnocentric, and sexist languge is totally absent.

IDS AMERICAN EXPRESS. Conducted a needs assessment to determine the types of diversity problems the organization possesses. It will use the needs assessment to measure diversity progress. The company has developed systematic training programs that link diversity, team building, and quality; all employees will be required to attend and to develop actions plans based on the skills and awareness acquired in the training. The training will have a number of phases built on learning from previous phases. IDS is moving toward self-directed teams and is providing more team-related compensation. A special program is being developed to assist people of color and women managers in career planning, counseling, and development. Several departments have developed a partner system that links up new employees with veterans to assist them in becoming effective members of the team; when appropriate, the coaches also help the new employee to adjust to the external community. This program will eventually be available to all employees. Many supervisor training programs have managing diversity components. An upper-middle level manager and staff make up a diversity/EEO/AA division. Specific weeks/months are set aside to celebrate the diversity of the organization. Most major departments have diversity councils. IDS's task force that is redesigning the company for the twenty-first century is expending considerable effort in linking diversity to the redesign strategy. IDS's field organizations are developing strategies to penetrate and capture the increasingly diverse customer base. Finally, IDS is developing a reward system based on employees exhibiting values and behaviors conducive to developing high-performance, diverse teams.

CONTINENTAL INSURANCE. The top fourteen officers, the president, and the chairman spent three days working on leadership and diversity issues. Part of the diversity training was to have professional actors and actresses role-playing specific diversity issues at Continental. After the exercise, the actors and actresses engaged the participants in a variety of ways that provided them with the opportunity to solve real problems that exist in their company. While diversity components are in many training programs, a separate diversity training program is being developed based on the above model; however, videotapes have been developed about the diversity problems rather than using live performance by actors and actresses. Continental, in partnership with ARMC is marketing the videos to other companies. Part of the profits will be used by Continental to develop new diversity programs. Continental has developed two programs to attract, retain, and promote people of color and women at all levels in the organization.

GENERAL FOODS. The Information Management Department has worked strenuously on developing the linkage among diversity, team building, and quality. The top fourteen managers spent four days over a six-month period learning to understand diversity and its linkage to quality. After six months, a two-day meeting was held with the top eighty or so managers to introduce and understand the concepts. Managers have four key areas on which their performance is rated: quality, team building, diversity, and outputs. Each area is given equal weight. Diversity is not just a check box; specific objectives are agreed upon and measured. Performance evaluations are multi-faceted—primary input is received from internal and external customers, and an employee attitude survey is administered to obtain direct report inputs on supervisors' evaluations. The organization also uses peer reviews and superior reviews.

The Beverage Technical Research Division has embarked on a long-term strategy of employee involvement to deal with diversity and other related issues. Five task forces have been formed. Each or every other Friday, normal work is put aside to work on diversity and other related issues. Every three to four months, the entire division gets together to review its progress and to develop new strategies where necessary.

BRITISH PETROLEUM. At its new Brussels-based European finance center, which has staff from thirteen different counties, BP has developed an elaborate, effective systematic way to create high performance teams. Its program had the following objectives:

- To provide team members with an awareness of culture differences and its impact on organizational structure and systems, management style, decision making, and interpersonal behavior.
- To help team members become aware of their different roles,

preferences, and strengths and how these can complement each other.

- To help team members develop methods of communicating swiftly and effectively with each other and with the various stakeholders in the European finance center.
- To develop a set of shared ground rules for maintaining team effectiveness when working together or apart.
- To begin the process of developing a shared vision for the team and a strategy for implementing this.

In addition, British Petroleum has founded small "cultural awareness teams" to make certain cultural issues do not interfere with the effective functioning of the organization.

MERCK AND STRIDE RITE. They have developed probably the most systematic, multifaceted family assistance programs. The key to the programs are their flexibility to recognize the diverse needs of their work force, especially (but not exclusively) in the areas of child care and elder care. Merck has also begun a Hispanic high school science competition program that will follow the academic careers of the winners and offer them internships and other initiatives to encourage their continued interest in Merck. The ultimate goal is that the students will come to work for Merck once they have graduated from college.

US WEST. Over fifteen years, US West has had numerous diversity training programs. During this period of time all officers, the president, and the chair of the board have attended these sessions on a regular basis. All employees (there are more than sixty thousand) are going through a new diversity training program. Diversity has been incorporated into the criteria for manager's bonuses. US West developed a special minority-women development program and has, over the years, done surveys that specifically focus on diversity issues. All employees have attended a one-day workshop on gay and lesbian issues; also, there are a number of support groups for women, people of color, gays, and lesbians. US West developed a training program to assist white males in coping and working in a diverse work force. In addition, the company has developed succession plans that are made up of diverse people. As a result, 25 percent of its top officers are women and people of color. It created a diversity center made up of compliant managers, EEO/AA programs, monitoring of external/internal requirements, and diversity administration and development (which, in cooperation with managers, handles employee and client diversity issues). A clearinghouse for complaints and grievances that resolves conflicts before they reach the legal department has been established. Finally, US West is catering to the needs of its Spanish-speaking clientele by providing sales literature, applications, contracts, and commercials in Spanish.

CAMPBELL SOUP. A division of Campbell Soup has ongoing training for employees who use English as a second language. The classes offered are generally provided in two-hour installments twice a week.

HILLHAVEN CORPORATION. Has hired staff people who teach English as a second language. They also conduct courses for people who speak English to better listen to those with accents and to teach them basic words in the dominant foreign languages spoken at the facilities. They have, furthermore, formed diverse teams to celebrate various racial and ethnic backgrounds. The team members are racially/culturally mixed and do not only represent the group being celebrated.

DUPONT. Diversity is part of the present criteria in which management-level people receive bonuses. Managers must fulfill all criteria, including environment, attitude, turnover, and other requirements—not just numbers—to receive the full bonus.

GENERAL MILLS. General Mills has established diverse marketing strategies to attract their local diverse cultures and regions. Part of this strategy includes promoting consistent community involvement and using a system for monitoring employees with diverse backgrounds to have access to their expertise and knowledge.

General Human Resources: Best Practices

This section contains efforts that are more directed at assisting all employees.

AT & T. Has developed a long-term, focused, systematic college relations program with top-level involvement to assure that it has an edge on its competitors in the recruitment of all employees, especially women and people of color.

JOHNSON & JOHNSON. Johnson & Johnson has incorporated work and family programs into their vision, stating that "we will be mindful of ways to help our employees fulfill their family responsibilities." They provide a child care center at the headquarters so that parents of mildly ill children can still come to work.

BANK OF ENGLAND. In conjunction with England's Opportunity 2000 program to increase the number of working women and to improve their working conditions, the bank is conducting an audit of all jobs to determine the viability of such working arrangements as flexible work hours, job sharing, telecommuting, part-time work, and temporary work.

LUDWIG BECK. This German retail chain has developed a flexible-hours program where employees can work between 60 and 163 hours a month in order to fit their child care needs.

ETHISAN. This subsidiary of Johnson & Johnson developed a vision statement around career development that was linked to the business strategy and long-range plans. These were linked to career development and job opportunities programs whose main components were self-assessment instruments; information about typical career fields in the company; a list of internal experts to contact for information and advice; career coaching for supervisors; and a required number of career discussions between supervisors and direct reports.

3M. Has developed a career resources department with three sections: career development, career transition, and career information systems. The career development section assists employees in assessing their strengths and weaknesses through various testing methods and assessment procedures and provides various seminars and workshops. It provides them with organizational and career information. Before attending any training or using the career development section's resources, employees go to a two-hour orientation to familiarize them with the basic career planning concepts and processes so that they can best select what resources they need to use. A key component of the program is the career directions workshop, which lasts for fourteen hours. In the workshop employees gain crucial knowledge about their culture (values and beliefs), personality type, interests, skills, and strengths and weaknesses. They analyze their current job as a stepping-stone to their next career move, their career options, and what their best next move or option might be. Other workshops assist employees in such techniques as interviewing skills and resumé writing. An extensive library offers numerous materials and videos about career planning and other related areas.

The career transition section was developed in response to constant organizational changes, restructuring, downsizing, and relocation of employees. Its main purpose is to assist employees and managers in adapting to these transitions. For example, during downsizing employees who are asked to or who volunteer to leave are counseled and assisted in job search techniques and networking. Also, they are assisted with the emotional difficulties of losing a job. The career information systems section aids managers in identifying internal qualified candidates for their job openings. There is also a job information system that is basically electronic job posting.

FEDERAL EXPRESS. Has developed a systematic mentoring program with an extensive training program for the mentors and protégés. The training assists those involved in developing skills in coaching and being coached. A key is to have the mentors and protégés reach consensus in the developmental needs and experiences the latter need to be successful in their career goals. Another key is to match up people of diverse backgrounds and assist them in understanding and appreciating their differences to form an effective relationship.

STEELCASE. Provides incentive pay based on individual achievement, as well as a large reward based on the performance of the company.

APPLE. Has a "hero/heroine" system to recognize those who design products for the company. Also, all employees at all levels of management and nonmanagement have stock options. Apple also has a program called Restart; employees who have served five continuous years receive a six-week sabbatical. Tandem (see below) provides the same sabbatical, but after only four years.

TANDEM. Offers a night on the town for all people who make a special contribution to complete important tasks. It also takes the top 10 percent of its performers to an exclusive resort once a year. These performers are nominated not only by supervisors but also peers; a key is to make certain there is a balance in terms of job function, departments, demographics, and locations.

WELLS FARGO BANK. Because of the overwhelming work load created for its employees due to acquisitions and mergers and because of a desire to create a team concept, employees were provided over a two-week period with the following rewards in the order listed: mugs inscribed with "Take a Break" containing a letter granting an extra day off before the end of the year in appreciation for effort (the program was presented immediately before the end of the holidays); a $100 bonus; an extra week's vacation for the following year.

UNUM CORPORATION. In addition to formal awards, UNUM encourages the following informal awards on an ad hoc basis:

1. Let people off early on Fridays.
2. Surprise people with refreshments.
3. Provide surprise casual lunches with guest speakers.
4. Give gift certificates for dinners.
5. Provide small gift from a company gift brochure.
6. Encourage managers to invite employees to their homes for barbecues and various recognition awards.
7. Have dress-down days.
8. Provide unique training opportunities to develop new skills.
9. Place employees on special important projects.

BRITISH TELECOM/ABBEY LIFE. Recognizing the limited opportunities they have to advance employees and the limitations they have on rewarding employees financially in terms of pay raises and bonuses, British Telecom and Abbey Life have developed a variety of awards for managers to show their appreciation and gratitude to employees who exhibit excellence in the implementation of quality and teamwork. These noncash benefits include such awards as attending conferences and conventions in desirable locations; special dinners that fete the contributors and their families; and gold pens, watches, ties, or scarves.

PROCTER & GAMBLE. Employees receive a certain amount of "flex dollars" based on their years of service and salary. The employees can select to spend the dollars in whatever proportions they desire. Some of the various areas are cash, extra vacation, IRAs, child care, elder care, medical, dental, or life insurance, vision care, and long-term care insurance.[11]

IBM. Every division has a work/family life council made up of representatives of that division. The council reports to the division executive and sends representatives to a regional and corporate council. Their purpose is to provide needs and issue feedback to divisional, regional, and corporate levels. The company provides a national day care referral service to employees; publishes a question-and-answer brochure on diversity to ensure employees understand the inclusive nature of their broad definition of diversity, communicate the extent of the company commitment, and provide examples of how to handle some situations and answer questions typically asked; and created a brochure describing diversity at IBM (used for recruiting and positive employee relations).

HUGHES AIRCRAFT COMPANY. Hughes provides its division office employees (charter members) the same information as home office employees, so that they are given the same opportunities to participate in activities and provide input. Hughes has developed a skills inventory to monitor the personal, professional, or educational skills of employees throughout home office and division offices. They also provide a mentoring program handbook to each interested business unit to be used as a guideline for starting their own mentoring programs.

As noted earlier, no company we know of is doing all of the above. To really manage the increasingly diverse work force and marketplace, however, all of these practices and programs must be implemented.

Conclusion

To build the successful company of the future, companies must first establish missions, values, norms, and behaviors. Then they must understand the current changing environment of their organizations. They must recognize that diversity is a complex business strategy that focuses not only on the employees but also on the customers, stake-holders, and influencers. They must recognize that diversity issues are tied into such other issues as the true nature of corporations, human nature, and the changing values of society. They must gauge their employees' attitudes through surveys and other methods. They must also understand that they have limited resources for recognizing and rewarding their employees. In sum, a total quality management, team-building, and diversity process must be implemented with the complete involvement of management and employees. As world competition increases, as the life cycle of products becomes shorter and shorter, and as customers become more demanding, we must recognize that employees are an organization's most important resource, and that employees at all levels make or break the company.

Employees must be fully trained, communicated with honestly, and fairly and innovatively rewarded. Only by fostering understanding among employees regarding their differences and creating the diverse, quality-oriented teams necessary to ensure quality products and services can corporations hope to be competitive in the 1990s and beyond. Diversity strategies, team-building commitments, and quality programs must be merged into one corporate strategy to achieve success in the global marketplace of the future. Companies who follow our advice will survive and prosper; companies who do not will expire.

Appendix A

Community Charter of the Fundamental Social Rights of Workers (Based on the Community Charter of 9 December 1989)

Freedom of Movement

Every worker of the European Community shall have the right to freedom of movement throughout the territory of the Community, subject to restrictions justified on grounds of public order, public safety or public health.

The right to freedom of movement shall enable any worker to engage in any occupation or profession in the Community in accordance with the principles of equal treatment as regards access to employment, working conditions and social protection in the host country.

Employment and Remuneration

Every individual shall be free to choose and engage in an occupation according to the regulations governing each occupation.

All employment shall be fairly remunerated.

Every individual must be able to have access to public placement services free of charge.

Improvement of Living and Working Conditions

The completion of the internal market must lead to an improvement in the living and working conditions of workers in the European Community. The improvement must cover, where necessary, the development of certain aspects of employment regulations such as procedures for collective redundancies and those regarding bankruptcies.

Every worker of the European Community shall have a right to a weekly rest period and to annual paid leave.

The conditions of employment of every worker of the European Community shall be stipulated in laws, a collective agreement or a contract of employment, according to the arrangements applying in each country.

Social Protection

Every worker of the European Community shall have a right to adequate social protection and shall, whatever his status and whatever the size of the undertaking in which he is employed, enjoy an adequate level of social security benefits, according to the arrangements applying in each country. Persons who have been unable either to enter or re-enter the labour market and have no means of subsistence must be able to receive sufficient resources and social assistance in keeping with their particular situation.

Freedom of Association and Collective Bargaining

Employers and workers of the European Community shall have the right of association in order to constitute professional organizations or trade union of their choice for the defence of their economic and social interests.

Employers or employers' organizations, on the one hand, and workers' organizations, on the other, shall have the right to negotiate and conclude collective agreements under the conditions laid down by national legislation and practice.

The right to resort to collective action in the event of a conflict of interests shall include the right to strike, subject to the obligations arising under national regulations and collective agreements.

Vocational Training

Every worker of the European Community must be able to have access to vocational training and to benefit therefrom throughout his working life.

Equal Treatment for Men and Women

Equal treatment for men and women must be assured. Equal opportunities for men and women must be developed.

Information, Consultation and Participation of Workers

Information, consultation and participation of workers must be developed along appropriate lines, taking account of the practices in force in the various Member States.

This shall apply in companies or groups of companies having establishments or companies in two or more Member States of the European Community.

Health Protection and Safety at the Workplace

Every worker must enjoy satisfactory health and safety conditions in his working environment.

The provisions regarding implementation of the internal market shall help to ensure such protection.

Protection of Children and Adolescents

The minimum employment age, subject to derogations limited to certain light work, must not be lower than the minimum school-leaving age and, in any case, not lower than 15 years.

Young people who are in gainful employment must receive equitable remuneration in accordance with national practice.

The duration of work must, in particular, be limited—without it being possible to circumvent this limitation through recourse to overtime—and night work prohibited in the case of a worker of under 18 years of age, save in the case of certain jobs laid down in national legislation or regulations.

Following the end of compulsory education, young people must be entitled to receive initial vocational training of a sufficient duration to enable them to adapt to the requirements of their future working life; for young workers, such training should take place during working hours.

Elderly Persons

Every worker of the European Community must, at the time of retirement, be able to enjoy resources affording him or her a decent standard of living.

Any person who has reached retirement age but who is not entitled to a pension or who does not have other means of subsistence, must be entitled to sufficient resources and to medical and social assistance specifically suited to his needs.

Disabled Persons

All disabled persons, whatever the origin and nature of their disablement, must be entitled to additional concrete measures aimed at improving their social and professional integration.

Appendix B

Equal Employment Opportunity Laws, Executive Orders, and Regulations

Many laws, executive orders, and regulations have been adopted to ensure equal opportunity protection. The following are some of those enacted by the federal government. Each is accompanied by a brief explanation.

Equal Pay Act of 1963

Prohibits gender-based pay differentials for equal work. Enforcement Agency: Equal Employment Opportunity Commission (EEOC)

Title VII, 1964 Civil Rights Act (as amended in 1972)

Prohibits job discrimination in employment based on race, religion, gender or national origin. Enforcement Agency: EEOC

Executive Order 11246 (1965)

Requires contractors and subcontractors performing work on federal or federally-assisted projects to prepare and implement affirmative action plans for minorities and women, persons with disabilities, and veterans. Enforcement Agency: Office of Federal Contract Compliance Programs (OFCCP)

Age Discrimination in Employment Act (1967)—ADEA

Prohibits age discrimination in any terms and conditions of employment, including areas such as hiring, promotion, termination, leaves of absence, and compensation. Protects individuals age forty and over. Enforcement Agency: EEOC

Rehabilitation Act of 1973

Prohibits contractors and subcontractors of federal projects from discriminating against applicants and/or employees who are physically or mentally disabled, if qualified to perform the job. This statute also requires the contractor to take affirmative action in the employment and advancement of individuals with disabilities. Enforcement Agency: OFCCP

The Vietnam Era Veterans Readjustment Assistance Act of 1972 and 1974

Requires government contractors and subcontractors to take affirmative action with respect to certain classes of veterans (of the Vietnam Era and Special Disabled Veterans). In connection with the affirmative action obligation, contractors and subcontractors are required to file the VETS-100 annual report of veterans employment and are required to prepare a written affirmative action plan. Enforcement Agency: OFCCP

The Immigration Reform and Control Act of 1986 (IRCA)

Prohibits employers from discriminating against persons authorized to work in the United States with respect to hire or termination from employment because of national origin or citizenship status. IRCA makes it illegal for an employer knowingly to hire an alien who is not authorized to work in the U.S. All new hires must prove their identity and eligibility to work in the U.S. Enforcement Agency: Immigration and Naturalization Service (INS)

The Americans with Disabilities Act of 1990, Title I

Prohibits employers from discriminating against qualified applicants and employees with disabilities in regard to any employment practices or terms, conditions, and privileges of employment. Enforcement Agency: EEOC

Civil Rights Act of 1991

Focuses on burdens of proof and remedies in cases of discrimination based on race, color, religion, gender, age, disability (under the ADA) and/or national origin. The Act grants to plaintiffs the right to a jury trial and makes available compensatory and punitive damages (capped at $300,000). Enforcement Agency: EEOC

Notes

Chapter 1

1. See Elizabeth H. Hastings and Philip K. Hastings (eds.), *Index to International Public Opinion*, New York: Greenwood Press, *1989–1990* and *1990–1991*.
2. Elizabeth H. Hastings and Philip K. Hastings (eds.), *Index to International Public Opinion, 1990–1991*, New York: Greenwood Press, 1992, pp. 185, 471–473.
3. Lee Smith, "Fear and Loathing of Japan," *Fortune*, February 26, 1990, pp. 50–60.
4. Joseph Mendes and Cindy Mikami, "Where People Live," *Fortune*, March 11, 1991, pp. 44–54.
5. T. R. Reid, "Low Birthrate Poses Risks for Japan's Future Prosperity," *Philadelphia Inquirer*, November 22, 1990, pp. 2–14.
6. Daniel Masler, "Japan's Working Wounded: In Limbo by the Window," *Across the Board*, 26(6), June 1988, pp. 22–26.
7. Edwin Whenmouth, "Is Japan's Corporate Style Changing?" *Industry Week*, October 3, 1992, pp. 33–35.
8. Jenny C. McCune, "Japan Says Sayonara to Womb-to-Tomb Management," *Management Review*, November 1990, pp. 12–15.
9. Catherine S. Manegold, "The Military Question," *Newsweek*, November 25, 1991, p. 45.
10. M. Silva and B. Sjögren, *Europe 1992 and the New World Power Game*, New York: John Wiley and Sons, 1990.
11. Silva and Sjögren, p. 16.
12. "Women in Statistics," *Commission of the European Communities*, no. 30, December 1989; also "The Dignity of Women at Work," parts I and II, *Commission of the European Communities*, 1988; and "The Community Law and Women," *Commission of the European Communities*, no. 25, 1986.
13. Joshua Hammer with Howard Manly and Marcus Mabry, "Business as Usual," *Newsweek*, January 27, 1992, p. 39.
14. U.S. Bureau of the Census, *Current Population Reports*, 1989, series P-60, no. 168.
15. U.S. Bureau of the Census, *Census of Population 1970*, vols. I and II; *1980 Census of Population*, vol. I, chap. C, *Current Population Reports*, May 1990, series P-20, no. 444 and earlier reports; and unpublished data.
16. U.S. Bureau of the Census, 1989.
17. "Annual Readers Poll," *Ebony*, April 1992, p. 34.

18. "Democracy's Next Generation II: A Study of American Youth on Race," *People for the American Way,* 1992.
19. Annetta Miller and Dody Taiantar, "Mommy Tracks," *Newsweek,* November 25, 1991, pp. 48–49.

Chapter 2

1. Wilhelm Heitmeyer, "Xenophobia: Modernization's Curse," *European Affairs,* 1991, p. 52.
2. Heitmeyer, p. 53.
3. See John F. Davidio and Samuel L. Gaertner (eds.), *Prejudice, Discrimination and Racism,* New York: Academic Press, 1986; also Robert M. Jiobu, *Ethnicity and Assimilation,* New York: State University of New York Press, 1988.
4. T. F. Pettigrew, "The Mental Health Impact." In *Impacts of Racism on White Americans,* ed. B. P. Bowser and R. G. Hunt, Newbury Park, Calif.: Sage Publications, 1981.
5. H. Ferguson, *Tomorrow's Global Executive.* Homewood, Ill.: Dow Jones-Irwin, 1988, p. 135.
6. Ferguson, p. 137.
7. Ferguson, p. 136.
8. "Foreign Acquisition," *Personnel Journal,* November 1991, pp. 100–101.

Chapter 3

1. See the following books for a wide spectrum of views about Japanese business practices: Pat Choate, *Agents of Influence: How Japan's Lobbyists in the United States manipulate America's Political and Economic System,* New York: Alfred A. Knopf, 1990; William J. Holstein, *The Japanese Power Game: What It Means for America,* New York: Charles Scribner's Sons, 1990; Bill Emmont, *The Sun Also Sets: The Limits to Japan's Economic Power,* New York: Times Books, 1989; Masaaki Imai, *Kaizen: The Key to Japan's Competitive Success,* New York: McGraw-Hill, 1986; James C. Morgan and J. Jeffrey Morgan, *Cracking the Japanese Market: Strategies for Success in the New Global Economy,* New York: Free Press, 1991; Karel Van Wolferen, *The Enigma of Japanese Power: People and Politics in a Stateless Nation,* New York: Vintage Books, 1990; J. Kotkin and Y. Kishimoto, *The Third Century: America's Resurgence in the Asian Era,* New York: Crown Publishing, 1988; F. Sugimoto and R. E. Mayer, *Constructs for Understanding Japan,* New York: Kegan Paul International, 1989; A. Morita, *Made in Japan,* New York: Penguin, 1988.
2. Karen Lowry Miller, "In Japan, the Little Guys Take the Big Hits," *Business Week,* February 24, 1992, p. 90B.
3. Ibid.
4. Karen Elliott House, "Japan's Decline, America's Rise," *Wall Street Journal,* April 21, 1992.

5. Alan Roland, *In Search of Self in India and Japan,* Princeton, N.J.: Princeton University Press, 1988.
6. Richard P. Miller, "Japan's Consumer Habits Reflect Their Cramped Living Conditions," *Market: Asia Pacific,* June 15, 1992, p. 8.
7. Saskia Sassen, "The Cost of Growth: In Japan, Telltale Signs of Social Distress," *International Herald Tribune,* January 11–12, 1992, p. 4.
8. B. Buell, "Japan's Silent Majority Starts to Mumble," *Business Week,* April 23, 1990, p. 54.
9. J. Stanley Brown, "The Japanese Approach to Labor Relations: Can It Work in America?" *Personnel,* April 1987, p. 26.
10. Yale E. Zussman, "Learning from the Japanese: Management in a Resource Scarce World," *Organizational Dynamics,* 11(3), Winter 1983, pp. 68–80.
11. Thomas J. Billesbach and Janet M. Rives, "Lifetime Employment: Future Prospects for Japan and the U.S.," *SAM Advanced Management Journal,* 50(4), Autumn 1985, p. 27.
12. F. J. Logan, "Executive Recruitment Japanese Style," *Across the Board,* September 1990, pp. 25–27.
13. Panos Mourdoukoutas and S. N. Sohng, "Japan's Low Unemployment: How They Do It?" *B & E Review,* October–December 1988, p. 19–21.
14. "Overworked: Japan's Way of Life, Death," *Philadelphia Inquirer,* April 22, 1991, p. A1.
15. Stanley J. Brown, p. 22.
16. Stanley J. Brown, p. 23.
17. Billesbach and Rives, p. 28.
18. Brown, p. 22.
19. Chuck Freadhoff, "U.S. Autoworkers Copy Japanese Practices," *Investor's Daily,* April 18, 1991, pp. 1, 36.
20. Billesbach and Rives, p. 27.
21. Edwin Whenmouth, "Is Japan's Corporate Style Changing?" *Industry Week,* October 3, 1992, pp. 33–35.
22. Jenny C. McCune, "Japan Says Sayonara to Womb-to-Tomb Management," *Management Review,* November 1990, pp. 12–15.
23. *World Opinion Update,* 13 (6), June 1989.
24. *World Opinion Update,* 13 (6), June 1989.
25. McCune, pp. 12–15.
26. Joann Lublin, "Japanese Are Doing More Job Hopping," *Wall Street Journal,* November 18, 1991, pp. B1–B5.
27. JPC News, *Productivity in Japan,* Autumn 1988, p. 3.
28. Yoshi Noguchi, "Dropping Out of Tokyo's Rat Race," *New York Times,* March 1, 1992.
29. "Japan Cares for Its Chemical Workers," *Chemical Week,* March 29, 1986, pp. 27–28.
30. Tomasz Mroczkowski and Masao Hanaoka, "Continuity and Change in Japanese Management," *California Management Review,* Winter 1989, pp. 39–53.
31. Daniel Masler, "Japan's Working Wounded: In Limbo by the Window," *Across the Board,* 26 (6), June 1988, pp. 22–26.

32. "The 1990 Survey on Human Resource Development," Recruit Company, Institute for Organizational Behavior.

Chapter 4

1. Edwin O. Reischaver, "History of Japan," *Academic Encyclopedia,* 1989, pp. 367, 369; also Ian Nish, "A Short History of Japan," New York: Praeger, 1968, p. 59.

2. "Japanese Women—Language of Stereotypes vs. Reality," *Focus Japan,* July 1992, p. 3.

3. Yumiko Ono, "Women's Movement in Corporate Japan Isn't Moving Very Fast," *Wall Street Journal,* June 6, 1991, pp. A1–A4.

4. Larry S. Carney and Charlotte G. O'Kelly, "Barriers and Constraints to the Recruitment and Mobility of Female Managers in the Japanese Labor Force," *Human Resource Management,* Summer 1987, p. 198.

5. Ken Schoolland, *Shogun's Ghost: The Dark Side of Japanese Education,* New York: Bergin and Garvey, 1990.

6. "Survey of Actual Condition of Life of Married and Employed Women," *Association for Women and Young Workers,* 1988; "The Labor Conditions of Women," *Ministry of Labor,* November 1989.

7. Carney and O'Kelly, p. 199.

8. Kathryn Ready and Paul Lansing, "Hiring Women Managers in Japan: An Alternative for Foreign Employers," *California Management Review,* sp. 88, 30 (3): 112–127.

9. Ono, pp. A1–A4.

10. Ready and Lansing, pp. 112–127.

11. Sumiko Iwao, *The Japanese Woman: Traditional Image and Changing Reality,* New York: Free Press, 1993, p. 194.

12. See "Women in Japan's Work World See Slow Change from Labor Shortage, Equal Employment Law," *Japan Economic Institute,* no. 33A, August 1991; Mary C. Bienton, "Gender Stratification in Contemporary Urban Japan," *American Sociological Review,* August 1989, vol. 54, pp. 549–564; "Women Workers in Japan," *Japan Institute of Labor,* 1990.

13. Robert Thomson, "Madonnas in Retreat," *Financial Times,* August 12, 1992, p. 6.

14. Sally Solo, "Japan Discovers Woman Power," *Fortune,* June 19, 1989, pp. 153–157.

15. Ready and Lansing, pp. 112–127.

16. Carney and O'Kelly, p. 201.

17. Yumiko Ono, pp. A1–A4.

18. Ready and Lansing, pp. 112–127.

19. "Women in Japan's Work World See Slow Change from Labor Shortage, Equal Employment Law," *Japan Economic Institute Report,* August 30, 1991, p. 8.

20. Japanese Ministry of Labor, "Women in Managerial Positions in Major Countries," 1991.

21. Carney and O'Kelly, pp. 193–216.
22. Ibid.
23. "Women in Japan's Work World," p. 23.
24. Carney and O'Kelly, p. 204.
25. Solo, pp. 153–157.
26. Carney and O'Kelly, "Barriers and Constraints to the Recruitment and Mobility of Female Managers in the Japanese Labor Force," *Human Resource Management,* Summer 1987, Vol. 26, Number 2, pp. 193–216.
27. Steven R. Weisman, "Tokyo Official Takes on Bastion of Sexism, and Loses," *New York Times,* January 6, 1990.
28. Karen Lowry Miller, "The 'Mommy Track,' Japanese-Style," *Business Week,* March 11, 1991, p. 46.
29. "Women in Japan's Work World," pp. 2–5.
30. "Women in Japan's Work World," p. 15.
31. Hirota Hisako, "Japanese Women Today," *Facts About Japan,* p. 5.
32. "Women Outnumber Men in Number of Newly Employed College Graduates," *International Press Division of Ministry of Foreign Affairs,* January 1990.
33. Japanese Ministry of Labor, March 1991.
34. Yumiko Ono, "Women's Movement In Corporate Japan Isn't Moving Very Fast," *Wall Street Journal,* , 217 (110), pp. A2–A4.
35. Carolyn Haynes, "Women's Concerns Transcend Borders and Cultures," *Japan Society Newsletter,* September 1992, p. 4.
36. General Affairs Agency, Statistics Bureau, *Special Survey on the Labor Force,* Tokyo: General Affairs Agency, 1990.
37. *Statistical Abstract of the United States 1991,* Washington, D.C.: U.S. Department of Commerce, Economics and Statistics Administration, Bureau of the Census, 1991.
38. Japan Institute of Labor, *Women Workers in Japan,* 1990, pp. 24, 26.
39. *UN Demographic Yearbook,* 1989.
40. Kay Itoi and Bill Powell, "Take a Hike, Hiroshi," *Newsweek,* August 10, 1992, pp. 38–39.
41. Ted Holden with Jennifer Weiner, "Revenge of the Office Ladies," *Business Week,* July 13, 1992, pp. 42–43.
42. Christopher J. Chipello, "Socialist Leader in Japan May Quit; LDP's Abe Is Dead," *Wall Street Journal,* May 16, 1991, p. A12.
43. David E. Sanger, "Tokyo Official Ties Birth Decline to Education," *New York Times,* June 27, 1990.
44. Chipello, p. A12.

Chapter 5

1. William H. Lash, "Unwelcome Imports: Racism, Sexism and Foreign Investment," *Michigan Journal of International Law,* 13 (1), Fall 1991, pp. 1–42.
2. F. Sugimoto and R. E. Moyer, *Constructs for Understanding Japan,* New York: Kegan Paul International, 1989, pp. 234–237.

3. Karl Schoenberger, "Issue of Japanese Racism Grows with Immigration," *Los Angeles Times,* January 1, 1990, p. A1, A20.
4. Kate Elwood, "Not All Foreigners Are Created Equal," *Japan Economic Journal,* November 3, 1990.
5. Schoenberger, p. A1, A20.
6. Elwood, p. 3.
7. Ibid.
8. Yuji Aida, "Trouble for U.S., Some in Japan Say," *Atlanta Journal Constitution,* May 12, 1991.
9. Urban C. Lehner, "Another Japanese Politician Criticizes U.S., Calling Management 'No Good'." *Wall Street Journal,* January 27, 1992, p. A6.
10. Bill Powell and Bradley Martin, "What Japan Thinks of Us," *Newsweek,* April 2, 1990, pp. 18–24.
11. T. R. Reid, "An Angry Japan Rejects Criticism by Gulf War Coalition," *New York Times,* March 21, 1991, p. A17.
12. George Friedman and Meredith LeBard, "Japan is One of the Wild Cards, and That's a Problem for the U.S.," *Philadelphia Inquirer,* October 27, 1991.
13. Lash, pp. 10–13.
14. "Japan and Anti-Semitism: The Proliferation of Anti-Jewish Literature," *ADL International Report,* April 1987.
15. Jonathan Schachter, "Japan Faces Up to Spread of Antisemitic Literature," *Jerusalem Post,* February 24, 1991.
16. J. Kotkin and Y. Kishimoto, *The Third Century: America's Resurgence in the Asian Era,* New York: Crown Publishing, 1988, pp. 199–200.
17. S. Duthie, "For Many Asians, Japanese Evoke Both Bitter Memories and Admiration," *New York Times,* August 10, 1990, p. A4.
18. Ibid.
19. See the following books for excellent perspectives about Americans working for Japanese: Robert M. March, *Working for a Japanese Company; Insights into the Multicultural Workplace,* New York: Kodanska International, 1992; Dennis Laurie, *Yankee Samurai: American Managers Speak Out About What It's Like to Work for Japanese Companies in the U.S.,* New York: Harper Business, 1992; David Gelsonliter, *Jump Start: Japan Comes to the Heartland,* New York: Farrar Strauss Group, 1990; Joseph J. Fucini and Suzy Fucini, *Working for the Japanese,* New York: Free Press, 1990.
20. "Seoul Tells Japan: Compensate Women," *International Herald Tribune,* January 22, 1992, p. 4.
21. David Sanger, "Of Sex and Lies: Japanese Teacher Debunks 'Comfort Women' Myths," *International Herald Tribune,* January 29, 1992, p. 3.
22. *World Opinion Update,* 15 (10), October 1990, pp. 110–111.
23. David E. Sanger, "A New Car for Malaysia," *New York Times,* March 6, 1991, pp. A1, D6.
24. Damon Darlin, "Debate over Museum Captures Conflict in South Korean Attitude Toward Japan," *Wall Street Journal,* October 21, 1991.

Chapter 6

1. J. Naisbitt and P. Aburdene, *Megatrends 2000,* New York: William Morrow, 1990, pp. 49–50.
2. "Europe Gets in Shape by Pushing Out Pink Slips," *Business Week,* March 2, 1992, p. 52.
3. Christopher Pares, "Mercedes-Benz to Cut 10,000 Jobs This Year," *Financial Times,* June 4, 1992, p. 17.
4. See the following publications for excellent statistics on the EC: "Demographic Statistics 1991," Statistical Office of the European Community, Eurostat, 1991; "A Social Portrait of Europe," published by the same source.
5. "A Social Portrait of Europe," pp. 12–13.
6. See the following books for a varied discussion of the EC and business: Spyros G. Markridakis and Associates, *Single Market Europe: Opportunities and Challenges for Business,* San Francisco, CA: Jossey-Bass, 1991; Michael Silva and B. Sjögren, *Europe 1992 and the New Power Game,* New York: John Wiley and Sons, 1990; Timothy M. Devinny and William C. Hightower, *European Market After 1992,* New York: Lexington Books, 1992.
7. Michael Meyer and Jennifer Meyer, "The Myth of German Efficiency," *Newsweek,* July 30, 1990.
8. Michael Spencer, "1992 and All That Civil Liberties in the Balance," *Civil Liberties Trust,* London, England, 1990; "Social Europe: The First Report on the Application of the Community Charter of Fundamental Social Rights of Workers," *Commission of the European Communities,* 1992; "Tripartite Symposium on Equality of Opportunity and Treatment for Men and Women in Industrialized Countries," *International Labour Office,* Geneva, Switzerland, 1990.
9. See books listed in end notes.
10. *Fortune,* April 6, 1992, p. 16.
11. Igor Reichlin with Sabrina Kiefer, Charles Hoots, and Jacek Dobrowlski, "Long Days, Low Pay and a Moldy Cot," *Business Week,* January 27, 1992, p. 44.
12. See note 8.
13. *Personnel,* October 1989, p. 22.
14. Everett M. Kassalow, "Employee Representation on U.S. German Boards," *Monthly Labor Review,* September 1989, pp. 39–40.
15. See note 8.
16. E. S. Browning, "Europe's Car Makers Struggle to Adopt Japan's Efficient Style, but Labor Balks," *Wall Street Journal,* November 22, 1991.
17. See note 8.
18. Michael Farr, "1992: The Workers' Stake," *International Management,* November 1989, pp. 50–54.

Chapter 7

1. Women's Studies International Forum Special Issue; *A Continent in Transition: Issues of Women in Europe in the 1990s,* 15 (1), New York: Pergamon Press,

1992; Michael Spencer, "1992 and All that Civil Liberties in the Balance," *Civil Liberties Trust*, London, England, 1990; "Social Europe: The First Report on the Application of the Community Charter of Fundamental Social Rights of Workers," *Commission of the European Communities*, 1992; "Tripartite Symposium on Equality of Opportunity and Treatment of Men and Women In Industrialised Countries," *International Labour Office*, Geneva, Switzerland, 1990.

2. *Women of Europe*, no. 69, June/July 1991, p. 117.

3. *Women of Europe*, no. 64, March/April 1990, p. 14.

4. A. B. Antal and C. Krebsbach-Gnath, "Women Managers in the Federal Republic of Germany." In Marilyn J. Davidson and Cary L. Cooper, eds., *Working Women: An International Survey*, New York: John Wiley, 1984.

5. Ibid.

6. *Women of Europe*, June 7, 1991, p. 18.

7. *Women of Europe*, June 7, 1991, p. 27.

8. OECD *Employment Outlook*, July 1989, p. 66.

9. *Women of Europe*, no. 69, June/July 1991, p. 12.

10. *Women of Europe*, no. 68, February/May 1991, p. 23.

11. *Women of Europe*, no. 64, March/April 1990, p. 35.

12. *Women of Europe*, no. 64, March/April 1990, p. 30.

13. Diane Summers, "Persuading Parties to Give Up Seats to Women," *Financial Times*, March 31, 1992, p. 10.

14. Christian Tyler, "The Strategists Fail to Locate the Majority of Voters," *Financial Times Weekend*, April 4, 1992, p. 6.

15. International Labour Organisation, "Tripartite Symposium on Equality of Opportunity and Treatment for Men and Women in Employment in Industrialised Countries," International Labour Office, Geneva, November 19–23, 1990.

16. "A Social Portrait of Europe," *Statistical Office of the European Communities: Eurostat*, 1991.

17. According to D. Meulders & V. Vanders Stricht, Belgian report, p. 48, as reported in the summary report, p. 64.

18. Ibid.

19. *Women of Europe*, June 7, 1991, p. 27.

20. Diane Summers, "Old Boy Network Remains Barrier to Career Women," *Financial Times*, November 1, 1992.

21. Ibid.

22. OECD *Employment Prospects 1988*, pp. 181–182.

23. *Women of Europe*, no. 68, February/May 1991, p. 16.

24. *Women of Europe*, no. 69, June/July 1991, p. 29.

25. International Labour Organisation, "Tripartite Symposium on Equality of Opportunity and Treatment for Men and Women in Industrialised Countries," International Labour Office, Geneva, November 19–23, 1990.

26. *Women of Europe*, no. 68, February-May 1991, p. 22.

27. *Women of Europe*, no. 66, September–November, 1990, p. 15.

28. *Equal Opportunity Review*, Industrial Relations Services, no. 42, March/April 1992.

29. Ibid.

30. Ibid.
31. Michael Spencer, "1992 and All That Civil Liberties in the Balance," *The Civil Liberties Trust,* London, England, 1990; "Social Europe: The First Report on the Application of the Community Charter of Fundamental Social Rights of Workers," *Commission of the European Communities,* 1992; "Tripartite Symposium on Equality of Opportunity and Treatment of Men and Women in Industrialised Countries," *International Labour Office,* Geneva, Switzerland, 1990; "Community Laws and Women," *Commission of the European Communities;* suppl. no. 25, 1986.
32. "Social Europe: First Report on the Application of the Community Center of the Fundamental Social Rights of Workers," Commission of the European Communities, Directorate-General for Employment, Industrial Relations and Social Affairs, January 1992.
33. "The Dignity of Women at Work: A Report on the Problem of Sexual Harassment in the Member States of the European Community," Office for Official Publications of the European Communities, 1988; "Condition of Work Digest: Combating Sexual Harassment at Work," vol. 11, *International Labour Office,* Geneva, Switzerland, 1992.
34. *Women of Europe,* no. 68, February-May 1991, p. 25.
35. *Women of Europe,* no. 69, June-July 1991, p. 33.
36. Ibid.
37. "Social Europe: First Report on the Application of the Community Charter of the Fundamental Social Rights of Workers," *Commission of the European Communities,* Directorate-General for Employment, Industrial Relations and Social Affairs, January 1992.
38. Ibid.
39. Jane Goldsmith, Policy and Outreach Officer, National Alliance of Women's Organizations, "The Impact of the Creation of the 1992 Single European Market on Black and Ethnic Minority Women in the UK," paper presented for Anita Pollack, MEP, London South West, March 1990.
40. Ibid.
41. Ibid.
42. *Women of Europe,* no. 65, May–July 1990, p. 18.
43. Jacqueline Andall, "Women Migrant Workers in Italy," *Women's Studies International Forum,* 15 (1), 1992, p. 41.
44. Ibid.
45. Ibid.
46. *Women of Europe,* June 7, 1991, p. 32.
47. Mary Bogan, "Staffing Targets Set to Help Women," *Financial Times,* April 27, 1992, p. 10; Mary Bogan, "An Opportunity Not to Be Missed," *Financial Times,* April 27, 1992, p. 10.

Chapter 8

1. J. Boucher et al., *Ethnic Conflict: International Perspective,* Newbury Park, Calif.: Sage Publications, 1987, pp. 120–139; "Minorities in Europe: What Self-Determination," *European Vision,* no. 8-19, Summer 1990.
2. See the following books for detailed discussions about potential and actual clashes in European business and in the world: Spyros J. Makridakis and Associates, *Single Market Europe: Opportunities and Challenges for Business,* San Francisco, Calif.: Jossey-Bass, 1991 (note especially chapters 8, 9, 10, and 11); Philip R. Harris and Robert T. Moran, *Managing Cultural Differences,* Houston: Gulf Publishing, 1991; Threnholme J. Griffin and W. Russell Daggatt, *The Global Negotiator,* New York: HarperBusiness, 1990; Christopher A. Bartlett and Sumantra Ghoshal, *Managing Across Borders,* Boston: Harvard Business School Press, 1989.
3. William Taylor, "The Logic of Global Business: An Interview with ABB's Percy Barnevik," *Harvard Business Review,* March/April 1991, pp. 106–114.
4. Bob Hagerty, "Companies in Europe Seeking Executives Who Can Cross Borders in a Single Bound," *Wall Street Journal,* January 25, 1991, p. B1, B5.
5. William Taylor, pp. 106–114.
6. Philip Kotler, "Analysis, Planning, Implementation and Control," *Marketing Magazine,* 7th ed., Englewood Cliffs, N.J.: Prentice Hall, 1991, p. 419.
7. "As the World Turns," *Wharton Alumnae Magazine,* Spring 1992.
8. Warren J. Keegan, *Multinational Marketing Management,* 3rd ed., Englewood Cliffs, N.J.: Prentice Hall, 1984, p. 115.
9. Alan Riding, "Anti-Japan Din in France Softens a Bit" *New York Times,* July 24, 1992, p. A13.
10. Alan Wheatley, "Japanese Competition Raises Fears in Europe," *Philadelphia Inquirer,* May 25, 1991, p. 5B.
11. Bill Powell, "A Case of Ja-Panic," *Newsweek,* June 24, 1991, p. 33.
12. Powell, p. 35.

Chapter 9

1. "Problems of Society in Europe," *Eurobarometer,* no. 30, December 1988, pp. 63–65.
2. Tony Horwitz and Craig Forman, "Clashing Cultures: Immigrants to Europe from the Third World Face Racial Animosity," *Wall Street Journal,* August 14, 1990, p. A1.
3. "Racial Violence and the Extreme Right," *Briefing on Europe,* January, 1992, p. 2.
4. Carla Rapaport, " 'Them:' How Europe's Hostility to Immigrants Hurts Its Drive for Unity and Greater Economic Power," *Fortune,* July 13, 1992, p. 96.
5. "A Social Portrait of Europe," Statistical Office of the European Communities: Brussels, Luxembourg, 1991; also "Continuous Reporting System on Migration," Directorate for Social Affairs, Manpower and Education, 1990.

6. David Lawday with John Marks, Alexander Stille, Douglas Stanglin, and Jennifer Fisher, "No Immigrants Need Apply," *U.S. News and World Report,* December 9, 1992, p. 46.
7. See note 5.
8. "Europe's Immigration Problems," *Forbes,* May 25, 1992, p. 86.
9. Alan Riding, "Europe's Growing Debate over Whom to Let Inside," *New York Times,* December 1, 1991, p. 2E.
10. *Migration News Sheet,* February 1992, pp. 2–3.
11. Craig R. Whitney, "Europe's Fortress: Immigrants Beware," *International Herald Tribune,* December 30, 1991, p. 4.
12. Paul Gordon, *Fortress Europe? The Meaning of 1992,* London, England: Runnymede Trust, 1989; also Bob Miles, "Racism and Migration in Europe in the 1990s," conference paper, University of Warwick Centre for Research in Ethnic Relations, England, 1989; "Europe: Variations on a Theme of Racism," *Race and Class,* 22 (3), January–March 1991.
13. Riding, p. 2E.
14. "Europeans to Tighten Borders," *Wall Street Journal,* November 1, 1991, p. A10.
15. Lawday et al., pp. 49–50.
16. "Fewer Foreigners Reside in France," *International Herald Tribune,* November 8, 1991.
17. "Europe's Immigration Problem," p. 88.
18. Judith Miller, "Strangers at the Gate," *New York Times Magazine,* September 15, 1991, p. 81.
19. "Extremists in Germany Step Up Attacks," *International Herald Tribune,* October 7, 1991, p. 1.
20. "Europe's Immigration Problems," p. 91.
21. Horwitz and Forman, p. A1.
22. Victor Smart, "Can Europe Cope?" *European,* August 9–11, 1991, p. 9.
23. Horwitz and Forman, p. A1.
24. George J. Church, "Surge to the Right," *Time,* January 13, 1992, p. 23.
25. Horwitz and Forman, p. A1.
26. Ibid.
27. Jacob Schreiber, "West European Antisemitism: Alarm and Encouragement," *Jerusalem Post,* June 15, 1990.
28. B. W. Nelon, "Lashed by the Flags of Freedom," *Time,* March 12, 1990, pp. 26–52; also R. Karklins, *Ethnic Relations in the USSR,* Boston, Mass.: Univen Hyman, 1986.

Chapter 10

1. "Pipelines of Progress: A Status Report on the Glass Ceiling," U.S. Department of Labor, U.S. Government Printing Office, Washington, D.C., 1992.
2. Tom Bovee, "Women Still Paid Less Than Men, Study Says," *Philadelphia Inquirer,* November 14, 1991, p. 9C.

3. Philip J. Hilts, "Women Still Behind in Medicine," *New York Times,* August 10, 1991.
4. Leslie Phillips, "Women on Senate Staffs Get Lower Pay," *USA Today,* December 10, 1991, p. 1A.
5. "Few Women Found in Top Public Jobs," *New York Times,* January 3, 1992.
6. Vineeta Anand, "Many Top Women Execs Closing in on No. 1 Spots," *Investor's Business Daily,* November 15, 1991.
7. Harriet Johnson Brackey, "Mutual Funds Take Stock in Female Managers," *USA Today,* March 23, 1992, p. B1.
8. Susan Chira, "Bias Against Girls Is Found Rife in Schools, with Lasting Damage," *New York Times,* February 12, 1992, p. 1.
9. David Shadovitz, "Jury Awards $17.6 Million in Sex Bias Suit," *Human Resource Executive,* November, 1991, p. 18.
10. Lou Cannon, "Women Win $157 Million Settlement," *Philadelphia Inquirer,* April 29, 1992, p. 1A.
11. "67 Navy Women Awarded Back Pay over Bias," *New York Times,* November 29, 1991.
12. Grada W. Bowman, "The Image of a Promotable Person in Business Enterprise," unpublished Ph.D. dissertation, New York University, 1962; Grada W. Bowman, "What Helps or Harms Promotability," *Harvard Business Review,* 42, 1964, pp. 6–26, 184–196.
13. M. Loden, *Feminine Leadership: On How to Succeed in Business Without Being One of the Boys,* New York: Times Books, 1985.
14. Barbara Kantrowitz with Todd Barrett and Karen Springen, Mary Hager, Lynda Wright, Genny Carroll, and Debra Rosenberg, "Striking a Nerve," *Newsweek,* October 21, 1991, pp. 34–40.
15. Jolene Sugarman, "The Spectra of Harassment," *Human Resource Executive,* April 1992, pp. 28–30.
16. Andrea Knox, "Harassment: What Employers Must Do," *Philadelphia Inquirer,* October 27, 1991, p. 7D.
17. Dennis Cauchon, "Harassment, Free Speech Collide in Florida," *USA Today,* November 20, 1991, p. 9A.
18. Sarah J. McCarthy, "Cultural Fascism," *Forbes,* December 9, 1991, p. 116.
19. Alan Deutschman, "Dealing with Sexual Harassment," *Fortune,* November 4, 1991, pp. 145–148.
20. Michele Ingrassia, "Workplace Experts Weigh Sex Harassment Issues," *Newsday,* October 12, 1991.
21. Walter Kiechel, III, "A Guide for the Expectant Executive," *Fortune,* September 9, 1991, pp. 191–192.
22. Julia Lawlor, "Bias Against Pregnancies Seen on Rise," *USA Today,* October 23, 1991, p. A1.
23. Julia Lawlor, "Survey: Good Maternity-Leave Plans are Hard to Find," *USA Today,* April 22, 1992, p. 1B.

Chapter 11

1. *Abstracts of the Reports of the U.S. Immigration Commission,* vol. 1, Washington, D.C.: U.S. Government Printing Office, 1911.
2. Celia W. Dugger, "U.S. Study Says Asian-Americans Face Widespread Discrimination," *New York Times,* February 29, 1992, p. 1.
3. Seth Mydans, "New Unease for Japanese Americans," *New York Times,* March 4, 1992, p. A11.
4. Vernon M. Briggs, Jr., *Mass Immigration and the National Interest,* Armonk, New York: M. E. Sharpe, 1992, p. 43.
5. *Abstracts of the Reports of the U.S. Immigration Commission,* p. 60.
6. U.S. Congress, Senate Committee on the Judiciary, *The Immigration and Naturalization System of the United States,* Washington, D.C.: U.S. Government Printing Office, 1950.
7. Elaine Sorenson, Frank D. Bean, Leighton Ku, and Wendy Zimmerman, *Immigrant Categories and the U.S. Job Market: Do They Make a Difference?,* Washington, D.C.: Urban Institute Press, 1992.
8. Gilbert Yochum and Vinod Agarwal, 1988. "Permanent Labor Certification for Alien Professionals, 1975–1982," *International Migration Review,* 22(2), pp. 265–281.
9. Briggs, p. 125.
10. Lourdes Lee Vaeriano, "Immigration Officials Sweeten Program to Lure Foreign Entrepreneurs to U.S.," *Wall Street Journal,* November 4, 1991, P. A13.
11. Briggs, p. 113.
12. Briggs, p. 42.
13. Reed Ueda, "The Permanently Unfinished Country," *The World & I,* October 1992, p. 44.
14. Ibid., p. 42–43.
15. "Special Report: The Challenge of Immigration," *The World & I,* October 1992, p. 22.
16. Juan J. Walte, "U.S. Haitian Refugee Policy Ruled Illegal," *USA Today,* July 30, 1992, p. 1A.
17. Michael J. Mandel, Christopher Farrell, Dori Jones Yang, Gloria Lau, Christina Del Valle, and S. Lynne Walker, "The Immigrants: How They're Helping to Revitalize the U.S. Economy," *Business Week,* July 13, 1992, pp. 114–115.

Chapter 12

1. Melvin Steinfeld, *Cracks in the Melting Pot: Racism and Discrimination in American History,* Beverly Hills, Calif.: Glencoe Press, 1970.
2. John E. Farley (ed.), *Majority-Minority Relations,* Englewood Cliffs, N.J.: Prentice-Hall, 1988; also Joe R. Flogin (ed.), *Racial and Ethnic Relations,* Englewood Cliffs, N.J.: Prentice-Hall, 1984; Robert Masao Jrobeu, *Ethnicity and Equality,* Albany: State University of New York, 1990; Irving Lewis Allen, *Unkind Words: Labeling from Redskin to WASP,* New York: Bergin and Garvey, 1990.

3. Dale McLemore, *Racial and Ethnic Relations in America,* Boston: Allyn and Bacon, 1983, p. 289.
4. Benjamin B. Ringer, *We the People and Others,* New York: Tavistock Publications, 1983, p. 948.
5. J. Kotkin and Y. Kishimoto, *The Third Century: America's Resurgence in the Asian Era,* New York: Crown Publishing, 1988, pp. 11–12.
6. Ibid.
7. J.W.V. Zanden, *American Minority Relations: The Sociology of Race and Ethnic Groups,* New York: Press Company, 1963, p. 207.
8. David M. Reimers et al., *Natives and Strangers: Ethnic Groups and the Building of America,* New York: Oxford University Press, 1979, p. 194.
9. D. K. Fellows, *A Mosaic of America's Ethnic Minorities,* New York: Wiley, 1972, p. 137.
10. Fellows, p. 140.
11. Fellows, p. 141.
12. E. Almquist, *Minorities, Gender, and Work,* Lexington, Mass.: Lexington Books, 1979, p. 43.
13. Almquist, pp. 122–129.
14. "A New Look at Asian Americans," *American Demographics,* October 1989, pp. 26–28.
15. Carla Rapoport, "The Big Split," *Fortune,* May 6, 1991, pp. 38–48.
16. Frank H. Wu, "Japan May Be the Target but Asian-Americans Hurt," *International Herald Tribune,* February 4, 1992, p. 6.
17. Ibid., p. 6.
18. Sam Fulwood, III, "Panel Faults Anti-Japan Politicking," *Philadelphia Inquirer,* February 29, 1992, p. A4.
19. A. P. Washington, "Rights Panel Cites Japan-Bashing as a Cause of Racial Bias in U.S.," *Investor's Business Daily,* March 2, 1992, p. 36.
20. Maxwell P. King, "Look Homeward, America, Rather Than Bash Japan," *Philadelphia Inquirer,* February 12, 1992, p. A12.
21. Wu, p. 6.
22. "Asian America," *America Demographics,* July 1991, pp. 16–18.
23. McLemore, p. 329.
24. Ibid., p. 373.
25. Ringer, pp. 142–144.
26. S. J. Makielski, Jr., *Beleaguered Minorities: Cultural Politics in America,* San Francisco: Freeman, 1973, p. 53.
27. W. E. Washburn, *Red Man's Land: White Man's Law,* New York: Charles Scribner's Sons, 1971, p. 95–96.
28. Ringer, p. 150.
29. James N. Baker, "Minority Against Minority," *Newsweek,* May 20, 1991, p. 28.
30. Seth Mydans, "L.A. Koreans and Blacks: Violence at Bottom Rung," *International Herald Tribune,* October 7, 1991.

Chapter 14

1. *Fortune,* November 4, 1992, p. 14.
2. K. Mannheim, *Ideology and Utopia,* New York: Harcourt, Brace, 1936, pp. 105–106.
3. K. E. Ferguson, *The Feminist Case Against Bureaucracy,* Philadelphia: Temple University Press, 1984, pp. 6–8.
4. R. K. Merton, "Bureaucratic Structure and Personality," *Social Forces,* 17, 1940, p. 564.
5. Marlene Caroselli, *Total Quality Transformations: Optimizing Missions, Methods, and Management,* Amherst, Mass.: Human Resource Development Press, 1991, p. 11.
6. P. Selznick, "A Theory of Organizational Commitments," in *Reader in Bureaucracy,* ed. R. K. Merton, A. P. Gray, B. Hockey, and H. C. Selvin, New York: Free Press, 1952, pp. 194–195.
7. G. Prezzolini, *Machiavelli,* New York: Farrar, Strauss and Giroux, 1967, p. 1.
8. R. W. White, *Lives in Progress,* New York: Holt, Rinehart, and Winston, 1952, pp. 9, 14.
9. H. Levinson, *Psychological Man,* Cambridge, Mass.: Levinson Institute, 1976, p. 37.
10. T. F. Pettigrew, "The Mental Health Impact," in *Impacts of Racism on White Americans,* ed. B. P. Bowser and R. G. Hunt, Beverly Hills, Calif.: Sage Publications, 1981, p. 108.

Chapter 15

1. "Managing Cultural Diversity: Implications for Organizational Competitiveness," *Academy of Management Executive,* vol. 5, 1991, pp. 45–56.
2. Richard L. Hoffman and Norman R. F. Maier, "Quality in Acceptance of Problem Solving by Members of Homogeneous and Heterogeneous Groups," *Journal of Abnormal and Social Psychology,* vol. 62, 1961, pp. 401–407.
3. Shaw, *Group Dynamics: The Psychology of Small Group Behavior,* New York: McGraw-Hill, 1981; Harry C. Triandis, Eleanor Hall, and Robert G. Ewen, "Member Homogeneity in Dyadic Creativity," *Human Relations,* vol. 18, 1965, pp. 33–54.
4. Dean Tjosvold, *Working Together to Get Things Done: Managing for Organization Productivity,* Lexington, Mass.: Lexington Books, 1986, p. 4.
5. Glenn M. Parker, *Team Players and Teamwork: The New Competitive Business Strategy,* San Francisco: Jossey-Bass, 1990.
6. Ernst and Young Quality Improvement Consulting Group, *Total Quality: An Executive's Guide for the 1990s,* Homewood, Ill.: Business One Irwin, 1990, p. 103.
7. Ibid., p. 6.
8. Marlene Caroselli, *Total Quality Transformations: Optimizing Missions, Meth-*

ods and Management, Amherst, Mass.: Human Resource Development Press, 1991, p. 155.

9. Ernst and Young, pp. 173, 218–220.

10. K. Sale, *Human Scale,* New York: Coward-McCann-Geoghehan, 1980, p. 403.

11. This information comes from various clients the authors' company works with, various publications, and numerous calls to consultants and companies. A key publication is D. Jamieson and J. O'Mara, *Managing Workforce 2000: Gaining the Diversity Advantage.* San Francisco, Calif.: Jossey-Bass, 1991. Others are Ann M. Morrison, *The New Leaders: Guidelines on Leadership Diversity in America.* San Francisco, Calif.: Jossey-Bass, 1992; Sandra Theiderman, *Bridging Cultural Barriers for Corporate Success: How to Manage the Multicultural Work Force,* Lexington, Mass.: Lexington Books, 1990; Sandra Theiderman, *Profiting in America's Multicultural Marketplace: How to do Business Across Cultural Lines,* Lexington, Mass.: Lexington Books, 1991.

Acknowledgments

To Sarah Barr, Julie Davis, and Soph Maifo for editing, researching, and revisions for Chapter 12. To Paulette Gerkovich for editing of Chapters 7 and 8, as well as for her work and inputs on numerous other chapters. To Sarah Barr, Susan Barr, Julie Davis, Paulette Gerkovich, Lori Jacobson, Soph Maifo, and Carol Nehls for endless typing and revisions. To Michele Fernandez, Lori Jacobson, and Soph Maifo for being there when I need them most. To Maureen T. McGinley for her insights, opinions, proofreading, editing, and moral support. To Heike Wipperfurth for her invaluable insights into, additions to, and editing of the European chapters, among others. To William Ray Brown for moral and other support. To Karen Cornelius for moral and staff support, as well as wisdom. To Mindy Printz for her inputs on the TQM material and for supplying tremendous amounts of data on the European Community and Japan.

Index